국가무형문화재 제76호 UNESCO 인류 무형문화유산

전통무예 택견

택견의 이해와 수련 II

마주 메기기 편

Korean Intangible Cultural Asset #76 UNESCO Intangible Cultural Heritage of Humanity

Traditional Martial Art TAEKGYEON

The Comprehension and Training of Taekgyeon II

Theory and Practice of Partner Training

일러두기 : 마주 메기기 편

이 '택견의 이해와 수련 II – 마주 메기기 편'은 기본 기술을 홀로 수련하는 '혼자 익히기'와 상대방과 서로 기술을 연습하는 '마주 메기기' 그리고 상대와 실질적인 대련을 통해 기술의 완성도를 더하는 '견주기'의 세 단계 중 '혼자 익히기 편'에서 다루지 않았던 마주 메기기를 중심으로 구성되었다.
이 책은 본래 '마주 메기기'의 세부 수련체계에 따라 막음질, 얼러 메기기, 마주차기, 마주걸이, 익힘수, 맞수, 결련수의 7 부분으로 구성하고자 하였다. 그러나 이어지는 '견주기'의 단계가 실제 자유 대련이기에 기술할 부분이 많지 않은 점과 '마주 메기기' 가 택견의 전체 수련단계에서 절반이 넘는 내용을 담고 있는 점 등을 고려해 이 '마주 메기기 편'에서는 막음질, 얼러 메기기. 마주차기, 마주걸이의 네 과정만을 담았다.
그리고 택견의 실제 '견주기'와 유사한 형태의 마주 메기기인 '익힘수', 익힘수를 보다 세련되게 세분화한 '맞수', 그리고 서기택견에서 사용하지 않는 살수인 '결련수'는 본때뵈기와 함께 이 '택견의 이해와 수련' 시리즈의 마지막인 '견주기 편'으로 구성하고자 한다.
'마주 메기기'는 낱개의 기본 기술을 실제로 상대방에게 사용해보는 과정이다. 동시에 자신이 그 기술에 당해봄으로써 택견의 기술들이 사람의 몸에 어떻게 작용하는지를 생생히 익히는 과정이기도 하다. 또한 '견주기'에서 상대의 움직임과 상황에 따라 각각의 기술들을 어떻게 적절하고 정확하게 사용해야할지 몸에 익히는 과정이다. 즉 '마주 메기기'는 몸에 익힌 기본 기술들을 자유롭게 활용할 수 있도록 깊이를 더하는 과정인 것이다.

Notice : Mah-joo Me-kee-kee (Partner Training)

This 'The Comprehension and Training of Taekgyeon II – Mah-joo Me-kee-kee' focuses on Mah-joo Me-kee-kee, which was not covered in 'Hone-jah Ik-hee-kee' section from the three stages of training that were 'Hone-jah Ik-hee-kee' which is learning the basic skills alone, 'Mah-joo Me-kee-kee' practicing the skills with each other, and the 'Kyeon-joo-kee' that adds the completeness of skills through practical sparring with the other.

This book was originally intended to consist of seven parts according to the detailed training system of 'Mah-joo Me-kee-kee': *Mahk-eum-jil, Eol-luh Me-kee-kee, Mah-joo-cha-kee, Mah-joo-guh-ree, Ik-heem-soo, Maht-soo, and Kyeol-lyeon-soo* However, considering the fact that the following 'Kyeon-joo-kee' stage is actually free sparring, so there are not many parts to describe, and that 'Mah-joo Me-kee-kee' contains more than half of the contents of Taekgyeon's entire training course, this 'Mah-joo Me-kee-kee' section contains only four processes: *Mahk-eum-jil, Eol-luh Me-kee-kee, Mah-joo-cha-kee and Mah-joo-guh-ree*.

In addition, 'Ik-heem-soo' (a type of Mah-joo Me-kee-kee similar to Taekgyeon's actual 'Kyeon-joo-kee'), 'Maht-soo' (a more refined breakdown of Ik-heem-soo) and 'Kyeol-lyeon-soo' (a dangerous technique that is not used by Seogi Taekgyeon) will be composed as 'Kyeon-joo-kee section', the last part of this series of 'The Comprehension and Training of Taekgyeon', along with 'Bohn-dae-bae-kee'.

'Mah-joo Me-kee-kee' is a process of actually using individual basic skills against another person. At the same time, it is also the process of vividly learning how Taekgyon's skills work on the human body by experiencing them. It is also a process of mastering how to use each skill properly and accurately, depending on the opponent's movements and circumstances in 'Kyeon-joo-kee'. In other words, 'Mah-joo Me-kee-kee' is a process of adding depth so that you can freely use basic skills that you have already mastered.

택견의 이해와 수련 II
The Comprehension and Training of Taekgyeon II

저자 신종근 · 양재식
번역 Guy Edward Larke
감수 정경화(택견 인간문화재)
사진 김규리
사진 모델 신종근 · 정연중 · 원창환
제작지원 사단법인 국가무형문화재 택견보존회, 한국문화재재단

Writer Shin, Joungkun / Yang, Jaesik
Translator Guy Edward Larke
Supervisor Jung, Kyunghwa(Human Cultural Asset of Taekgyeon)
Photographer Kim, Gyuri
Model Shin, Joungkun / Jung, Yeonjoong / Won, Changhuan
Supporter Taekgyeon Preservation Society / Korea Cultural Heritage Foundation

발행일 2021년 2월 11일
발행인 이진숙
펴낸곳 충남대학교출판문화원 주소 대전광역시 유성구 대학로 99
전화 042-821-6045 홈페이지 http://www.cnupress.co.kr E-mail cnupress@cnu.ac.kr

ISBN 979-11-6503-104-6 03690
정가 20,000원

국가무형문화재 제76호 UNESCO 인류 무형문화유산 **전통무예 택견**

Korean Intangible Cultural Asset #76 UNESCO Intangible Cultural Heritage of Humanity **Traditional Martial Art TAEKGYEON**

택견의 이해와 수련 II

마주 메기기 편

The Comprehension and Training of Taekgyeon II

Theory and Practice of Partner Training

신종근 · 양재식

충남대학교출판문화원

서문

택견의 이해와 수련 - 혼자익히기 편(2017. 11. 01. 발간)이 나오고 다음 해에 바로 택견의 이해와 수련의 2권인 마주메기기 편을 바로 집필하기 시작했지만 역시 게으름으로 인해 3년이라는 시간이 지나고서야 발간하게 되어 다시 한번 핑계를 대지 않을 수 없다.

많은 택견인들이 마주 메기기에서 다양한 부분이 보충된 교재가 빨리 나오길 바란다는 재촉이 있어서 필자 역시 곤혹스러웠지만 그래도 마주메기기 편을 많은 분들이 기다린다는 생각에 조금 더 심혈을 기울이다 보니 이제야 발간되게 되었다.

이 책은 택견의 이해와 수련 - 혼자익히기 편의 다음 차례인 마주메기기의 과정으로 막음새, 막음질, 얼름새, 얼러메기기의 수련 과정을 정리하고 설명하였다.

막음새와 얼름새에서는 자세의 정확성과 정면사진과 측면사진을 첨부하여 동작을 조금 더 잘 알 수 있게 하였고 막음질과 얼러 메기기에서는 기술의 설명 뿐만 아니라 기술과 기술 사이의 연결성도 세심히 알 수 있게 하였다.

올해는 개인적으로 필자에게는 국가무형문화재 제76호 택견국가전수조교로(2020.7.29.인정) 인정되고 발간되는 첫 번째 책이다 보니 더욱 애착이 간다.

뿐만 아니라 코로나 19로 인해 대면으로 택견을 보급하기가 어려운 시기이고 특히 외국인들에게 택견을 전수하기는 거의 불가능한 시기에 국,영문 혼용 마주메기기 편 택견교재가 발간되어서 기쁘기 한이 없다.

이 책이 나오기까지 많은 분들의 도움이 있었지만 지면의 한계로 인해 몇 분만 소개하게 되는 것이 송구스럽다.

우선 교재의 감수를 해주신 택견인간문화재 정경화 선생님께 깊이 감사드리며 사)국가무형문화재 택견보존회 김안수 회장님을 비롯한 이사님들과 전 회원에게도 고마운 마음을 전하고 싶다. 또한 사진 촬영을 위해 고생한 김규리 전수생과 마주 메기기의 과정의 정확한 동작을 위해 동작을 시연한 정연중, 원창환 이수자에게 감사드린다. 마지막으로 영문번역을 해준 무예저널리스트 가이 라크에게도 지면을 통해 감사의 마음을 전하며 공동집필을 함께한 양재식 박사에게 감사의 마음을 전하고 싶다.

2020. 11.

저자 신종근 올림

택견의 이해와 수련이라는 제목으로 우리 국가무형문화재 제76호 택견을 쉽게 설명하고 이해할 수 있는 책을 처음 써낸 시기가 2017년 10월 이었다. 혼자서 택견을 수련하는 혼자익히기 과정을 다룬 '택견의 이해와 수련 : 혼자익히기 편'에 이어 상대방과 기술을 주고받는 연습을 하는 '마주 메기기 편'을 쓰고자 시작한지 어느덧 3년째가 되어서야 마무리가 되었다.

첫 번째를 써 보았으니 쉬워지겠지 라는 생각은 어느새 저 멀리 도망가 버린 한참 뒤였다. 나중에 이 글을 보면 3년이나 걸린 집필 작업의 핑계가 대단하구나 하는 생각이 들지 모르겠지만, 올해는 특히 코로나 19로 전 세계가 고생하고 있고 이것이 이 책의 사진 촬영 작업과 글쓰기의 진행에 많은 부담을 주기도 하였다. 그럼에도 불구하고 꾸역꾸역 마무리를 지을 수 있었던 건 함께 글을 써주신 신종근 전수교육조교와 번역을 맡아준 가이, 그리고 사진 촬영에 힘써준 깜직한(?) 정연중, 원창환, 김규리 후배들 덕일 것이다. 또한 이 책이 나올 수 있는 자양분을 전해준 사단법인 국가무형문화재 택견보존회와 한국문화재재단의 도움 역시 잊을 수가 없다. 그리고 바쁜 출판 일정과 작은 예산에도 많은 도움을 주신 충남대학교출판문화원에도 별도의 인사를 꼭 전하고 싶다.

이제 총 세권으로 기획한 '택견의 이해와 수련'이 반절을 후딱 넘어 버렸지만, 세 번째 책을 시작해야 한다는 계획이 두려움으로 다가온다. 부디 세 번째 책에서는 정신없고 막막하고 바쁘고 피곤한 시간이 적어지길 빌며, 이 책을 만나실 모든 분들께 건강과 안녕을 기원하는 마음을 전해드린다.

2020. 11.

저자 양재식

역자 서문

Why an updated textbook, many might ask. There are many answers. for myself, I grew up surrounded by the martial arts and a wide selection of books and magazines as well. I believe I learned almost as much as well. I think I learned almost as much from textbooks and well-prepared articles as I did in the training halls.

Many argue that books cannot teach martial arts. Perhaps not by books alone, but for an existing martial artist, they are gold.

Throughout history, there have been treatises and textbooks on all aspects of combat around the world. Korea can look to the Muye Dobo Tongji for an example.

These media also were instrumental in me moving to Asia 20 years ago. I came for one reason only to learn more martial arts. I became a writer 15 years ago to save dying martial arts systems from disappearing. One of the arts I was drawn to was Taekgyeon. I saw the art as a gentleman's art. It is very intricate, with many layers of complexity. Grandmaster Jeong's original text was very well done and I proudly display an autographed copy on myself. However, a more detailed version with an emphasis on educating the international martial arts community was needed, so with my master Yang Jae-Sik, we began a long series of discussions leading to the works you now hold in your hands.

It is a work of blood, sweat, tears, and love. Once you read through the pages, you will see why.

Sincerely,

Master Guy Edward Larke

목차

택견의 이해와 수련 II

Index

The Comprehension and Training of Taekgyeon II

Chapter 03

마주 메기기의 이해와 수련
Understanding Mah-joo Me-kee-kee and Its Practice

1. 막음질
Mahk-eum-jil

2. 얼러 메기기
Eol-luh Me-kee-kee

3. 마주차기
Mah-joo-cha-kee

4. 마주걸이
Mah-joo-guh-ree

III. 마주 메기기의 이해와 수련

무술 혹은 무예라 불리는 기술 및 수련체계를 대하는 대부분의 사람들이 우선적으로 떠올리는 것은 실전성일 것이다. 실제로 누군가와 마주한 상황에서 그 무술(혹은 무예)이 주장하는 만큼의 효과를 낼 수 있는가의 문제인 것이다. 그리고 이러한 의문에 부응하기 위하여 대부분의 무술(무예)들은 가상의 상대 혹은 실제 동료와 함께 짝을 이루어 기술을 수련하는 과정이 존재한다.

이런 과정을 일반적으로 상대연습(相對練習)이라고 한다. 하지만 택견에서는 한자식 표현을 사용할 수밖에 없는 용어를 제외하고는 거의 모든 부분에서 순우리말로 되어있어 다소 생소할 수도 있으나 다른 분야에서 일컫는 상대연습을 '마주 메기기' 라고 부른다.

택견의 경우는 혼자 익히기의 기본 기술을 수련한 후, 바로 마주 메기기로 불리는 짝을 이루는 기술 수련 과정이 시작된다. 마주 메기기라는 이름은 '어떤 대상에 대해 정면으로 향하여'라는 의미를 지니는 '마주'와 민요 등의 전통 노래를 '두 편이 주고받을 때 먼저 부르다' 혹은 '둘이 마주잡고 톱질할 때 밀어 주다'의 뜻을 가진 '메기다'의 명사형인 '메기기'의 합성어로 추정하는 것이 대부분의 견해를 차지한다. 즉, 한사람이 상대를 '마주'하고 기술을 '메기'면 상대방이 그 기술을 받고 다시 되돌아'메기'는 수련과정을 순우리말로 명료하게 표현한 것이다.

마주 메기기를 수련하는데 있어서 주의할 점은 첫째, 상대를 하는 두 사람이 서로의 공격과 방어 기술을 미리 알고 있기 때문에 자신의 공격에 대한 상대의 반응을 생각하느라 선제 공격 기술을 제대로 구사하지 않는 경우가 있다는 것이다. 이렇게 하게 되면 마주 메기기를 통해 실전의 기술을 익힐 수가 없게 되므로 선제공격은 항상 실전과 다름없이 이루어져야만 한다. 둘째, 마주 메기기라고 해서 단편적인 공격과 방어의 기술을 습득하는 것에만 너무 치우쳐서는 안 되며, 품의 자세나 품밟기의 움직임에서 자연스럽게 공격이나 방어로 이어지도록 연습하는 것 또한 매우 중요하다. 다시 말해, 품밟기와 공방의 기술이 분리되어서 따로따로 이루어진다는 느낌이 들어서는 안 된다.

III. Understanding Mah-joo Me-kee-kee and Its Practice

The first thing most people would think of when dealing with techniques and training system called martial arts would be practicality. Indeed, it is a question of whether the martial art can produce as much effect as it claims in a face-to-face confrontation with someone. And to meet this question, most martial arts have a process of training skills in pairs with virtual opponents or actual partners.

This process is commonly referred to as partner-training. However, in Taekgyeon, almost every term is in pure Korean except for the terms that are inevitable to use Chinese characters, which may be somewhat unfamiliar. The partner-training, as is referred to in other styles, is called 'Mah-joo Me-kee-kee' in Taekgyeon.

In the case of Taekgyeon, after mastering the basic skills of Hone-jah Ik-hee-kee (solo training), the process of training in pairs called Mah-joo Me-kee-kee (partner training). Most views are that the word 'Mah-joo Me-kee-kee' is a combination of the word 'Mah-joo' which means'facing forward for a subject' and the word 'Me-kee-kee' a noun form of 'Me-kee-da' which means 'to sing first' when the two groups sing traditional songs such as folk songs in a turn-taking way or 'to push' when two people hold the saw face to face and saw. In other words, the training process when a person faces (Mah-joo) an opponent and demonstrates (Me-kee-da) a skill, the other person receives the skill and then turns it back is clearly expressed in Korean.

There are things to be careful about training Mah-joo Me-kee-kee. First, the two opposing people know each other's attack and defense skills in advance, so they sometimes do not use preemptive attack techniques properly to think about the other's response to the attacks. If this happens, you will not be able to learn the skills necessary for a real match through Mah-joo Me-kee-kee, so preemptive attacks must always be carried out as if they were for real. Second, when you train Mah-joo Me-kee-kee, you should not be too biased towards acquiring the techniques of fragmentary attack and defense. It is also very important to practice naturally leading to attack or defense from the posture of Poom or the movement of Poom-bahl-kee. In other words, it should not feel that Poom-bahl-kee and the techniques of attack and defense are separated and performed separately.

1. 막음질

택견의 방어 기술을 중점적으로 수련하는 과정인 막음질은 기본 자세를 수련하는 막음새와 상대의 공격 기술을 실제로 막는 연습을 주고받는 막음질의 두 부분으로 구성된다.

혼자서 방어를 위한 기본 동작을 익히는 막음새는 '막다'의 명사형인 '막음'과 '모양, 상태, 정도의 뜻을 더하는 접미사'인 '-새'가 결합된 단어로 보는 것이 타당하다. 따라서 막음새는 '막는 모양'을 뜻하는 명칭이 된다. 이러한 '-새'의 쓰임새는 태권도의 '품새'에서도 동일하게 나타난다.

막음질의 '-질'은 '그 신체 부위를 이용한 어떤 행위의 뜻을 더하는 접미사'로 '막음질'은 막는 행위를 뜻하는 명칭이 된다. 비슷한 예로는 '주먹질'등의 표현이 있다.

막음새는 막음다리, 한 손 내려막고 세워막기, 치막고 가로막기, 두 손 내어막고 두 손 치켜막기 의 네 가지 동작을 품밟기와 조화시켜 혼자 연습한다.

막음질은 다리를 이용한 발질과 활갯짓(손)을 이용한 손질의 두 부분으로 구성된다. 다리를 이용한(발질) 4 가지 막는 동작과 활갯짓을 이용한(손질) 12 동작을 짝을 이룬 상대의 공격에 맞추어 실제로 활용하는 수련을 한다.

막음질은 막음새(막음거리)와 막음질(메기고 받기)로 이루어져 있기에 방어기술 전체를 의미하는 막음질과 실제 방어를 연습하는 막음질(메기고 받기)이 혼동될 수 있으나, 막음질=막음새+막음질 이라는 점을 기억하여 필요에 따라 구분할 필요가 있다.

1. Mahk-eum-jil

Mahk-eum-jil, the training process of focusing on Taekgyeon's defense skills consists of two parts: Mahk-eum-sae, which trains basic stance, and Mahk-eum-jil, which exchanges exercises that actually block opponents' attack skills.

It is reasonable to regard Mahk-eum-sae, which train basic movements for defense by themselves, as a combination of 'Mahk-eum', a noun for 'Mahk-da', which means block and '-sae', a suffix that adds meaning of shape, condition and degree. Therefore, the word Mahk-eum-sae means 'shape of blocking'. This use of '-sae' is the same in Taekwondo's 'Poom-sae'.

'-Jil' from Mahk-eum-jil is a suffix that adds the meaning of an act using that body part, and 'Mahk-eum-jil' is the name for the act of blocking. A similar example is the expression of 'Joo-Muk-jil.

Mahk-eum-sae is a self training movement in which four movements of Mahk-eum-dah-ree, Han-sohn Nae-ryo-mahk-go Say-wuh-mahk-kee, Chi-mahk-go Gah-roh-mahk-kee, and Doo-sohn Nae-eo-mahk-go Doo-sohn Chi-kyeo-mahk-kee are practiced by harmonizing with Poom-bahl-kee.

Mahk-eum-jil consists of two parts: Bahl-jil (footwork) using the legs and Sohn-jil using Hwahl-get-jit (hand). Practical training is conducted to match the attack of the paired opponent with four blocking movements using legs (Bahl-jil) and the 12 movements using Hwahl-get-jit (Sohn-jil).

Since Mahk-eum-jil includes Mahk-eum-sae (Mahk-eum-guh-ree) and Mahk-eum-jil (Me-kee-go Baht-kee), it means all the defense techniques but can be confused with Mahk-eum-jil (Me-kee-go Baht-kee) that practices the actual defenses. However, it is necessary to remember that Mahk-eum-jil = Mahk-eum-sae (Mahk-eum-guh-ree) + Mahk-eum-jil (Me-kee-go Baht-kee) and distinguish it as necessary.

(1) 막음새(막음거리)

막음새는 '바로 → 절 → 원품'의 순서에 따라 시작을 준비한다.

막음새는 품밟기에 조화된 손 및 다리의 움직임으로 구성된다. 수련할 때 주의할 점은 품밟기를 할 때 막음새 동작을 하기 직전에는 평소의 품밟기보다 자세를 낮추어야 한다는 것이다. 그리고 막는 동작을 하는 순간 살짝 무릎을 튕겨 일어나는 느낌으로 막음새를 수련해야 한다.

이때, 여타의 무술처럼 자세를 낮추고 힘을 주어 상대의 동작을 막아 멈춘다기보다는 무릎을 굼실대는 반동을 이용해 스프링처럼 튕겨 흘려낸다는 느낌을 유지해야 한다.

막음새를 수련할 때 잘못 하는 것 중 하나가 품으로 이동할 때는 일어선 자세로 있다가 방어동작을 취하기 전에 앉았다 일어나는 것으로 알고 있다는 것이다. 그러나 올바른 동작은 품으로 움직일 때는 자세를 낮추고 이동한 후, 방어동작 직전에 자세를 약간 더 낮추었다가 일어나면서 막는 것이다. 즉 활시위가 당겨져 있는 것처럼 항상 낮은 자세를 취하고 있다가 상대의 공격에 곧바로 방어의 동작을 할 수 있어야 한다. 이러한 낮추어진 채로 움직이는 품의 자세는 막음질 때도 동일하게 적용해야 한다.

(1) Mahk-eum-sae (Mahk-eum-guh-ree)

Mahk-eum-sae prepares to start after the orders of 'Baro → Jeol → → Won-poom'.

Mahk-eum-sae consists of the movement of the hands and legs in harmony with Poom-bahl-kee. One thing to be careful about when you are training is that you should lower your posture than usual Poom-bahl-kee just before you do the Mahk-eum-sae movement during the Poom-bahl-kee. When you do the blocking action, you have to train Mahk-eum-sae with a slight bounce of your knees.

At this time, rather than stopping the opponent's movement by lowering your posture and applying force like any other martial art, you should maintain the feeling of using a spring-like bounce from the knees.

One of the things you could do wrong when practicing Mahk-eum-sae is standing up when you move in the form of Poom, then sit down and stand up again before doing any defensive moves. So the correct movement is to lower your posture when moving in the form of Poom, after moving, lower the posture a little more just before the defensive action, and then stand up to block the attack. In other words, you should always be in a low position as if the bow string was pulled, and be able to immediately defend against the opponent's attack. The posture of Poom moving in this lowered position should be applied equally to Mahk-eum-jil.

① 막음다리

막음다리는 서서익히기의 무릎올려재기 동작을 이용하여 상대의 공격을 막는 자세를 혼자서 연습하는 과정이다.

첫째, 원품으로 선 상태에서 오른다리로 체중을 이동하며, 왼팔은 긁기 동작을 준비한다. 둘째, 왼팔로 긁기를 마무리함과 동시에 왼 다리를 90°로 접어 정면을 향해 들어올린다. 이때, 오른팔을 뻗어 오른 손으로 왼쪽 무릎을 덮어준다. 여기까지가 막음다리의 한 동작이다. 셋째, 두 팔을 자연스럽게 내리며, 왼발을 품 째밟기의 형태로 왼쪽으로 어깨 폭의 1.5배 정도로 넓게 내딛는다. 넷째, 오른손으로 긁기를 준비하며 왼 다리로 체중을 이동한다. 끝으로 오른손으로 긁기를 마무리하며 오른다리를 정면을 향해 90°로 들어올린다. 왼손은 오른 무릎을 짚어준다.

> 막음다리를 할 때, 첫 동작은 원품에서 막음다리 동작을 바로 취하게 되지만, 두 번 째 이후부터는 들어 올린 다리를 품 째밟기의 형태로 넓게 내딛으며 반복한다. 즉 첫 시작을 제외하고는 아래 그림의 2-1에서 2-3의 동작이 지속적으로 반복되는 것이다.
> 막음다리에서 긁기 동작과 무릎을 덮는 동작을 취하는 양 팔은 몸통과 얼굴을 방어하기 위한 준비동작으로 이해할 수 있다.

1-1

1-2

1-3

① Mahk-eum-dah-ree

Mahk-eum-dah-ree is a process in which one practices the posture of blocking an opponent's attack by himself using Moo-reup-ohl-ryuh-jae-kee move of Suh-suh-Ik-hee-kee.

First, move your weight on your right leg from Won-poom, and prepare your left arm for Guhl-kee. Second, finish Guhl-kee with your left arm and at the same time, fold your left leg 90° to lift it forward. At this time, stretch out your right arm and cover your left knee with your right hand. This is one movement of Mahk-eum-dah-ree. Third, with both arms naturally lowered, the left foot is stepped forward 1.5 times the width of the shoulder to the left in the form of Poom Jae-bahl-kee. Fourth, move your weight to your left leg, preparing Guhl-kee with your right hand. Finally, finish Guhl-kee with your right hand and lift the right leg to 90° to the front. The left hand is placed on the right knee.

When you do Mahk-eum-dah-ree, the first movement is performed immediately from Won-poom, but from the second step, the raised leg is taken a wide step in the form of Poom Jae-bahl-kee and repeated. That is, except for the first start, the 2-1 to 2-3 moves in the figures below are repeated continuously. Both arms, which take the action of Guhl-kee and covering the knee in Mahk-eum-dah-ree, can be understood as a preparatory move to defend the body and face.

2-1

2-2

2-3

② 한손 내려막고 세워막기

한손 내려막고 세워막기는 품 길게 밟기를 하며 앞쪽으로 좌(우)품을 내딛는 순서에 맞으로 내려막기를, 뒤쪽으로 물러나 우(좌)품을 내딛는 순서에 세워막기를 하는 동작이다. 두 가지 방어 동작을 품 길게 밟기의 박자와 조화를 이루어 실시한다.

첫째, 원품에서 자세를 낮추며 좌품을 내딛는다. 이때, 왼손은 손등이 자신의 오른쪽 귀를 덮도록 들어올린다. 둘째, 좌품을 내딛는 동시에 가볍게 튕겨 일어나며, 왼 손바닥이 왼쪽 바깥을 향하도록 가볍게 내리 휘두른다(내려막기). 이때, 왼 팔은 자신의 몸통 방향을 기준으로 왼쪽 45°, 아래쪽 45°를 향하도록 한다. 손목은 힘을 빼고 한손 긁기나 제치기처럼 자연스럽게 나부끼도록 한다. 여기까지가 품 길게 밟기의 '하나'에 해당하는 박자이다. 셋째. 내려막기 한 팔을 자연스럽게 풀어주며 자세를 낮추고 왼발을 뒤쪽 45°부분에 내딛는다. 동시에 오른팔을 자신의 좌측 겨드랑이까지 가볍게 들어올린다. 넷째, 우품을 내딛음과 동시에 가볍게 튕겨 일어나며 겨드랑이까지 들어 올린 오른 팔뚝을 손등이 바깥을 향하도록 회전시켜 세워준다(세워막기). 이때 오른손이 자신의 눈높이 정도에 위치하도록 하며, 오른 팔뚝은 자신의 몸통을 기준으로 위쪽 45°, 오른쪽 45°를 향하도록 한다. 손목은 마찬가지로 자연스럽게 나부끼게 한다. 이때가 품 길게 밟기의 '넷'에 해당하는 박자이다. 다섯째, 세워막기 한 팔을 자연스레 풀어주고 품 길게 밟기를 하며 앞쪽으로 이동하여 다시 좌품에서의 내려막기를 실시한다.

1-1	1-2	2-1

② Han-shon Nae-ryo-mahk-goh Say-wuh-mahk-kee

Han-shon Nae-ryo-mahk-goh Say-wuh-mahk-kee is a movement in which you perform Nae-ryo-mahk-kee with Maht at the moment of stepping forward of Jwa(Woo)-poom while performing Poom Keel-gay-bahl-kee, and perform Say-wuh-mahk-kee at the moment of stepping backward of Woo(Jwa)-poom. Two defensive moves are performed in harmony with the beat of Poom Keel-gay-bahl-kee.

First, lower your posture and step Jwa-poom from Won-poom. At this time, your left hand is lifted so that the back of the hand covers your right ear. Second, as soon as step down into Jwa-poom, you bounce off lightly and swing your left hand down lightly with the palm facing out to the left(Nae-ryo-mahk-kee). At this point, the left arm is positioned 45° to the left and 45° downwards in front of the body. Relax your wrist and let it flow naturally, like Han-sohn Guhl-kee or Jay-chee-kee. This is the beat equivalent to the 'one' of Poom Keel-gay-bahl-kee. Third, lower your posture while relaxing the arm which performed Nae-ryo-mahk-kee naturally and step your left foot back 45°. At the same time, lift your right arm lightly up to your left armpit. Fourth, as soon as you take a step of Woo-poom, lightly bounce up and rotate your right arm with the back of the hand facing outwards and lift it up(Say-wuh-mahk-kee). At this point, the right hand should be positioned at your eye level, and the right forearm should be facing 45° up and 45° to the right, relative to the body position. The wrist should also naturally flow. This is the beat equivalent to the 'four' of Poom Keel-gay-bahl-kee. Fifth, naturally release the arm which performed Say-wuh-mahk-kee, step Poom Keel-gay-bahl-kee and move forward to perform another Nae-ryo-mahk-kee from Jwa-poom.

2-2

side of 1-2

side of 2-2

한손 내려막고 세워막기는 품 길게 밟기와 마찬가지로 시작하는 품을 좌품으로 연습한 후, 반드시 시작하는 품을 우품으로 바꾸어 연습하여 좌우를 고르게 수련한다.
내려막기를 할 때 팔꿈치를 완전히 펴게 되면 팔꿈치에 상대의 발차기가 적중할 경우, 상당한 부상이 발생할 수 있다. 따라서 팔꿈치를 가볍게 굽힌 상태에서 팔뚝의 안쪽 근육부위가 상대의 발차기를 막을 수 있도록 한다. 물론 내려막기의 기본은 자신의 손바닥을 이용해 상대의 발차기를 방어하는 것이지만, 실제 견주기에서 방어를 하게 될 경우에는 손바닥과 팔뚝 전체를 이용한다는 느낌으로 하는 것이 효과적이다.
세워막기를 할 때에도 자신의 팔뚝 바깥쪽 근육으로 상대의 공격을 막아야 한다. 간혹, 팔을 비틀어 팔뚝의 뼈를 이용해 상대의 공격을 막는 경우가 생긴다. 이는 태권도 등 강한 힘으로 상대의 공격을 방어하는 무예를 익힌 사람들이 주로 취하는 습관적인 행동이다.
그러나 택견의 경우, 상대의 공격을 '막아서 멈춘다'라기 보다는 무릎이 움직이는 탄력을 이용해 '튕겨 흘려낸다'는 개념으로 방어를 한다. 따라서 힘을 주고 뼈로 막기보다는 팔뚝 바깥쪽의 근육을 이용해 가볍게 튕겨내는 느낌이 들도록 실시해야 한다. 이는 내려막기에서도 마찬가지이다.
내려막기와 세워막기를 할 때 모두, 방어를 하는 팔은 자신의 몸통을 기준으로 45°바깥을 향한다고 설명하였다. 그러나 몸통 자체가 품밟기를 하며 자연스럽게 양쪽 옆으로 틀어지게 되므로 실제 동작을 정면에서 보게 되면 위 사진과 마찬가지로 몸통의 바깥쪽 라인에 걸치게 된다. 이보다 안쪽에서 방어를 하게 되면 몸통에 공격을 허용하게 되고, 바깥을 향하게 되면 방어해야할 부위가 넓어져 실수를 하게 되니 유의하여야 한다.

when you practice Han-sohn Nae-ryo-mahk-goh Say-wuh-mahk-kee, you start from Jwa-poom just like you practice Poom Keel-gay-bahl-kee. Then, practice by changing the starting part from Woo-poom and training left and right evenly.

If the elbow is fully extended when you perform Nae-ryo-mahk-kee, significant injury can occur if the opponent's kick hits the elbow. Thus, with the elbow lightly bent, let the inner muscle area of the forearm prevent the opponent from kicking. Of course, the basis of Nae-ryo-mahk-kee is to use your palm to defend your opponent's kick, but if you are to defend yourself in the actual Kyeon-joo-kee, it is effective to use your palm and forearm as a whole.

Even when you perform Say-wuh-mahk-kee, you should block the opponent's attack with the muscles outside your forearm. Occasionally, there are cases people twist their arm to use the bone in their forearm to prevent the opponent's attack. This is a habitual behavior usually taken by those who have mastered the martial arts of defending the opponent's attack with strong force such as Taekwondo.

But in the case of Taekgyeon, rather than 'block and stop' the opponent's attack, you use the moving momentum of the knee to defend yourself with the concept of 'bouncing off'. Therefore, rather than applying pressure and blocking it with bones, the muscles on the outside of the forearm should be used to make it feel like it is bouncing lightly. The same goes for Nae-ryo-mahk-kee.

In the both cases of performing Nae-ryo-mahk-kee and Say-wuh-mahk-kee, it is explained that the defensive arm is facing outside 45° of your body. However, the body itself naturally turns to both sides of the body while stepping Poom-bahl-kee, so if you look at the actual movement from the front, the arms will hang on the outer line of the body as shown in the figures above. It is important to note that if you defend from the inside more than this line, you will be attacked in your torso, and if you do so from the outside, you will make mistakes due to being wide open to attack.

③ 치막고 가로막기

치막고 가로막기 역시 품 길게 밟기를 하며 그 박자에 맞추어 치막기와 가로막기를 실시한다.

첫째, 원품에서 자세를 낮추며 좌품을 내딛는다. 이때, 왼손은 오른쪽 겨드랑이 앞으로 들어 올린다. 둘째, 좌품을 내딛는 동시에 가볍게 튕겨 일어나며 왼 손바닥이 자신의 머리를 막도록 가볍게 회전시켜 들어 올린 후, 이마 위에서 멈춘다(치막기). 이때, 왼 손바닥은 자신의 이마를 기준으로 위쪽 45°앞을 향하도록 한다. 손목은 힘을 빼고 활갯짓 치돌리기를 할 때처럼 자연스레 나부끼며 움직인다. 셋째. 치막기 한 팔을 자연스럽게 풀어주며 자세를 낮추고 왼발을 뒤쪽 45°부분에 내딛는다. 동시에 오른팔을 자신의 오른쪽 겨드랑이 앞으로 가볍게 들어올린다. 넷째, 우품을 내딛음과 동시에 가볍게 튕겨 일어나며 겨드랑이까지 들어 올린 오른 팔뚝을 세운 채 허리를 좌측으로 틀어준다(가로막기). 이때 오른손이 자신의 눈높이 정도에 위치하도록 하며, 오른 팔뚝은 허리의 회전에 더해 자신의 좌측 머리와 가슴을 막을 수 있는 위치까지 가볍게 밀어준다. 손목은 마찬가지로 자연스럽게 나부끼게 한다. 다섯째, 가로막기 한 팔을 자연스레 풀어주고 품 길게 밟기를 하며 앞쪽으로 이동하여 다시 좌품에서의 치막기를 실시한다.

1-1	1-2	2-1

③ Chi-mahk-goh Gah-roh-mahk-kee

Chi-mahk-goh Gah-roh-mahk-kee is also performed at the beat of Poom Keel-gay-bahl-kee.

First, lower your posture and take a step of Jwa-poom from Won-poom. At this time, the left hand is lifted forward near the right armpit. Second, as soon as you step down into Jwa-poom, bounce up lightly, and lift your left hand up lightly and rotate so that the left palm protects your head(Chi-mahk-kee). At this point, the left palm should be forward 45° above your forehead. Relax your wrist and let it flow naturally, like performing Hwahl-get-jit Chee-dohl-lee-kee. Third, lower your body while relaxing the arm which performed Chi-mahk-kee naturally and step your left foot back 45°. At the same time, lift your right arm lightly forward up to your right armpit level. Fourth, as soon as you take a step of Woo-poom, lightly bounce up and twist your waist to the left with your right forearm raised(Gah-roh-mahk-kee). At this point, the right hand should be positioned at your eye level, and the right forearm should be gently pushed to the position where it can defend the left side of your head and chest in addition to the rotation of the waist. The wrist should also naturally flow. Fifth, naturally release the arm which performed Gah-roh-mahk-kee, step Poom Keel-gay-bahl-kee and move forward to perform Chi-mahk-kee from Jwa-poom again.

2-2

side of 1-2

side of 2-2

치막고 가로막기 역시, 자세를 낮췄다 튕겨 일어나는 무릎의 탄력을 이용해 상대의 공격을 튕겨 흘려낸다. 상대의 공격을 방어할 때는 자신의 팔뚝에 부딪혀 멈추게 하는 느낌이 아니라 튕겨지며 흘러 나가는 느낌이 들도록 해야 한다.
이를 위해서는 무릎을 튕겨 일어나는 동작과 막는 동작을 취하는 순간, 그리고 상대의 공격이 내 방어에 부딪히는 순간이 절묘하게 맞아떨어져야 한다. 그래야 막는 동작에 자신이 일어나는 탄력을 더하여 적절히 상대의 공격을 튕겨 흘릴 수 있는 것이다. 따라서 막음새와 뒤에 이어지는 막음질을 연습할 때에는 막는 순간을 제외하고는 지속적으로 무릎을 굽혀 낮은 자세를 유지함으로써 적절한 순간에 튕겨 일어날 준비가 되어있어야 한다.
치막기를 할 때는 막는 순간의 손의 위치가 중요하다. 대개의 경우, 상대의 공격이 다가오면 자신도 모르게 움츠러들어 막는 손을 이마에 바짝 붙여 방어를 하게 된다. 이렇게 되면 상대의 공격이 자신의 얼굴에 바로 닿게 되므로 항상 이마 위쪽으로 45˚, 앞쪽으로 45˚를 유지해야 한다(그림 side of 1–2).
가로막기를 할 때에는 팔보다는 허리의 회전으로 상대의 공격을 흘려 내듯이 막아야 한다. 또한 손의 위치가 자신의 얼굴보다 앞쪽에 위치하도록, 팔뚝을 앞쪽 45˚방향으로 세워주어야 한다(그림 side of 2–2). 얼굴에 너무 가까운 위치에서 막게 되면 상대의 공격에 조금이라도 밀리는 순간 공격을 허용하게 되기 때문이다.

Chi-mahk-goh Gah-roh-mahk-kee also uses the elasticity of the knees when you bounce up from the lower position to bounce off the opponent's attack. When defending an opponent's attack, you should make it feel like it's bouncing and flowing out, not hitting your forearm and stopping it.
To do this, the moment you bounce your knees up and take an action to block the attack, and the moment your opponent's attack hits your own defense, must be exquisitely matched. Only then you can properly bounce off the opponent's attack by adding the momentum you take in the blocking motion. Therefore, when practicing Mahk-eum-sae and Mahk-eum-jil that follows it, be prepared to bounce up at the appropriate moment by continuously bending your knees and maintaining a low position, except at the point of contact for defense.
When performing Chi-mahk-kee, the position of the hand at the moment of block is important. In most cases, when the opponent's attack approaches, he or she unwittingly shrinks and holds his or her hand close to his or her forehead to defend himself or herself. This will bring the opponent's attack directly into his or her face, so the arm must always be kept 45° above the forehead and 45° forward (Figure side of 1-2).
When performing Gah-roh-mahk-kee, use the rotation of the waist rather than the arm to block the opponent's attack. The forearm should be raised 45° to the front, so your hand is positioned in front of your face (Figure side of 2-2). If you block too close to your face, you will allow yourself to be attacked as soon as you arm is pushed back by your opponent.

④ 두손 내어막고 두손 치켜막기

두손 내어막고 두손 치켜막기는 품 길게 밟기의 박자에 맞추어 엇갈린 두손을 이용해 허리 아래와 머리 위를 번갈아 막는 동작이다.

첫째, 원품에서 자세를 낮추며 좌품을 내딛는다. 이때, 두 손을 늘어뜨린 채 양쪽 겨드랑이 앞으로 들어올린다. 둘째, 좌품을 내딛는 동시에 가볍게 튕겨 일어나며, 두 손의 손목부분이 엇갈리도록 정면 아래 방향을 향해 밀어내린다. 이때 양손의 손바닥은 바닥을 향해야 한다. 또한 엉덩이는 가볍게 뒤쪽으로 빼주어 급소 부위가 공격에 닿지 않도록, 양손이 충분히 아래쪽으로 내려가도록 한다(내어막기). 셋째. 두손 내어막기 한 팔을 자연스럽게 풀어주며 자세를 낮추고 왼발을 뒤쪽 45°부분에 내딛는다. 동시에 두 손을 양쪽 겨드랑이까지 가볍게 들어 올린다. 넷째, 우품을 내딛음과 동시에 가볍게 튕겨 일어나며 겨드랑이까지 들어 올린 두 손을 손목이 엇갈리도록 하여 머리 위 45°를 향해 뻗어준다(치켜막기). 이때 양 손의 손바닥이 하늘을 향해야 한다. 다섯째, 치켜막기 한 팔을 자연스레 풀어주고 품 길게 밟기를 하며 앞쪽으로 이동하여 다시 좌품에서의 내어막기를 실시한다. 수차례 연습이 끝난 후, 품을 바꾸어 우품에서 시작하는 품 길게 밟기와도 조화시켜 연습하여야 한다.

1-1

1-2

2-1

④ Doo-sohn Nae-eo-mahk-goh Doo-sohn Chi-kyeo-mahk-kee

Doo-sohn Nae-eo-mahk-goh Doo-sohn Chi-kyeo-mahk-kee is a movement that blocks below the waist and over the head alternately using crossed hands at the beat of Poom Keel-gay-bahl-kee.

First, lower your posture and step forward Jwa-poom from Won-poom. At this time, lift both arms to the front of the armpits with both hands hanging down. Second, bounce off lightly at the same time as you step down Jwa-poom and push down the two hands in the direction below the front to cross the wrists. The palms of both hands must face the floor. Also, lightly pull the hips back so that the vital areas are not open to attack and both hands are low enough(Nae-eo-mahk-kee). Third, naturally relax your arms that performed Doo-sohn Nae-eo-mahk-kee and lower your posture and put your left foot at 45° to the back. Lift both hands lightly up to both armpits at the same time. Fourth, as soon as you take a step of Woo-poom, lightly bounce up and extend your hands from the armpits level to 45° above the head with your wrists crossed(Chi-kyeo-mahk-kee). At this time, the palms of both hands should face the sky. Fifth, naturally release the arm which performed Chi-kyeo-mahk-kee, step Poom Keel-gay-bahl-kee and move forward to perform Nae-eo-mahk-kee from Jwa-poom again. After several exercises, you should change Poom and practice in harmony with Poom Keel-gay-bahl-kee starting from Woo-poom.

2-2

side of 1-2

side of 2-2

두손 내어막기와 두손 치켜막기에서는 두 손의 손목이 엇갈린 상태에서 양 손바닥이 막는 방향을 향하도록 하는 것이 중요하다. 내어막기를 할 때에는 두 손바닥이 바닥을, 치켜막기를 할 때에는 하늘을 향하게 함으로써 손바닥이나 엇갈린 양 손목의 안쪽 근육으로 상대의 공격을 받아야 한다. 그렇지 못하면 엇갈린 손목뼈나 손날의 뼈로 공격을 막게 되는데, 이는 상당한 부상을 일으킬 수 있다.
특히, 두손 내어막기의 경우, 나중의 수련과정에서 상대의 발차기를 방어하는 동시에 양 손목을 꺾어 상대의 발목을 걸어 잡고 공격으로 전환하게 되는데, 이를 위해서도 양손의 바닥이 바닥을 향하도록 방어하는 것이 중요하다.

When performing Doo-sohn Nae-eo-mahk-kee and Doo-sohn Chi-kyeo-mahk-kee, it is important to make sure that both palms face the direction of blocking with the wrists crossed. Make sure that your palms are facing the floor when you perform Nae-eo-mahk-kee, and your palms are facing up to the sky when you perform Chi-kyeo-mahk-kee to take the opponent's attack with your palms or the muscles on the inside of your wrists. Otherwise, you will block the attacks with your wrist bone or the bone on the edge of your hand, which can cause considerable injury.
Particulary, in the case of Doo-sohn Nae-eo-mahk-kee, as soon as you block the opponent's kick with your wrists, you drop the hands to grab the opponent's ankle and turn the block into an attack in the later training courses. For this, it is also important to defend with the palms facing down.

(2) 막음질 (메기고 받기)

막음질은 '바로 → 절 → 원품 → 서거라 → 거리 맞추고'의 구령에 따라 준비 자세를 취한 후 시작하게 된다.

첫째, 상대와 마주보고 선 후, '바로' 구령에 맞추어 바로자세를 취한다. '절'의 구령에 맞추어 상대에게 예를 표한 후, '원품'의 구령에 따라 상대를 마주보고 원품으로 선다. 둘째, '서거라'의 구령에 따라 좌품 자세를 취한다. 셋째,'거리 맞추고'의 구령에 따라 상대의 공격이 자신의 몸에 닿을 정도로 거리를 조절한 후, 원품 상태로 서서 막음질 수련의 시작을 준비한다. 이때 두 팔을 앞으로 쭉 뻗어 서로의 어깨에 가볍게 닿는 정도의 거리가 적당하다.

> 막음질은 막음새에서 연습한 개별의 방어 동작을 상대와 함께 실제로 사용해보는 수련과정이다. 막음질은 방어를 위한 동작들의 수련 과정이므로 항상 방어자가 중심이 되어 수련을 실시한다. 대개 먼저 공격을 시작하는 사람을 윗대로 정하고 나중에 공격을 시작하는 사람을 아랫대로 정해 공격과 방어를 번갈아 수련하며, 윗대의 공격이 정해진 회수만큼 끝나면 아랫대의 공격을 윗대가 방어하게 된다. 이를 '메기고 받기'라고 부른다.
> 막음질에서는 공격을 하는 사람이 먼저 시작하므로 윗대로 칭해지기는 하지만 아랫대로 칭해지는 방어자가 왼발을 먼저 움직일 수 있도록 공격자가 공격하는 다리나 손의 방향을 정해주어야 한다.

1-1

1-2

1-3

(2) Mahk-eum-jil (Me-kee-go Baht-kee)

Mahk-eum-jilis started after taking a ready stance following the command of 'Baro → Jeol → Won-poom → Suh-guh-ra → Guh-ri-mat-chu-go'.

First, stand face to face with the opponent, and then stand-up straight with the command of 'Baro'. To express one's gratitude to the other in accordance with the command of the 'Jeol' and stand in Won-poom facing the other according to the command of the 'Won-poom'. Second, take a posture of Jwa-poom according to the command of 'Suh-guh-ra'. Third, under the command of 'Guh-ri-mat-chu-go', adjust the distance to the point where the opponent's attack reaches your body, and then stand in Won-poom stance to prepare for the start of Mahk-eum-jil training. At this time, the distance from the opponent is enough to lightly touch each other's shoulders when both arms are stretched forward.

Mahk-eum-jil is a set of practicing Mahk-eum-sae motions with a partner. Since Mahk-eum-jil is a training process for defensive movements, the training is always centered on defenders. Usually, the person who starts the attack first is set as Wit-dae and the person who starts the attack later is set as Ah-raet-dae to train the attack and defense alternately, and when Wit-dae finishes the attack as much as the set number of times, Wit-dae will defend the attack from Ah-raet-dae. It is called 'Me-kee-go Baht-kee'.
In Mahk-eum-jil, the attacker is called Wit-dae because he/she starts first, but the person should set the direction of the attacker's leg or hand so that the defender, who is called Ah-raet-dae, can move the left foot first.

2	3-1	3-2

막음질 유의사항

① 막음질은 방어자가 중심이 되는 수련과정이므로 방어자에게 맞춰서 수련한다.
② 시작 공방에서 방어자가 처음 방어동작을 취할 때는 왼발이 뒤로 물러서면서 방어한다.
③ 한 가지 기술 당 보편적으로 4회~8회 반복 연습한다.
④ 공격자는 공격을 실시할 때 실전에 가까운 속도로 공격한다.(마주메기기라는 생각에 천천히 공격하게 되면 방어자의 방어 기술이 향상되기 어렵다.)
⑤ 공격과 공격 사이에 약간의 시간적 여유를 주면서 수련한다.(상대가 방어의 예비 자세를 취하도록)
⑥ 공방을 마무리할 때 공격자는 뒤의 발을 앞으로 끌어당기면서 원품의 자세를 취하고, 방어자는 앞발을 뒤로 끌어당기면서 원품의 자세를 취한 후, 공격과 방어를 바꾸어서 실시한다.
⑦ 방어자가 뒤로 물러나면서 방어할 때, 물러나는 자세는 항상 품의 형태로 낮은 자세를 유지하면서 물러나고 낮은 자세에서 일어나는 동시에 곧바로 방어의 동작을 취하여야 한다.

Matters to be attended to Mahk-eum-jil

① Mahk-eum-jil is a training course centered on the defender, so it is trained with the defender in mind.

② When a defender first takes defensive moves in the starting match, his/her left foot steps back and defends.

③ Repeat 4 to 8 times per skill.

④ Attackers strike at almost the same speed as an actual attack when carrying out the attack (It is difficult for defenders to improve their defense skills if they attack slowly, thinking it is Mah-joo Me-kee-kee).

⑤ Train with some delay between one attack and a following attack (To allow the opponent to take a preparatory position on the defense).

⑥ At the end of the match, the attacker takes the position of Won-Poom by pulling the back foot forward, and the defender takes the position of 'One-Poom' by pulling the front foot back, changing the attack and defense positions.

⑦ When the defender defends as he/she steps back, he/she must always remain in a lower position in the form of 'Poom' and take a defensive action immediately while standing up from the low position.xz

(2-1) 발질

① 막음다리

앞서 설명한 택견의 품 즉, 좌품, 우품 및 원품을 번갈아 딛는 동작을 품밟기라 칭한다. 그리고 이 품밟기 과정에서 나타나는 발자국의 모양이 한자의 물건 품(品)자와 유사하다는 이유에서 품밟기라는 이름이 유래된 것으로 여겨진다.

품밟기는 택견의 구성요소 3가지 중 단연 으뜸으로 공방에 있어서 택견의 독특한 몸짓을 나타내는 발놀림이다. 굼실대며 율동적인 택견의 몸짓을 구사하기 위해서는 이 품밟기가 원활해야한다. 품밟기는 기량의 향상이 눈에 보이지 않기 때문에 상당히 지루한 수련과정이지만 지속적으로 끊임없이 수련해야만 본인이 원하는 자신만의 품을 밟을 수 있게 된다.

품밟기는 택견의 기본 스텝으로 내밟기와 길게 밟기, 째밟기의 세가지 기본형으로 이루어진다. 이 중, 내밟기의 수련이 가장 주가 되며, 이 내밟기를 앞뒤로 이어붙인 형태가 길게 밟기, 좌우로 늘인 형태가 째밟기가 된다. 길게 밟기와 째밟기가 내밟기의 응용에 가까운 형태라는 점에서 대체로 품밟기라 하면 이 내밟기를 지칭하는 경우가 많다. 대신 길게 밟기와 째밟기는 반드시 '길게 밟기' 혹은 '째밟기'라고 부른다.

1-1	1-2	2

(2-1) Bahl-jil

① Mahk-eum-dah-ree

Mahk-eum-dah-ree is a technique that defends against the opponent's attack in the form of blocking the route of the opponent's Bahl-jil in advance with Moo-reup-ohl-ryuh-jae-kee. At the beginning, Wit-dae attempts a left Jae-cha-kee so that Ah-raet-dae can lift the left leg first to block the kick. The attacker attacks in turn left and right and the defender usually defends about eight consecutive times, and practices by changing Wit-dae and Ah-raet-dae under the command of 'Suhn-soo Bah-kweo' which means 'change players'.

First, when Ah-raet-dae is confirmed to be ready, Wit-dae attacks with a left Jae-cha-kee. At this time, Ah-raet-dae lower his/her knees slightly and waits for the opponent to kick. Second, Ah-raet-dae moves his/her weight on the right leg, raising the left leg timing the kick's speed to reach the body to block the opponent's Jae-cha-kee. Third, after the Jae-cha-kee is blocked, Wit-dae takes a step forward with the left foot in the form of stepping. Ah-raet-dae prepares for the next defense, putting down the left foot of Mahk-eum-dah-ree in the form of a step backwards.

Wit-dae is then performs Jae-cha-kee with the right foot, while Ah-raet-dae blocks with a right leg Mahk-eum-dah-ree. Repeat as many times as agreed upon, or until Ah-raet-dae can no longer go back; then stand in Won-poom, adjusting the distance under the command of 'Geu-mahn'. According to the command, 'Shun-soo Bah-kweo (change players)', they will change the roles of attacker and defender.

3-1	3-2	next

막음다리로 상대의 째차기를 막을 때는 들어 올린 무릎이 자기 몸의 안쪽을 향하도록 비스듬한 각도를 유지해야 한다. 들어 올린 다리의 대각선 방향에서 날아오는 상대의 째차기와 각도를 맞추어 자신의 다리와의 접촉 면적을 최대화함으로써 막는 다리에 전해지는 충격을 고루 분산시키기 위함이다. 또한 다리를 들어 막는 순간에도 중심을 안정되게 유지하여 실제 견주기에서 상대의 발차기 한 다리가 앞으로 내려졌을 때, 바로 낚시걸이 등의 공격으로 연결할 수 있도록 준비하여야 한다.

When blocking the opponent's Jae-cha-kee with Mahk-eum-dah-ree, you should keep the raised knee facing the inside of your body at an angle. The purpose is to maximize the contact area with your leg by aligning the opponent's Jae-cha-kee from the diagonal direction of the raised leg to evenly disperse the impact of the blocking leg. In addition, the center should be kept stable even when you lift your leg to block, so that when the leg of the opponent's kick is lowered forward in actual sparring, it can be connected directly to another attack such as Nak-shee-guh-ree.

② 너울거리

너울거리는 막음다리 헤치기라고도 불리는 기술로 막음다리로 활갯짓 헤치기를 하듯이 상대의 공격을 방어하는 기술이다. 첫 시작에 윗대는 아랫대가 왼쪽 다리부터 들어 막을 수 있도록 오른발 후려차기를 해준다.

첫째, 아랫대의 준비가 확인되면 윗대가 오른발 후려차기를 실시한다. 이때 아랫대는 무릎을 살짝 낮추며 상대의 후려차기를 기다린다. 둘째, 아랫대는 오른 다리 쪽으로 체중을 이동하며 상대의 후려차기가 자신의 몸에 닿는 속도를 고려하여 왼다리를 들어올려 자신의 몸 안쪽에서 밖으로 휘두르며 상대의 후려차기를 밖으로 걷어낸다. 셋째, 윗대는 후려차기가 막힌 후, 오른발을 걷기의 형태로 한발 전진하며 내딛는다. 아랫대는 너울거리 한 왼발을 뒤쪽으로 걷기의 형태로 내려놓으며 다음 방어를 준비한다.

이어서 윗대는 왼발로 후려차기를 하며 아랫대는 오른발 너울거리로 막아준다. 서로 약속한 회수만큼 혹은 아랫대가 더 이상 뒤로 가지 못할 정도까지 반복한 후, '그만'이라는 구령에 따라 원품으로 서서 다시 거리를 맞춘다. '선수 바꿔'라는 구령에 따라 서로 공방의 역할을 바꿔 실시한다.

1-1

1-2

2-1

② Neoh-wul-guh-ree

Neoh-wul-guh-ree is also called Mahk-eum-dah-ree Hay-chee-Kee, a technique that defends attacks as if performing Hwahl-get-jit Hay-chee-Kee with Mahk-eum-dah-ree. At the beginning, Wit-dae kicks Hoo-ryuh-cha-kee with his/her right foot so that Ah-raet-dae can block lifting his/her left leg first.

First, once Ah-raet-dae is ready, Wit-dae performs Hoo-ryuh-cha-kee with his/her right foot. At this time, Ah-raet-dae lowers the knees slightly and waits for the opponent to kick. Second, Ah-raet-dae moves the weight towards the right leg, raising the left leg, swinging it out from the inside to the outside of the body to block the kick, in accordance with the speed at which the opponent's kick touches the body. Third, after the kick is blocked, Wit-dae takes a step forward as if walking with the right foot. Ah-raet-dae lay down the left leg in the form of a backward step, preparing for the next defense.

Wit-dae then performs Hoo-ryuh-cha-kee with his/her left foot, while Ah-raet-dae blocks with a right foot Neoh-wul-guh-ree. Repeat as many times as agreed upon, or until Ah-raet-dae can no longer go back, then stand in Won-poom, adjusting the distance under the command of 'Geu-mahn'. when the command is called 'Shun-soo Bah-kweo'(change players), they will change the roles of attacker and defender.

2-2	3	next

너울거리로 상대의 후려차기를 막을 때는 들어 올린 다리를 안에서 밖으로 휘둘러 상대의 후려차기를 밖으로 튕겨내야 한다. 날아오는 상대의 후려차기와 맞닿는 첫 순간에는 각도를 맞추어 자신의 다리와의 접촉 면적을 최대화함으로써 막는 다리에 전해지는 충격을 고루 분산시켜야한다. 후려차기를 튕겨낸 후에는 상대의 벌어진 정면 복부를 바로 공격할 수 있도록 중심을 안정되게 유지하여야 한다. 특히 상대의 후려차기를 튕겨낼 때에는 때려서 튕긴다기보다는 내 다리에 붙은 상대의 다리를 끌어당겨 뒤로 던진다는 느낌으로 해야 한다.

When you block the opponent's Hoo-ryuh-cha-kee with Neoh-wul-guh-ree, you have to swing your raised leg from the inside-out to bounce the opponent's kick away. At the first moment of contact with the flying opponent's Hoo-ryuh-cha-kee, the impact on the blocked leg should be evenly distributed by adjusting the angle to maximize the contact area with your leg. After bouncing the Hoo-ryuh-cha-kee away, you have to keep the balance stable so that you can attack the opponent's abdomen immediately. In particular, when you deflect the opponent's Hoo-ryuh-cha-kee, you should feel like you are pulling the opponent's leg and throwing it backwards rather than hitting it.

③ 발등걸이

발등걸이는 엄지발가락이 안쪽을 향하게 발목을 꺾어 발 바깥쪽을 날을 세운 뒤, 이 날을 이용하여 아래로 옆발질 하듯이 상대의 발목을 찍어 차 발차기를 막는 동작이다.

첫째, 아랫대의 준비가 확인되면 윗대가 왼발 걸어차기를 실시한다. 이때 아랫대는 무릎을 살짝 낮추며 상대의 걸어차기를 기다린다. 둘째, 아랫대는 오른 다리 쪽으로 체중을 이동하며 상대의 걸어차기가 다가오는 속도를 고려하여 왼 무릎을 몸 안쪽으로 높게 들어 올려 자신의 몸 중심에서 왼발의 발날을 찍어 내리듯이 상대의 발목을 아래로 차 내린다. 셋째, 윗대는 걸어차기가 막힌 후, 오른발을 걷기의 형태로 한발 전진하며 내딛는다. 아랫대는 발등걸이 한 왼발을 뒤쪽으로 걷기의 형태로 내려놓으며 다음 방어를 준비한다. 이어서 윗대는 오른발로 걸어차기를 하며 아랫대는 오른발 발등걸이로 막아준다.

1	2-1	2-2

③ Bahl-deung-guh-ree

Bahl-deung-guh-ree is a movement to block the opponent's kick by hitting the opponent's ankle as if you were performing side kick downward using the knife edge of your foot.

First, when Ah-raet-dae is ready, Wit-dae performs Guh-duh-cha-kee with his/her left foot. At this time, Ah-raet-dae lowers his/her knees slightly and waits for the opponent to kick. Second, Ah-raet-dae moves his/her weight on his/her right leg, lifting his/her left knee high towards the inside the body, considering the speed at which the opponent's Guh-duh-cha-kee is approaching, and kicks towards the opponent's ankle, as if he/she were stamping the knife edge of his/her left foot from the center of his/her body. Third, after being blocked, Wit-dae takes a step forward in the form of stepping with the right foot. Ah-raet-dae prepares for the next defense, putting down his/her left foot performed Bahl-deung-guh-ree in the form of a backward step. Wit-dae then performs Guh-duh-cha-kee with his/her right foot, while Ah-raet-dae blocks with a right foot Bahl-deung-guh-ree.

3

4-1

4-2

발등걸이를 할 때는 자신의 무릎을 가능한 높이 올린 상태에서 상대의 발목을 겨냥해 경쾌하게 찍어차야 한다. 무릎의 높이가 낮으면 상대의 발목을 정확히 차기 어렵기 때문이다. 또한 경쾌한 느낌으로 찍어준 후에는 원래대로 무릎을 튕겨 올리며 중심을 유지해 연속적인 공격 및 방어 동작을 대비해야 한다.
또한 그림 4-1과 4-2처럼 공격의 좌우를 바꾸어서 오른발 걷어차기에 왼발 발등걸이로 연습하기도 한다.

When you perform Bahl-deung-guh-ree, you should keep your knees up as high as possible and chop at the opponent's ankle lightly. If your knee is low, it is difficult to kick the opponent's ankle accurately. After chopping with the kick, you should bounce your knee back and keep the balance to prepare for continuous offensive and defensive movements.
In addition, as shown in figure 4-1 & 4-2, change the left and right sides of the attack and defense to practice right-foot Guh-duh-cha-kee with left-foot Bahl-deung-guh-ree.

④ 무릎걸이

무릎걸이는 엄지발가락과 무릎이 바깥을 향하도록 하고 무릎을 접은 채로 깎음다리처럼 다리를 높게 들어 올려 걷어차기 하는 상대의 무릎을 찍어 누르듯이 밟아 막는 동작이다. 첫 시작에 윗대는 아랫대가 왼쪽 다리부터 들어 막을 수 있도록 왼발 걷어차기를 해준다.

첫째, 아랫대의 준비가 확인되면 윗대가 왼발 걷어차기를 실시한다. 이때 아랫대는 무릎을 살짝 낮추며 상대의 걷어차기를 기다린다. 둘째, 아랫대는 오른 다리 쪽으로 체중을 이동하며 상대의 걷어차기가 다가오는 속도를 고려하여 왼무릎을 높이 들어 올려 다가오는 상대의 무릎 혹은 그 윗부분을 내려 밟아준다. 셋째, 윗대는 걷어차기가 막힌 후, 왼발을 걷기의 형태로 한발 전진하며 내딛는다. 아랫대는 무릎걸이 한 왼발을 뒤쪽으로 걷기의 형태로 내려놓으며 다음 방어를 준비한다. 이어서 윗대는 오른발로 걷어차기를 하며 아랫대는 오른발 무릎걸이로 막아준다.

1	2-1	2-2

④ Moo-reup-guh-ree

Moo-reup-guh-ree is a movement in which the big toe and knee face outward, and with the knee folded, the leg is lifted high like in Gahk-gum-dah-ree and the foot pressed down on the knee of the opponent who performed Guh-duh-cha-kee. At the beginning, Wit-dae performs Guh-duh-cha-kee with his/her left foot so that Ah-raet-dae can lift his/her left leg to block first.

First, when Ah-raet-dae is ready, Wit-dae performs Guh-duh-cha-kee with his/her left foot. At this time, Ah-raet-dae lowers his/her knees slightly and waits for the opponent to kick. Second, Ah-raet-dae moves his/her weight on his/her right leg, lifting his/her left knee high, considering the speed at which the opponent's kick is approaching, and stepping on the opponent's knee or upper part. Third, after his Guh-duh-cha-kee is blocked, Wit-dae takes a step forward with his/her left foot. Ah-raet-dae lays down the left leg in a backward step after performing Moo-reup-guh-ree, and prepares for the next defense. Wit-dae then performs Guh-duh-cha-kee with his/her right foot, while Ah-raet-dae blocks with a right-foot Moo-reup-guh-ree.

3

4-1

4-2

무릎걸이를 연습할 때 걷어차기를 하는 공격자는 무릎을 완전히 펴지 않도록 주의한다. 걷어차기 동작이 완전히 이루어져 무릎이 다 펴진 순간 무릎걸이가 닿게 되면 무릎관절에 큰 충격이 가해지기 때문이다.
무릎걸이를 하는 방어자는 상대의 무릎을 내리 밟아 막기 위해 상대의 무릎보다 훨씬 높게 자신의 무릎을 들어 올려야 한다. 특히 막는 부위가 무릎이나 그 위쪽인 만큼, 상대가 발차기를 시작하는 순간을 미리 예측하고 높게 들어 올려 묵직하게 내리 밟으며 찍어 눌러야 한다.
실전에서의 상황을 가정하여 그림 4-1, 4-2처럼 오른발로 걷어차기를 하고 왼발로 막는 연습도 실시한다.

When practicing Moo-reup-guh-ree, the attacker who performs Guh-duh-cha-kee should be careful not to fully stretch out his/her knee. This is because the knee joint will be severely impacted if Moo-reup-guh-ree touches the knee at the moment of the knee is fully extended as Guh-duh-cha-kee is fully completed.

The defender who performs Moo-reup-guh-ree should lift his/her knee much higher than that of his/her opponent to step down on his/her knee to block. In particular, since the area to block is on the knee or above, the defender should predict the moment when the opponent starts kicking, raise it high, and press it down with a heavy step.

Assuming the situation in the actual sparring, practice Guh-duh-cha-kee with your right foot and blocking with your left foot (figure 4-1 & 4-2).

(2-1) 손질

① 활개 내려막기

활개 내려막기는 옆구리를 향하는 상대의 후려차기를 활갯짓을 이용하여 위에서 아래로 손을 내리며 몸의 바깥쪽으로 쳐내어 막는 동작이다. 이때, 손목으로 상대의 발차기 공격을 휘어 감으면서 막는다는 기분으로 실시한다. 첫 시작에 윗대는 아랫대가 왼쪽 다리를 뒤로 빼고 우품 상태에서 막을 수 있게 왼발 후려차기를 해준다.

첫째, 아랫대의 준비가 확인되면 윗대가 왼발 후려차기를 실시한다. 이때 아랫대는 무릎을 살짝 낮추며 왼발을 뒤로 빼어 우품을 만들고 오른손의 손등이 왼쪽 귀 위로 가도록 들어 올려 상대의 후려차기를 기다린다. 둘째, 아랫대는 자세를 살짝 낮춘 우품 상태에서 가볍게 튕겨 일어나며 오른손 손바닥이 바깥을 향하도록 하여 오른쪽 옆구리 앞으로 휘둘러 내리며 손바닥의 장심 부위로 상대의 정강이를 찰싹 때리듯이 막아준다. 이때 오른팔은 몸통의 옆이 아닌 정면에서 오른쪽 45°앞을 향한다. 셋째, 윗대는 후려차기가 막힌 후, 왼발을 걷기의 형태로 한발 전진하며 내딛는다. 아랫대는 오른발을 뒤쪽으로 내딛어 좌품을 만들고 자세를 낮추어 다음 방어를 준비한다. 이어서 윗대는 오른발로 후려차기를 하며 아랫대는 왼손 활개 내려막기로 막아준다.

1-1

1-2

2

(2-1) Sohn-jil

① Hwahl-gay Nae-ryo-mahk-kee

Hwahl-gay Nae-ryo-mahk-kee is a movement in which you block your opponent's Hoo-ryuh-cha-kee towards your side by lowering your hand from top to bottom to knock it outside of the body, using Hwahl-get-jit. At this time, it is carried out with the wrist to prevent the opponent's kick by winding it around the limb. At the beginning, Wit-dae performs Hoo-ryuh-cha-kee with his/her left foot so that Ah-raet-dae can pull the left leg back and block the kick in Woo-poom.

First, when Ah-raet-dae is ready, Wit-dae performs Hoo-ryuh-cha-kee with his/her left foot. At this time, Ah-raet-dae lowers his/her knees slightly and pulls the left foot back to make Woo-poom, while the back of the right hand is lifted to be above the left ear to wait for the opponent's kick. Second, Ah-raet-dae springs up lightly from a slightly lowered stance of Woo-poom with the right palm facing outward, swinging it downwards in front of the right side to block the opponent's shin (as if you are giving a slap on the shin) with the center of the palm. At this time, the right arm faces 45° to the right from the front, not from the side of the torso. Third, after his Hoo-ryuh-cha-kee is blocked, Wit-dae takes a step forward with his/her left foot. Ah-raet-dae takes a back step with his/her right foot to form Jwa-poom and lowers the posture to prepare for the next defense. Wit-dae then performs Hoo-ryuh-cha-kee with his/her right foot, while Ah-raet-dae blocks with a left-hand Hwahl-gay Nae-ryo-mahk-kee.

3

4-1

4-2

막음질의 경우는 방어자가 먼저 움직여 막는 동작을 완전히 익힐 수 있도록 공격자가 배려를 해야 한다. 그리고 택견의 동작들은 왼발이 먼저 움직이는 것을 기준으로 한다. 따라서 손을 활용한 막음질을 연습할 때는 방어자가 왼발을 먼저 뒤로 빼는 자세 즉, 우품을 만들 수 있도록 공격자가 맞춰주어야 한다. 그래서 활개 내려막기에서는 공격자가 왼발 후려차기를 하고 방어자가 왼발을 뒤로 뺀 우품에서 오른손 활개 내려막기를 하게 되는 것이다.
손질을 이용한 막기는 자세를 낮춘 좌품이나 우품에서 튕겨 일어나며 하게 된다. 이때 중요한 점은 힘으로 상대의 공격을 그 자리에 막아 세우는 느낌이 아니라 일어서는 탄력을 이용해 툭 털어내듯이 막아야 한다는 것이다. 즉, 상대의 공격을 멈춰 세우는 게 아니라 팔로 이루어진 스프링으로 충격을 해소한 후, 털어내듯이 상대의 힘을 흘리는 느낌으로 막아야 한다.
또한 손질을 이용한 막음질에서 중요한 것은 막는 위치가 자신의 몸통 바로 앞이나 옆이 아닌 더 먼 곳에서 이루어져야 한다는 것이다. 달리 말하자면 어깨를 기준으로 복부의 앞쪽와 옆쪽으로 45°의 가상 공간을 만들고 그 공간을 막아주어야 한다는 것이다. 이는 혼자익히기에서 배웠던 45°의 활개 움직임이 막음질에서도 그대로 살아나야 한다는 뜻이다. 몸에서 너무 가까운 위치에서 상대의 공격을 막고자 하면 조금이라도 실수가 생겼을 때, 상대의 공격이 자신의 몸에 닿아 충격이 전달되기 때문이다.
내려막기를 실시하는 팔은 팔꿈치가 완전히 펴지지 않도록 주의해야 한다. 팔이 완전히 펴진 상태에서 상대의 발차기가 팔꿈치에 맞으면 작은 충격에도 관절에 부상이 올 수 있기 때문이다. 또한 팔을 어깨에서부터 안쪽으로 비틀어 팔의 옆 뼈가 아닌 전완근 쪽으로 방어할 수 있도록 해야 한다. 이는 상대의 공격을 힘으로 막아 세우는 것이 아니라 흘려내듯이 튕겨낸다는 관점에서 뼈를 사용하기 보다는 근육을 이용해 충격을 흡수하기 위함이다.

In the case of Mahk-eum-jil, the attacker should be considerate of the defender so that he/she can fully master the movement of the defense first. Taekgyeon's movements are based on the left foot moving first. Therefore, when practicing Mahk-eum-jil using hands, the attacker should be considerate so that the defender can pull his/her left foot back first to make the stance of Woo-poom. So in Hwahl-gay Nae-ryo-mahk-kee, the attacker performs a left-foot Hoo-ryuh-cha-kee and the defender performs a right-hand Hwahl-gay Nae-ryo-mahk-kee from the stance of Woo-poom with his left foot pulled back.

Blocking using Sohn-jil takes place by springing up from a lowered stance of Jwa-poom or Woo-poom. The important thing is that we should use the momentum of the springing up to block as if you are shaking off the opponent's attack instead of simply blocking. In other words, instead of stopping the opponent's attack, you should relieve the shock with springing of the arm and then shaking it off with a feeling of shedding off the opponent's strength.

Also, what's important in Mahk-eum-jil using Sohn-jil is that the blocking position should be made not just in front of or next to your body, but in a further place. In other words, you should create a virtual space of 45° to the front and side of your abdomen based on your shoulders, and defend that space. This means that the 45°Hwahl-gay movement, which was learned from Hone-jah Ik-hee-kee, should also be shown in Mahk-eum-jil. This is because if you make even a small mistake when you try to block your opponent's attack from a position too close to your body, the opponent's attack will touch your body and deliver a shock to your system.

You should be careful not to fully out stretch your arm when you perform Nae-ryo-mahk-kee. This is because if the opponent's kick is hit by the elbow while the arm is fully extended, the elbow can be injured even in a small impact. The arm should also be twisted inward from the shoulder so that it can be defended with forearm muscles, not by the side bones of the arm. This is not to block the opponent's attack with force, but to absorb the shock using muscles rather than using bones from the point of view of deflecting the attack away.

② 곁들어 내려막기

곁들어 내려막기는 옆구리를 향하는 상대의 째차기나 후려차기를 두 손을 모두 이용하여 한손은 얼굴을, 한손은 옆구리를 방어하는 동작이다. 이때, 옆구리를 막는 손은 활개 내려막기의 동작을 취하고, 얼굴을 막는 손은 가로막기의 형태를 기본으로 손바닥이 얼굴을 막을 수 있도록 밀어준다. 첫 시작에 윗대는 아랫대가 왼쪽 다리를 뒤로 빼고 우품 상태에서 막을 수 있게 오른발 째차기를 해준다.

첫째, 아랫대의 준비가 확인되면 윗대가 오른발 째차기를 실시한다. 이때 아랫대는 무릎을 살짝 낮추며 왼발을 뒤로 빼어 우품을 만들고 왼손과 오른손을 얼굴 앞에 교차시켜 들어 올린 채로 상대의 째차기를 기다린다. 두 손 중 오른손이 바깥쪽으로 위치해야 오른쪽 옆구리를 방어하기 위한 내려막기 동작이 수월하다. 둘째, 아랫대는 자세를 살짝 낮춘 우품 상태에서 가볍게 튕겨 일어나며 오른 손으로 활개 내려막기를 해 상대의 째차기를 막아준다. 왼손은 오른쪽 볼 앞에서 얼굴로 향할지 모르는 발차기를 손바닥으로 막아주는 동작을 취한다. 셋째, 윗대는 째차기가 막힌 후, 오른발을 걷기의 형태로 한발 전진하며 내딛는다. 아랫대는 오른발을 뒤쪽으로 내딛어 좌품을 만들고 자세를 낮추어 다음 방어를 준비한다. 이때 얼굴을 막은 왼손을 왼쪽 바깥으로 활갯짓 치돌리기 하듯이 회전시키며 내려막기 한 오른손을 밀어올려 얼굴 앞에서 자연스럽게 교차되도록 들어올린다. 이어서 윗대는 왼발로 째차기를 하며 아랫대는 오른손으로는 가로막기의 변형된 형태로 얼굴을, 왼손은 활개 내려막기로 옆구리를 막아준다. 경우에 따라 후려차기로 연습하기도 한다.

1-1

1-2

2-1

② Gyeot-deul-uh Nae-ryo-mahk-kee

Kyeot-deul-uh Nae-ryo-mahk-kee is a movement to defend the opponent's Jae-cha-kee or Hoo-ryuh-cha-kee against your side, using both hands. One hand defends the face and the other defends the side. At this time, the hand that blocks the side takes the action of Hwahl-gay Nae-ryo-mahk-kee, while the hand that blocks the face pushes the palm to block the face in the form of Gah-roh-mahk-kee. At the start, Wit-dae kicks a right foot Jae-cha-kee so that Ah-raet-dae can block it in a stance of Woo-poom with his/her left leg pulled back.

First, once Ah-raet-dae is ready, Wit-dae performs right foot Jae-cha-kee. At this time, Ah-raet-dae lowers his/her knees slightly and pulls his/her left foot back to make Woo-poom, and with his/her left and right hands crossed in front of his/her face, waits for the opponent to perform Jae-cha-kee. It is easier to do Nae-ryo-mahk-kee to defend the right side only when the right hand is positioned outwards of the two hands. Second, Ah-raet-dae is lightly spring up from Woo-poom, and performs Hwahl-gay Nae-ryo-mahk-kee with his/her right hand to block the opponent's Jae-cha-kee. His/her left hand takes an action to block the kick that may come to the face with the palm of the hand to block in front of his/her right cheek. Third, after the kick is blocked, Wit-dae takes a step forward with the right foot. Ah-raet-dae steps his/her right foot back to form Jwa-poom and lowers his/her posture to prepare for the next defense. At this time, the left hand that covers the face is rotated outwards to the left like Hwahl-get-jit Chee-dohl-lee-kee, and the lower

2-2

3-1

3-2

두 손 곁들어 내려막기는 한쪽 손에 다른 손이 '곁들여져' 막기 때문에 곁들어 내려막기라고 부른다는 의견과 막는 동작 직전에 얼굴 앞에 두 손을 교차시킬 때 '겨드랑이(곁)를 들어 올려' 준비하기 때문에 곁들어 내려막기라고 불린다는 두 가지 의견이 있다. 두 가지 의견 모두 나름의 타당성을 지니고 있어 어느 의견이 정확한지는 애매하며 두 가지 모두 설명하는 경우가 많다.
곁들어 내려막기를 한번 한 후, 얼굴 쪽을 막은 손을 활갯짓 치돌리기의 형태로 돌려 반대편의 옆구리를 막은 손목 밑으로 집어넣어 얼굴 앞으로 끌어올리며 다음 동작을 준비하는 것은 활갯짓의 흐름 속에서 연속적인 방어동작을 연습한다는 데 의미가 있다. 과거에는 이러한 연속동작 없이 그냥 얼굴 앞으로 양 손을 들어 올려 연습하기도 하였는데 지금의 형태가 보다 원래의 동작에 가까우며 '활갯짓의 연장선 속에서의 방어 동작'이라는 의미에도 적합하다고 볼 수 있을 것이다.
곁들어 내려막기 동작을 수련하는 과정에서 흔히, 얼굴을 막는 손의 역할을 대충하고 넘어가는 경우가 있다. 그러나 두 손 곁들어 내려막기의 기본 공격이 째차기라는 것은 발차기의 궤적을 통해 옆구리를 노리는 것인지 얼굴을 노리는 것인지 파악하기 어려운 상황을 가정하는 것이라 볼 수 있다. 째차기는 발차기가 나오는 중간에 무릎의 각을 변화시켜 변화를 주기 쉽기 때문이다. 따라서 곁들어 내려막기를 연습할 때는 이러한 상황을 감안하여 얼굴을 막는 손에도 반드시 집중하여 온전한 동작을 수련할 수 있도록 하여야 한다.

right hand that performed Nae-ryo-mahk-kee is pushed up so that it naturally crosses in front of the face. Then, Wit-dae performs Jae-cha-kee with his/her left foot, Ah-raet-dae defends the face with the right hand in the form of modified Gah-roh-mahk-kee, and the left hand defends the side with Hwahl-gay Nae-ryo-mahk-kee. In some cases, Hoo-ryuh-cha-kee is made instead of Jae-cha-kee.

There are two opinions that why Doo-sohn Kyeot-deul-uh Nae-ryo-mahk-kee is called like that. One is because one hand sides with the other when they block an attack, and the other is because it's prepared to raise the arms when you cross your hands in front of your face just before the blocking movement. Both opinions have their own validity, so it is unclear which ones are correct, so both are often explained.

After doing Kyeot-deul-uh Nae-ryo-mahk-kee, turn the hand that defended the face in the form of Hwahl-get-jit Chee-dohl-lee-kee and put it under the wrist that defended the side of the other side to bring it up to the front of the face and prepare for the next move. This is meaningful in practicing a series of defensive movements in the course of Hwahl-get-jit. In the past, people practiced with both hands raised in front of their faces without such continuous movements, but the current form is closer to the original movement and is suitable for the meaning of 'defensive action in the extension of Hwahl-get-jit'.

In the course of training Kyeot-deul-uh Nae-ryo-mahk-kee, there are often cases where the role of the hand defending the face is roughly played. However, the fact that the basic attack on the defense action of Doo-sohn Kyeot-deul-uh Nae-ryo-mahk-kee is a Jae-cha-kee assumed to be a difficult situation to determine whether the kick is aimed at the side or the face through the trajectory of the kick. This is because Jae-cha-kee is easy to alter if you change the angle of the knee in the middle of the kick. Therefore, when practicing Kyeot-deul-uh Nae-ryo-mahk-kee, it is necessary to focus on the hand that defends the face so that the entire movement should be trained.

③ 활개 발회목잡기

활개 발회목잡기는 복부를 향하는 상대의 는질러차기를 잡아대기의 형태로 방어하며 상대의 발목을 잡아채는 동작이다. 첫 시작에 윗대는 아랫대가 왼쪽 다리를 뒤로 빼고 우품 상태에서 막을 수 있게 왼발 는질러차기를 해준다.

첫째, 아랫대의 준비가 확인되면 윗대가 왼발 는질러차기를 실시한다. 이때 아랫대는 무릎을 살짝 낮추며 왼발을 뒤로 빼어 우품을 만들고 오른손을 오른쪽 45°정면 아래방향으로 뻗어 잡아대기를 준비한 채로 상대의 는질러차기를 기다린다. 둘째, 아랫대는 가볍게 튕겨 일어나며 허리의 회전을 이용하여 는질러차기 한 상대의 왼 발목 바깥쪽을 오른손 손목의 안쪽을 이용하여 튕기듯 왼편 몸 바깥쪽으로 걷어낸다. 그리고 상대의 다리를 몸 바깥으로 충분히 걷어낸 후 손목을 접어 상대의 발목을 잡아챈다. 셋째, 아랫대가 잡아챈 발목을 놓아주면 윗대는 왼발을 걷기의 형태로 한발 전진하며 내딛는다. 아랫대는 오른발을 뒤쪽으로 내딛어 좌품을 만들고 자세를 낮추어 다음 방어를 준비한다. 이어서 윗대는 오른발로 는질러차기를 하며 아랫대는 왼손으로 잡아대기를 하며 는질러차기는 막은 후 잡아챈다.

1-1

1-2

2

③ Hwahl-gay Bahl-hoe-mohk-jahp-kee

Hwahl-gay Bahl-hoe-mohk-jahp-kee is a movement that grabs the ankle and defends against the opponent's Neun-jil-luh-cha-kee toward the abdomen in the form of Jahb-ah-dae-kee. At the start, Wit-dae performs Neun-jil-luh-cha-kee with his/her left foot so that Ah-raet-dae can block it in a stance of Woo-poom with his/her left leg pulled back.

First, once Ah-raet-dae is ready, Wit-dae performs Neun-jil-luh-cha-kee with his/her left foot. At this time, Ah-raet-dae lowers his/her knees slightly and pull his/her left foot back to make Woo-poom, and waits for the opponent to kick Neun-jil-luh-cha-kee with his/her right hand extended downwards 45° to the right to be ready for Jahb-ah-dae-kee. Second, Ah-raet-dae springs up lightly and uses the rotation of the waist to hit the outside of the opponent's left ankle, which performed Neun-jil-luh-cha-kee, and deflects (parries) to the left using the inside of the right wrist. Then, after sufficiently moving the opponent's leg away from the body to the left, folds his/her wrist to grab the opponent's ankle. Third, if Ah-raet-dae let the ankle go, Wit-dae takes a step forward with his/her left foot. Ah-raet-dae takes his/her right foot back to form Jwa-poom and lowers the stance to prepare for the next defense. Wit-dae is then performs Neun-jil-luh-cha-kee with his/her right foot, and Ah-raet-dae blocks the Neun-jil-luh-cha-kee with a left hand Jahb-ah-dae-kee and then snatches it.

3

next-1

next-2

활개 발회목잡기에서 중요한 것은 허리의 회전을 이용하여 상대의 는질러차기를 몸 바깥으로 걷어내는 것이다. 팔의 힘만으로는 상대의 공격을 충분히 치워내지 못하므로 밀려들어오는 상대의 발차기에 충격을 받게 된다.
또한 회목잡기를 할 때에는 무엇보다 상대의 발차기를 자신의 몸통 바깥으로 우선 걷어낸 후, 잡아채야 한다는 것을 반드시 지켜야 한다. 연습과정에서는 공격자가 는질러차기에 충분히 힘을 싣지 않아 방어자가 발차기를 몸 바깥으로 충분히 걷어내지 않고 잡아채도 발차기에 맞지 않게 된다. 이런 경우 좋지 않은 습관이 몸에 익을 수 있으므로 주의해야 한다.
활개 발회목잡기를 연습할 때는 상대의 다리 바깥쪽을 밀어 걷어내고 잡아챔으로서 방어 후 방어자의 몸이 공격자의 바깥쪽에 서게 된다, 이는 안쪽에서 잡을 경우 방어자의 몸이 상대의 품안으로 들어가 오히려 눌리게 될 수 있기 때문이다. 실전에서 안쪽과 바깥쪽을 구분하지 못하고 잡아대기를 했을 경우에는 이점을 기억하여 안쪽에서 잡았을 때, 상대에게 눌리지 않도록 하여야 한다. 물론 활개 발회목잡기가 안정감 있게 마무리 된 후, 상대의 중심을 방어자의 의지대로 이동시키며 연속 공격을 위해 상대의 품안으로 들어가는 것은 전혀 문제가 되지 않는다.
발회목잡기로 상대의 발질을 잡을 때는 엄지손가락까지 모두 모아서 손바닥 전체로 잡아채야한다. 엄지손가락이 벌어져 있으면 손가락을 다칠 수도 있다. 또한 상대의 발차기를 주먹 쥐듯이 잡는 것이 아니라 손바닥 전체로 감아버리는 형태가 되어야 한다. 왜냐하면 상대의 발차기가 어디로 들어올지 알 수가 없으므로 크게 원을 그리듯이 상대의 발차기를 잡아채야하기 때문이다. 즉 잡아대기를 연습할 때와 동일한 형태가 되어야 한다.

What is important in Hwahl-gay Bahl-hoe-mohk-jahp-kee is to use the rotation of the waist to push away the opponent's Neun-jil-luh-cha-kee from the body. The strength of the arm alone does not totally newtralize the opponent's attack enough, so you will be affected by the rushing opponent's kick.

Also, when you do Hoe-mohk-jahp-kee, it is important to keep in mind that the opponent's kick should be removed from the body first before snatching it. During the practice, the attacker does not put enough power to his/her Neun-jil-luh-cha-kee, so even if the defender catches the kick without properly removing it from the body, he/she does not get hit by the kick. In this case, you should be careful as bad habits may develop.

When practicing Hwahl-gay Bahl-hoe-mohk-jahp-kee, the defender pushes the outside of the opponent's leg out then snatches it, so after the defense, the defender stands outside of the attacker. This is because if the defender grabs the leg from the inside, the defender's body can enter the opponent's arms and be squashed by the opponent. If you cannot distinguish between the inside and the outside when you perform Jahb-ah-dae-kee in actual sparring, remember this and make sure that you are not be squashed by the opponent when you grab it from the inside. Of course, it is not a problem at all to move the opponent's center to the will of the defender and enter the opponent's arms for a series of attacks after the Hwahl-gay Bahl-hoe-mohk-jahp-kee has been completed in a stable manner.

When you grab the opponent's Bahl-jil with Bahl-hoe-mohk-jahp-kee, you have to close all your fingers up including your thumb and grab it with the entire palm of your hand. If your thumb is open, you can hurt your finger. Also, it should be shaped as if you are wrapping the opponent's kicks with the whole palm of the hand, rather than clenching it like a fist. This is because you don't know where the opponent's kick will come to, so you have to grab the opponent's kick as if you are making a big circle. That is, it should be the same form as when you practice Jahb-ah-dae-kee.

④ 활개 바닥으로 막기

활개 바닥으로 막기는 낮게 들러오는 상대의 걷어차기를 활개 바닥, 즉 손바닥으로 막는 동작이다. 첫 시작에 윗대는 아랫대가 왼쪽 다리를 뒤로 빼고 우품 상태에서 막을 수 있게 왼발 걷어차기를 해준다.

첫째, 아랫대의 준비가 확인되면 윗대가 왼발 걷어차기를 실시한다. 이때 아랫대는 무릎을 살짝 낮추며 왼발을 뒤로 빼어 우품을 만들고 오른손을 오른쪽 겨드랑이 앞으로 끌어올린 채로 상대의 걷어차기를 기다린다. 둘째, 아랫대는 가볍게 튕겨 일어나며 허리를 살짝 숙이고 엉덩이를 뒤로 조금 빼며 걷어차기 한 상대의 왼 발목을 오른손 바닥으로 내리 누르듯이 막는다. 이때 손모양은 칼재기와 같이 엄지만 벌린 채로 손아귀 바닥으로 막아준다. 셋째, 윗대는 걷어차기가 막히면 왼발을 걷기의 형태로 한발 전진하며 내딛는다. 아랫대는 오른발을 뒤쪽으로 내딛어 좌품을 만들고 자세를 낮추며 왼손을 겨드랑이로 끌어올려 다음 방어를 준비한다. 이어서 윗대는 오른발로 걷어차기를 하며 아랫대는 왼손으로 활개 바닥으로 막기를 한다.

1-1

1-2

2-1

④ Hwahl-gay Ba-dahk-eu-roh Mahk-kee

Hwahl-gay Ba-dahk-eu-ro Mahk-kee is a move that blocks the opponent's Guh-duh-cha-kee, which is a type of low kick, with the palm of the hand (Hwahl-gay Ba-dahk). At the start, Wit-dae performs Guh-duh-cha-kee with his/her left foot so that Ah-raet-dae can block it in Woo-poom with his/her left leg pulled back.

First, once Ah-raet-dae is ready, Wit-dae performs Guh-duh-cha-kee with his/her left foot. At this time, Ah-raet-dae lowers his/her knees slightly and pull his/her left foot back to make Woo-poom, and waits for the opponent to kick Guh-duh-cha-kee with his/her right hand raised forward in front of his/her right armpit. Second, Ah-raet-dae springs up lightly and slightly lowering the waist and pulling the hips back at the same time, then blocking the opponent's left ankle as if pressing down on the floor with the palm of the right hand. At this time, the hand is shaped like Kahl-jae-kee, with only the thumbs open. Third, after his Guh-duh-cha-kee is blocked, Wit-dae" takes a step forward with his/her left foot. Ah-raet-dae takes a back step with his/her right foot to form Jwa-poom and lower the posture and raise the left hand to the armpit to prepare for the next defense. Wit-dae then performs Guh-duh-cha-kee with his/her right foot, while Ah-raet-dae blocks with a left-hand Hwahl-gay Ba-dahk-eu-ro Mahk-kee.

2-2	3	next

활개 바닥으로 막기에서 주의할 점은 상대의 발목을 내리누를 때, 팔의 움직임이 일직선이 되지 않아야 한다는 것이다. 스트레이트처럼 일직선으로 손이 뻗어질 경우, 상대의 다리 힘에 밀려 팔꿈치에 무리가 갈수 있기 때문이다. 따라서 손을 위에서 아래로 휘둘러 책상을 내려치듯 상대의 발목을 막아주어야 한다.
손의 모양은 칼재기처럼 엄지손가락만 벌린 채, 나머지 네 손가락은 모아주어야 한다. 엄지손가락을 벌린 손아귀가 정면을 향하도록 하여 손바닥으로 상대의 발목을 찰싹 때리며 누르는 느낌으로 동작을 실시한다.

One thing to be careful about in Hwahl-gay Ba-dahk-eu-ro Mahk-kee is that the arm's movement should not be in a straight line when you press down on the opponent's ankle. This is because if your arms are stretched out in a straight line, you can strain your elbow due to the opponent's leg force. Therefore, you should swing your hands from top to bottom to block the opponent's ankles as if you are hitting the desk.
The shape of the hand should be like Kahl-jae-kee," with only the thumb open, while the other four fingers should be gathered together. Make the thumb-opened grip face the front, and use the palm of the hand to hit the opponent's ankle and push it.

⑤ 두손 내어막기

두손 내어막기는 복부를 향하는 상대의 걷어차기를 X자 형태로 엇갈린 두 손의 손바닥을 이용하여 눌러 막는 동작이다. 첫 시작에 윗대는 아랫대가 왼쪽 다리를 뒤로 빼고 우품 상태에서 막을 수 있게 오른발 걷어차기를 해준다.

첫째, 아랫대의 준비가 확인되면 윗대가 오른발 걷어차기를 실시한다. 이때 아랫대는 무릎을 살짝 낮추며 왼발을 뒤로 빼어 우품을 만들고 두 손을 양쪽 겨드랑이 앞으로 끌어올린 채로 상대의 걷어차기를 기다린다. 둘째, 아랫대는 가볍게 튕겨 일어나며 엉덩이를 뒤로 조금 뺀 상태에서, 두 손을 X자 형태로 교차시키며 전방 45°아래로 밀어 내린다. 이때 두 손의 손바닥을 지면을 바라보아야 하며 엇갈린 두 손의 장심 또는 손목 안쪽 부위로 상대의 발목을 내리 눌러 막아준다. 셋째, 윗대는 걷어차기가 막힌 후, 왼발을 걷기의 형태로 한발 전진하며 내딛는다. 아랫대는 오른발을 뒤쪽으로 내딛어 좌품을 만들고 자세를 낮추며 두 손을 겨드랑이 앞으로 올려 다음 방어를 준비한다. 이어서 윗대는 왼발로 걷어차기를 하며 아랫대는 좌품 상태에서 두손 내어막기를 한다.

1-1	1-2	2

⑤ Doo-sohn Nae-uh-mahk-kee

Doo-sohn Nae-uh-mahk-kee is a movement to block the opponent's Guh-duh-cha-kee toward the abdomen using the palms of two hands which are crossed in an X-shaped form. At the start, Wit-dae performs Guh-duh-cha-kee with his/her right foot so that Ah-raet-dae can block it in a stance of Woo-poom with his/her left leg pulled back.

First, once Ah-rat-dae is ready, Wit-dae performs Guh-duh-cha-kee with his/her right foot. At this time, Ah-raet-dae lowers his/her knees slightly and pull his/her left foot back to make Woo-poom, and waits for the opponent to kick Guh-duh-cha-kee with his/her both hands raised forward in front of his/her armpits. Second, Ah-raet-dae springs up lightly and pulls the hips back a little, then cross his/her hands in an X shape and push them down the front 45°. At this time, the palm of the two hands should be facing the ground, and the opponent's ankle should be pressed down to be blocked with the inside of the wrist or the center of the palms of the two crossed hands. Third, after his Guh-duh-cha-kee is blocked, Wit-dae takes a step forward with his/her left foot. Ah-raet-dae takes a back step with his/her right foot to form Jwa-poom and lower the posture and raise both hands in front of the armpits to prepare for the next defense. Wit-dae then performs Guh-duh-cha-kee with his/her left foot, while Ah-raet-dae blocks with Doo-sohn Nae-uh-mahk-keein the stance of Jwa-poom.

3

next-1

next-2

두손 내어막기를 할 때 우선 확인해야 할 것은 방어를 하는 순간 허리를 뒤로 살짝 빼며 허리를 약간 숙여주는 것이다. 이는 활개 바닥으로 막기에서와 유사한 자세인데 상대의 걷어차기로부터 급소(낭심)를 보호하기 위한 것이다.
두 번째 확인 사항은 막는 두 손의 손바닥이 지면을 향해 수평으로 펼쳐져야 한다는 것이다. 이는 손바닥의 장심이나 손목의 안쪽으로 상대의 걷어차기를 막을 수 있도록 하는 것이다. 만약 손날이 바닥을 향하게 된다면, 상대의 걷어차기를 손 옆의 뼈나 손목의 뼈로 막게 되어 상당히 큰 충격과 부상을 얻을 수 있다.
두손 내어막기는 나중에 두 손으로 상대의 발목을 엇갈리게 잡아 비틀어 넘어뜨리는 반격으로 활용하기도 한다.

The first thing to check when you do Doo-sohn Nae-uh-mahk-kee is to slightly pull your hips back and bend your waist a little when you defend. This posture is similar to that of Hwahl-gay Ba-dahk-eu-ro Mahk-kee to protect the groin from the opponent's Guh-duh-cha-kee.
The second thing to check is that the palms of the two blocking hands should be spread horizontally toward the ground. This allows you to block the opponent's Guh-duh-cha-kee in the center of the palms or the inside of your wrist. If the knife edges of the hand are facing the ground, you will block the opponent's Guh-duh-cha-kee with the bones of the hands or wrists, which can cause quite a shock and injury.
Doo-sohn Nae-uh-mahk-kee is also used as a counterattack in which the opponent's ankle is grabbed with two hands that are crossed, then twisted and knocked down.

⑥ 세워막기

세워막기는 목으로 들어오는 상대의 덜미잽이를 팔뚝의 바깥쪽으로 막는 동작이다. 첫 시작에 윗대는 아랫대가 왼쪽 다리를 뒤로 빼고 우품 상태에서 오른손으로 막을 수 있게 오른손과 오른발로 덜미잽이를 해준다.

첫째, 아랫대의 준비가 확인되면 윗대가 오른발을 정면으로 길게 내딛으며 아랫대의 목을 향해 오른손 가로밀기(덜미잽이)를 실시한다. 이때 아랫대는 무릎을 살짝 낮추며 왼발을 뒤로 빼어 우품을 만들고 오른손을 왼쪽 어깨 앞으로 끌어올리며 상대의 공격을 기다린다. 둘째, 아랫대는 가볍게 튕겨 일어나며 팔꿈치를 축으로 팔뚝을 바깥쪽으로 돌려 상대의 덜미잽이를 팔뚝 바깥부위의 근육으로 막아준다. 이때 방어를 하는 팔은 손목이 눈높이 정도에 오도록 한다. 셋째, 윗대는 덜미잽이가 막히면 오른발을 뒤로 당겼다가 걷기의 형태로 한발 전진하며 내딛는다. 아랫대는 오른발을 뒤쪽으로 내딛어 좌품을 만들고 자세를 낮추며 왼손을 오른쪽 어깨 앞으로 올려 다음 방어를 준비한다. 이어서 윗대는 왼쪽 덜미잽이를 하며 아랫대는 왼손으로 세워막기를 한다.

1-1	1-2	2

⑥ Say-wuh-mahk-kee

Say-wuh-mahk-kee is a movement that blocks the opponent's Duhl-mee-jae-bee coming into the neck with the outside of the forearm. At the start, Wit-dae performs Duhl-mee-jae-bee with his/her right hand and right foot so that Ah-raet-dae can block it with his/her right hand in a stance of Woo-poom with his/her left leg pulled back.

First, once Ah-raet-dae is ready, Wit-dae will take a long step forward with his/her right foot and perform Gah-roh-mil-kee (Duhl-mee-jae-bee) toward the neck of Ah-raet-dae with his/her right hand. At this time, Ah-raet-dae lowers his/her knees slightly and pull his/her left foot back to make Woo-poom, and waits for the opponent's attack with his/her right hand raised forward in front of his/her left shoulder. Second, Ah-raet-dae springs up lightly and turns his/her forearm outward to block the opponent's Duhl-mee-jae-bee with muscles on the outside of the forearm. At this time, the wrist of the arm that is defending should be at the eye level. Third, when his Duhl-mee-jae-bee is blocked, Wit-dae pulls back his/her right foot then takes a step forward. Ah-raet-dae takes a back step with his/her right foot to form Jwa-poom and lowers the posture, while raising the left hand in front of his/her right shoulder to prepare for the next defense. Wit-dae then performs Duhl-mee-jae-bee with his/her left hand, while Ah-raet-dae blocks with Say-wuh-mahk-keewith his/her left hand.

3-1

3-2

next

세워막기를 할 때, 팔뚝의 위치는 막음새에서 배운 자세 그대로 유지하도록 한다. 대개 상대의 공격이 다가오면 몸이 움츠려들어 자신의 눈 바로 앞에서 혹은 팔뚝 높이가 낮아진 상태에서 막게 되는데, 이 경우 상대의 공격이 방어한 팔을 밀고 들어올 수 있으므로 주의한다.
또한 상대의 공격을 걷어내기 위해 팔뚝을 과도하게 밖으로 밀어내지 않도록 한다. 막음새에서 배운 위치에서 팔을 멈추지 않고 상대의 공격을 밀어내려 할 경우, 공격 박자를 속이는 동작에 걸리게 되면 팔이 과도하게 벌어져 상대의 공격을 허용하게 된다. 따라서 세워막기를 할 때는 정확한 위치에서 동작을 멈추고 상대의 공격을 기다리는 연습도 이루어져야 한다.
세워막기 역시 막음질의 기본개념-튕기듯이 흘려낸다-에 걸맞게 튕겨 일어나는 무릎의 탄력을 팔까지 전달하여 목으로 향하는 상대의 공격이 자신의 팔에 닿았을 때, 위쪽으로 밀려나가는 느낌이 나도록 집중하여 실시한다.
세워막기의 공격자는 나아가며 익히기의 동작처럼 덜미잽이(가로밀기)를 최대한 깊숙이 해주고, 그 다음 공격으로 이어질 때는 나아가며 익히기에서의 품밟기 형태로 발을 끌어들였다가 걷기로 놓고 다음 공격을 실시해야 한다. 그러지 않으면 방어자가 세워막기를 정확히 습득할 수가 없다. 치막기와 가로막기에서도 동일하게 깊숙이 공격해 주어야 한다.

When performing Say-wuh-mahk-kee, keep the position of the forearm as it was learned in Mahk-eum-sae. Usually, when an opponent's attack approaches, the defender often shrinks and blocks it right in front of his/her eyes or with his/her forearm lowered. In this case, care must be taken as the opponent's attack may push and come through the weak defending arm.

Also, don't push your forearm too far out to get rid of the opponent's attack. If you try to push the opponent's attack without stopping the arm from the position you learned in Mahk-eum-sae, your rhythm will be broken by your opponent's timing, which will result in excessive spread of the arm and allow the opponent's attack. Therefore, when you do Say-wuh-mahk-kee, you have to practice stopping the movement at the correct position and waiting for the opponent's attack.

When you perform Say-wuh-mahk-kee, make sure to deliver the elasticity from the knee that springs up to your arm to suit the basic concept of Mahk-eum-jil, which is to bounce it out. So when the opponent's attack on your neck touches your arm, focus and defend it so that you feel like it is being pushed upwards.

The attacker of Say-wuh-mahk-kee should make his/her Duhl-mee-jae-bee (Gah-roh-mil-kee) as deep as possible as the movement of Nah-ah-gah-myuh Ik-hee-kee. If the attack leads to the next attack, the foot should be drawn in the form of Poom-bahl-kee of Nah-ah-gah-myuh Ik-hee-kee and then put down in Guht-kee. Then the next attack should be carried out. Otherwise, the defender will not be able to acquire Say-wuh-mahk-kee accurately. He/she must attack deeply in the same way in the Chee-mahk-kee and Gah-roh-mahk-kee.

⑦ 치막기

치막기는 목을 향하는 상대의 덜미걸이를 활개 치돌리기의 형태로 막는 동작이다. 첫 시작에 윗대는 아랫대가 왼쪽 다리를 뒤로 빼고 우품 상태에서 막을 수 있게 왼손과 왼발로 덜미걸이를 해준다.

첫째, 아랫대의 준비가 확인되면 윗대가 왼발을 멀리 내딛으며 왼손으로 세워밀기(덜미걸이)를 실시한다. 이때 아랫대는 무릎을 살짝 낮추며 왼발을 뒤로 빼어 우품을 만들고 오른손으로 타원을 그리며 왼쪽 어깨 앞으로 들어올려 상대의 덜미걸이를 기다린다. 둘째, 아랫대는 가볍게 튕겨 일어나며 왼쪽 어깨 앞에 있던 손을 자신의 이마 45° 상방으로 밀어 올려 상대의 덜미잽이를 막아준다. 이때, 손바닥이 하늘을 향하도록 팔뚝을 틀어주어 손목 안쪽 근육으로 방어한다. 셋째, 윗대는 덜미걸이가 막히면 왼발을 뒤로 당겼다가 걷기의 형태로 한발 전진하며 내딛는다. 아랫대는 오른발을 뒤쪽으로 내딛어 좌품을 만들고 자세를 낮추며 왼손을 오른쪽 어깨 앞으로 올려 다음 방어를 준비한다. 이어서 윗대는 오른쪽 덜미걸이를 하며 아랫대는 왼손으로 세워막기를 한다.

1-1	1-2	1-3

⑦ Chee-mahk-kee

Chee-mahk-kee is a move that blocks the opponent's Duhl-mee-guh-ree toward the neck with Hwahl-gay Chee-dohl-lee-kee. At the start, Wit-dae performs Duhl-mee-guh-ree with his/her left hand and left foot so that Ah-raet-dae can block it in a stance of Woo-poom with his/her left leg pulled back.

First, once Ah-raet-dae is ready, Wit-dae will take a long step forward with his/her left foot and perform Say-wuh-mil-kee (Duhl-mee-guh-ree) with his/her left hand. At this time, Ah-raet-dae lowers his/her knees slightly and pull his/her left foot back to make Woo-poom, and waits for the opponent's Duhl-mee-guh-ree with his/her right hand raised in an ellipse to the front of his/her left shoulder. Second, Ah-raet-dae springs up lightly and pushes the hand in front of the left shoulder up to 45° above his/her forehead to block the opponent's Duhl-mee-guh-ree. At this time, turn the forearm so that the palm faces the sky to defend the attack with the inner muscles of the wrist. Third, when his Duhl-mee-guh-ree is blocked, Wit-dae pulls back his/her left foot then takes a step forward. Ah-raet-dae takes a back step with his/her right foot to form Jwa-poom and lowers the posture, while raising the left hand in front of his/her right shoulder to prepare for the next defense. Wit-dae then performs Duhl-mee-guh-ree with his/her right hand, while Ah-raet-dae blocks with Say-wuh-mahk-keewith his/her left hand.

2	3	next

치막기는 활개 치돌리며 품밟기의 활개짓이 자신의 이마 앞에서 멈추는 형태로 방어를 해준다. 이때, 손목이 자신의 이마 위에서 45° 앞쪽에 오도록 멈춰주어야 한다. 상대의 공격을 걷어내고자 휘두르게 되면 적절한 위치에서 벗어나 자신의 얼굴이 공격에 노출된다. 또한 초보의 경우 팔을 너무 위로 올려 손목의 위치가 자신의 정수리 위에까지 오도록 막는 경우가 있는데, 이때는 상대의 공격이 방어하는 팔의 앞을 스쳐지나 고스란히 자신의 얼굴로 내려올 수 있음을 주의하여야 한다.

Chee-mahk-kee is a defensive move that uses Hwahl-get-jitof Hwahl-gay Chee-dohl-lee-myuh Poom-bahl-kee, but stops in front of your forehead to defend yourself. At this time, you have to stop your wrist at 45° above the forehead. If you swing to remove the opponent's attack, your face will be exposed to the attack as it is away from the proper position. Often with beginners, the arm is raised too high for his/her wrist to reach the top of his/her head when defending themselves. In this case, it should be noted that the opponent's attack could pass through the front of the defending arm and come straight down to his/her face.

⑧ 가로막기

가로막기는 목으로 들어오는 상대의 칼잽이를 팔뚝의 안쪽으로 걷어내어 막는 동작이다. 첫 시작에 윗대는 아랫대가 왼쪽 다리를 뒤로 빼고 우품 상태에서 오른손으로 막을 수 있게 왼손과 왼발로 칼잽이를 해준다.

첫째, 아랫대의 준비가 확인되면 윗대가 왼발을 정면으로 길게 내딛으며 아랫대의 목을 향해 왼손 칼재기(칼잽이)를 실시한다. 이때 아랫대는 무릎을 살짝 낮추며 왼발을 뒤로 빼어 우품을 만들고 오른손을 오른쪽 겨드랑이 앞으로 끌어올리며 상대의 공격을 기다린다. 둘째, 아랫대는 가볍게 튕겨 일어나며 오른 팔뚝을 세운 후, 허리의 회전을 이용하여 왼쪽으로 휘둘러 상대의 칼잽이를 팔뚝 안쪽 부위로 걷어내어 막는다. 이때 방어를 하는 팔은 90° 정도로 접어 손목이 눈높이 정도에 오도록 한다. 셋째, 윗대는 칼잽이가 막히면 왼발을 뒤로 당겼다가 걷기의 형태로 한발 전진하며 내딛는다. 아랫대는 오른발을 뒤쪽으로 내딛어 좌품을 만들고 자세를 낮추며 왼손을 왼쪽 겨드랑이 앞으로 올려 다음 방어를 준비한다. 이어서 윗대는 오른쪽 칼잽이를 하며 아랫대는 왼손으로 가로막기를 한다.

1-1	1-2	2

⑧ Gah-roh-mahk-kee

Gah-roh-Mahk-kee is a defensive move that removes the opponent's Kahl-jae-bee coming to the neck with the inside of the forearm. At the start, Wit-dae performs Kahl-jae-bee with his/her left hand and left foot so that Ah-raet-dae can block it with his/her right hand in a stance of Woo-poom with his/her left leg pulled back.

First, once Ah-raet-dae is ready, Wit-dae will take a long step forward with his/her left foot and perform Kahl-jae-kee (Kahl-jae-bee) toward the neck of Ah-raet-dae with his/her left hand. At this time, Ah-raet-dae lowers his/her knees slightly and pulls his/her left foot back to make Woo-poom, and waits for the opponent's attack with his/her right hand raised forward in front of his/her right armpit. Second, Ah-raet-dae springs up lightly and straight up his/her right forearm, then swings it to the left using the rotation of the waist to remove the opponent's Kahl-jae-bee with the inside of the forearm. At this time, fold the defending arm at 90° so that the wrist is at the eye level. Third, when his Kahl-jae-bee is blocked, Wit-dae pulls back his/her left foot then takes a step forward. Ah-raet-dae takes a back step with his/her right foot to form Jwa-poom and lowers the posture, while raising the left hand in front of his/her left armpit to prepare for the next defense. Wit-dae then performs Kahl-jae-bee with his/her right hand, while Ah-raet-dae blocks with Gah-roh-Mahk-kee with his/her left hand.

next-1

next-2

next-3

가로막기로 상대의 칼잽이를 막을 때에는 항상 상대 팔의 바깥쪽에서 안쪽으로 막아야 한다. 상대의 팔 안쪽에서 바깥쪽으로 막게 되면, 방어 후에 자신의 몸이 틀어진 채로 상대의 품안에 그대로 남아 있어 바로 다른 공격을 당하게 된다.
또한 상대의 칼잽이를 막을 때에는 튕겨 내거나 막아 세운다기보다, 상대 팔의 옆면을 밀어내어 비껴나가도록 상대 힘의 방향을 바꿔준다는 느낌으로 해야 한다.

When blocking the opponent's Kahl-jae-bee with Gah-roh-Mahk-kee, always block from the outside of the opponent's arm to the inside. If you block the opponent's attack from the inside to the outside of the opponent's arm, you will find yourself in the opponent's arms with your body twisted after the defense and face another attack.
Also, when you block the opponent's Kahl-jae-bee, you should feel that it changes the direction of the opponent's force to push the side of the opponent's arm away rather than bounce it off or simply block it.

⑨ 떼밀기

떼밀기는 상대의 몸을 밀어내는 동작이다. 윗대가 공격하고 아랫대가 방어하는 대부분의 막음질과 달리 윗대가 손바닥을 이용하여 상대의 몸을 밀어내는 공격에 가까운 동작을 한다. 이때 아랫대는 별다른 움직임 없이 윗대가 미는 힘에 가볍게 저항하며 왼발부터 뒷걸음질을 한다.

첫째, 아랫대의 준비가 확인되면 윗대는 오른발로 체중을 이동하며 아랫대의 가슴 한가운데에 칼재기의 형태로 왼쪽 손바닥을 가져다 댄다. 둘째, 윗대는 왼발을 앞으로 길게 내딛으며 아랫대의 가슴을 밀어낸다. 이때, 아랫대는 가볍게 버티며 뒤로 한걸음 물러난다. 이렇게 가슴 한가운데를 밀어낼 경우는 복장밀기(그림 1~3)라고 하며 오른손으로 상대의 왼쪽 옆구리를 밀게 되면 허구리밀기(그림 4~5)라 부른다. 셋째, 윗대는 상대를 충분히 밀어내고 난 후, 왼발을 뒤로 당겼다가 걷기의 형태로 한발 전진하며 내딛는다. 아랫대는 밀려난 형태 그대로 다시 중심을 잡으며 서서 다음 동작을 기다린다. 이어서 윗대는 오른발을 길게 내딛으며 상대의 가슴을 밀어내고, 아랫대는 가볍게 저항하며 한발 물러난다. 허구리밀기에서는 왼손과 왼발로 상대의 오른 옆구리를 밀어준다.

1	2	3

⑨ Dde-mil-kee

Dde-mil-kee is a move that pushes the opponent's body away. Unlike most of Mahk-eum-jil that Wit-dae attacks and Ah-raet-dae defends, Wit-dae uses the palm to push the opponent's body away. At this time, Ah-raet-dae lightly resists the force of Wit-dae and steps backward from the left foot without any particular movement.

First, when Ah-raet-dae is ready, Wit-dae moves his/her weight on the right foot and brings the left palm in the form of Kahl-jae-kee in the middle of Ah-raet-dae's chest. Second, Wit-dae will take a long step forward with his/her left foot and pushes the chest of Ah-raet-dae. At this time, Ah-raet-dae holds out lightly and takes a step back. If you push out the middle of the chest like this, it's called Bohk-jang-mil-kee, (Figure 1 to 3) and if you push the opponent's left side with your right hand, it's called Huh-koo-ree-mil-kee (Figure 4 to 5). Third, after sufficiently pushing the opponent away, Wit-dae pulls the left foot back then takes a step forward. Ah-raet-dae gets his/her balance back as he/she was pushed out and waits for the next move. Wit-dae then takes a long step with his/her right foot and pushes the opponent's chest, while Ah-raet-dae takes a step back with slight resistance. In Huh-koo-ree-mil-kee, Wit-dae pushes the opponent's right side with his/her left hand and left foot.

4

5

6

떼밀기는 복장밀기와 허구리밀기의 두 가지로 연습한다. 복장밀기(그림 1~3)는 상대의 가슴 한가운데를 밀어내는 동작이다. 칼재기의 형태로 상대의 가슴 한가운데에서 목에 가까운 쪽으로 장심을 대고 팔 힘이 아닌 체중의 이동을 이용해 상대의 몸을 정면으로 밀어낸다.
허구리밀기(그림 4~6)는 상대의 옆구리를 밀어낸다. 허구리밀기를 오른손으로 할 때는 오른손 엄지의 뿌리 부분이 상대의 명치에 닿게 한다. 그리고 나머지 네 손가락이 상대의 왼쪽 갈비뼈를 감싼 상태에서 상대의 갈비뼈를 옆으로 벌리는 느낌으로 밀어낸다. 허구리밀기도 발을 내딛으며 체중을 이용해 밀어낸다.
밀리는 아랫대는 별다른 동작 없이 가볍게 저항한 후, 자연스럽게 왼발부터 한발씩 물러나면 된다. 그리고 윗대는 아랫대가 왼발부터 밀리도록 복장밀기에서는 왼손부터, 허구리밀기에서는 오른손부터 밀어준다.
이렇게 상대를 공격하는 것 같은 떼밀기가 막음질에 속하는 이유는 상대를 때리거나 넘어뜨리는 것이 아니라 상대의 움직임을 자신의 통제 아래에 두기위해 또는 상대가 공격을 하지 못하도록 거리를 벌리기 위해 사용하기 때문이다.

There are two types of Dde-mil-kee: Bohk-jang-mil-kee, and Huh-koo-ree-mil-kee. Bohk-jang-mil-kee (Figure 1 to 3) is a movement that pushes the opponent in the middle of his/her chest. It is a form of Kahl-jae-bee. You put your palm on the middle of the opponent's chest close to the throat, and push him/her straight back using the movement of your weight, not arm strength.

Huh-koo-ree-mil-kee (Figure 4 to 6) is the motion of pushing the opponent's side. When you perform Huh-koo-ree-mil-kee with your right hand, the root of your right thumb should touch your opponent's solar plexus. Then, with the other four fingers wrapped around the opponent's left rib, and push as if you open the opponent's ribs to the side. This push is also using the weight taking a step forward.

Ah-raet-dae who is pushed back can resist lightly without any movement and naturally step back from his left foot. Wit-dae starts to push with left hand when he/she performs Bohk-jang-mil-kee and starts with the right hand to perform Huh-koo-ree-mil-kee, so that Ah-raet-dae can be pushed from his/her left foot.

The reason why Dde-mil-kee, which seems to be attacking the opponent, is belong to Mahk-eum-jilis because it is used to put the opponent's movements under his/her control or to widen the distance from the opponent to prevent him/her from attacking rather than to hit or knock the opponent down.

⑩ 덜미잽이

막음질의 덜미잽이는 나아가며 익히기의 덜미잽이 동작을 상대와 연습하는 동작이다. 덜미잽이는 아랫대가 먼저 왼발을 움직이며 왼손으로 상대의 목에 덜미잽이를 하고 윗대는 목이 끌려가는 방향에 따라 오른발부터 내딛으며 끌려오게 된다.

첫째, 윗대의 준비가 확인되면 아랫대가 오른발로 체중을 이동하며 왼손을 가로밀기의 형태로 뻗어 상대의 목을 감아 잡는다. 이때 윗대의 목을 손목에서 손바닥까지 모두 이용해 감싸듯이 잡아줘야 한다. 둘째, 아랫대는 체중을 이동할 때 살짝 굽혔던 오른다리로 바닥을 밀며 그 반동을 이용해 왼발을 뒤로 한걸음 내딛는다. 또한 그 힘을 이용하여 상대의 목을 자신의 왼쪽 어깨 앞쪽으로 끌어당겨온다. 이때 윗대는 가볍게 저항하며 목이 끌려가는 방향대로 오른발을 내딛는다. 셋째, 아랫대는 윗대의 목을 끌어온 자리에서 균형을 유지하며 일어선다. 윗대 역시 끌려온 자리에서 그대로 일어선다. 이어서 아랫대는 왼쪽다리를 살짝 굽히며 체중을 이동하고 오른손으로 상대의 목을 감싸 잡은 후, 오른쪽으로 덜미잽이를 한다. 윗대는 가볍게 저항하며 왼발을 내딛고 끌려간다.

1-1	1-2	2

⑩ Duhl-mee-jae-bee

Duhl-mee-jae-bee of Mahk-eum-jil is a move to practice Duhl-mee-jae-bee from Nah-ah-gah-myuh Ik-hee-kee with the opponent. Ah-raet-dae moves first with the left foot and performs Duhl-mee-jae-bee to the opponent's neck with the left hand. Wit-dae steps forward from the right foot depending on the direction in which his/her neck is pulled.

First, when Wit-dae is ready, Ah-raet-dae moves his/her weight on his/her right foot and stretches out his/her left hand in the form of Gah-roh-mil-kee to hold the opponent's neck. At this time, Ah-raet-dae should hold the neck of Wit-dae as if he/she was wrapping it with the entire hand. Second, Ah-raet-dae pushes on the floor with the right leg, which was slightly bent when moving the weight, and uses that rebound to take a step back. Also uses that power to pull the opponent's neck toward of his left shoulder. At this time, Wit-dae lightly resists and takes the right foot in the direction in which the neck is pulled. Third, Ah-raet-dae stands up while maintaining balance in the position where the neck of Wit-dae is pulled to. Wit-dae also stands up from where he/she was taken. Subsequently, Ah-raet-dae bends the left leg slightly, moving the weight, holding the opponent's neck with the right hand, and then performs Duhl-mee-jae-bee to the right. Wit-dae is dragged with his left foot stepping forward, resisting lightly.

3

next-1

next-2

덜미잽이 역시 떼밀기처럼 상대의 움직임을 자신의 통제 아래에 두고자 하는 기술이기 때문에 막음질에 속한다. 막음질의 덜미잽이에서 특이한 점은 나아가며 익히기에서는 앞으로 전진하며 연습했던 동작을 뒤로 후진하면서 하게 된다는 점이다. 물론 나아가며 익히기에서도 덜미잽이 동작의 마무리는 상대의 목을 끌고 들어오는 형태라는 점을 기억할 필요가 있다.
막음질의 덜미잽이에서 중요한 점은 덜미잽이가 가로밀기 후 잡아채오는 동작으로 구성된다는 것이다. 따라서 상대의 목을 가로밀기의 손날을 이용하여 대각선 방향으로 살짝 밀어준 후 잡아채야 상대의 중심이 흔들려 끌고 오기가 쉽다는 것이다.
덜미잽이로 상대의 목을 끌어당길 때는 목을 잡은 손의 팔꿈치를 먼저 구부려 당기면서 실시해야 한다. 즉 팔꿈치가 먼저 반응하여 상대의 목을 끌어당긴다는 기분으로 상대의 목을 잡아채는데, 이때 목을 끌어당기는 힘은 손이나 팔의 힘보다는 앞발을 뒤로 내딛으며 자세를 낮추는 힘과 골반을 회전하는 힘을 이용해야 한다.

Duhl-mee-jae-bee is also part of Mahk-eum-jil because it is a technique that wants to put the opponent's movement under his/her control like Dde-mil-kee. What's unique about Duhl-mee-jae-bee in Mahk-eum-jil is moving backward unlike we learned it while moving forward in Nah-ah-gah-myuh Ik-hee-kee. Of course, it is important to remember that in Nah-ah-gah-myuh Ik-hee-kee, the finishing touch of Duhl-mee-jae-bee is the form of pulling the opponent's neck in, rather than pushing.

What's important in Duhl-mee-jae-bee from Mahk-eum-jil is that it consists of the movements for snatching after performing Gah-roh-mil-kee. Therefore, it is easy to drag the opponent's neck if you grab after pushing it diagonally using the knife edge of the hand from Gah-roh-mil-kee to shake the opponent's balance.

When pulling the opponent's neck with Duhl-mee-jae-bee, it should be done by bending and pulling the elbow of the hand that grabbed the neck first. In other words, the elbow reacts first and grabs the opponent's neck with the feeling that it pulls his/her neck. At this time, the force to pull the neck should not be the force of the hand or arm, but the force to lower the position while the front foot is put back and the pelvis rotated.

⑪ 덜미걸이

막음질의 덜미걸이는 덜미잽이와 같이 나아가며 익히기의 덜미걸이 동작을 상대와 연습하는 동작이다. 덜미걸이는 아랫대가 먼저 왼발을 움직이며 오른손으로 상대의 목에 덜미걸이를 하고 윗대는 목이 끌려가는 방향에 따라 오른발부터 내딛으며 끌려오게 된다. 아랫대의 손 움직임이 덜미잽이와는 반대로 이루어진다.

첫째, 윗대의 준비가 확인되면 아랫대가 오른발로 체중을 이동하며 오른손을 세워밀기의 형태로 뻗어 상대의 목을 감아 잡는다. 이때 윗대의 목을 손목에서 손바닥까지 모두 이용해 감싸듯이 잡아줘야 한다. 둘째, 아랫대는 체중을 이동할 때 살짝 굽혔던 오른다리로 바닥을 밀며 그 반동을 이용해 왼발을 뒤로 한걸음 내딛는다. 또한 그 힘을 이용하여 상대의 목을 자신의 가슴 앞쪽으로 끌어당겨온다. 이때 윗대는 가볍게 저항하며 목이 끌려가는 방향대로 왼발을 내딛는다. 셋째, 아랫대는 윗대의 목을 끌어온 자리에서 균형을 유지하며 일어선다. 윗대 역시 끌려온 자리에서 그대로 일어선다. 이어서 아랫대는 왼다리를 살짝 굽히며 체중을 이동하고 왼손으로 상대의 목을 감싸 잡은 후 오른쪽으로 누르듯 당기며 덜미걸이를 한다. 윗대는 가볍게 저항하며 왼발을 내딛고 끌려간다.

1-1	1-2	2

⑪ Duhl-mee-guh-ree

Duhl-mee-guh-ree of Mahk-eum-jil is a move to practice Duhl-mee-guh-ree from Nah-ah-gah-myuh Ik-hee-kee with the opponent as you do Duhl-mee-jae-bee. Ah-raet-dae moves first with the left foot and performs Duhl-mee-guh-ree to the opponent's neck with the right hand. Wit-dae steps forward from the right foot depending on the direction in which his/her neck is pulled. The hand movement of Ah-raet-dae is the opposite of that of Duhl-mee-jae-bee.

First, when Wit-dae is ready, Ah-raet-dae moves his/her weight on his/her right foot and stretches out his/her right hand in the form of Say-wuh-mil-kee to hold the back of the opponent's neck. At this time, Ah-raet-dae should hold the neck of Wit-dae as if he/she was wrapping it with the entire hand. Second, Ah-raet-dae pushes on the floor with the right leg, which was slightly bent when moving the weight, and uses that rebound to take the left foot a step back. Also uses that power to pull the opponent's neck toward his/her chest. At this time, Wit-dae lightly resists and takes the left foot in the direction in which the neck is pulled. Third, Ah-raet-dae stands up while maintaining balance in the position where the neck of Wit-dae is pulled to. Wit-dae also stands up from where he/she was taken. Subsequently, Ah-raet-dae bends the left leg slightly, moving the weight, holding the opponent's neck with the left hand, and then performs Duhl-mee-guh-ree to pull as you are pressing down to the right. Wit-dae is dragged with his/her left foot stepping forward, resisting lightly.

3

next-1

next-2

덜미걸이 역시 나아가며 익히기의 동작을 상대와 연습하지만, 덜미잽이와 팔다리의 움직임이 서로 반대가 된다. 먼저 오른손으로 상대의 목을 감아 잡고 왼발을 뒤로 내딛으며 밖에서 안쪽으로 당겨온다. 덜미잽이는 안에서 바깥쪽으로 당겨온다. 오른손을 쓸 때는 오른발을 뒤로 내딛는다. 이러한 차이는 가로밀기와 세워밀기의 공격방향의 차이로 인해 발생한다.
덜미잽이와 덜미걸이 모두 가로밀기와 세워밀기의 기본을 지켜 상대의 목을 대각선 방향으로 살짝 밀어준 후, 당겨 와야 한다. 다리 움직임을 통한 체중이동을 이용해야 하는 것 역시 마찬가지다.
덜미걸이로 상대의 목을 끌어당길 때는 목을 잡은 손의 하박 부분을 상대 가슴에 밀착시키며 팔꿈치가 상대와 자신의 가슴 중앙에 오도록 하여 끌어당긴다. 덜미잽이와 마찬가지로 팔의 힘으로 당기기보다는 자세를 낮추는 힘과 더불어 골반을 회전하는 힘을 더해 상대의 덜미를 제압한다.

Duhl-mee-guh-ree also practices the movement of Nah-ah-gah-myuh Ik-hee-kee with the opponent, but the movement of arms and legs is opposite from Duhl-mee-jae-bee. First, hold the opponent's neck with your right hand and pull inside from the outside, stepping back with your left foot. Duhl-mee-jae-bee is a movement that pulls outward from the inside. When you use your right hand, put your right foot back. This difference is caused by differences in the direction of attacks between Gah-roh-mil-kee and Say-wuh-mil-kee.

Both Duhl-mee-jae-bee and Duhl-mee-guh-ree should follow the basics of Gah-roh-mil-kee and Say-wuh-mil-kee, slightly pushing the opponent's neck diagonally, and then pulling it. Also, you have to move your weight through leg movements.

When pulling the opponent's neck with Duhl-mee-guh-ree, the forearm of the hand that holds the neck is attached to the opponent's chest, and pull the neck with the elbow is in the center of the opponent's and your chest. Just like Duhl-mee-jae-bee, it overpowers the opponent's back of the neck by adding the power to lower the posture and the power in rotating the pelvis, rather than pulling with the force of the arm.

⑫ 곁들어 뒤로 내려막기

곁들어 뒤로 내려막기는 곁들어 내려막기의 변형 동작이다. 곁들어 내려막기가 우품일 때 오른쪽을, 좌품일 때 왼쪽을 막는 반면, 곁들어 뒤로 내려막기는 우품일 때 왼쪽, 좌품일 때 오른쪽을 막는다. 이는 돌개차기처럼 강한 발차기를 자신의 몸에서 먼 곳에서 막아내기 위한 움직임이다. 시작에서 윗대는 왼발로 째차기를 해주며 아랫대는 우품에서 이를 곁들어 내려막기 한다. 두 번째부터 윗대는 째차기를 돌개차기로 해준다.

첫째, 아랫대의 준비가 확인되면 윗대가 왼발 째차기를 실시한다. 이때 아랫대는 무릎을 살짝 낮추며 왼발을 뒤로 빼어 우품을 만들고 왼손과 오른손을 얼굴 앞에 교차시켜 들어 올린 채로 상대의 째차기를 기다린다. 두 손 중 왼손이 바깥쪽으로 위치해야 동작이 수월하다. 둘째, 아랫대는 자세를 살짝 낮춘 우품 상태에서 가볍게 튕겨 일어나며 자신의 몸을 왼쪽으로 90°정도 회전시킨다. 그리고 그 탄력을 활용하여 왼손으로 활개 내려막기를, 오른손으로 가로막기를 하며 상대의 째차기를 자신의 왼쪽으로 튕겨내며 막아준다. 셋째, 윗대는 째차기가 막힌 후 왼발을 걷기의 형태로 한발 전진하며 내딛는다. 아랫대는 오른발을 뒤쪽으로 내딛어 좌품을 만들고 자세를 낮추어 다음 방어를 준비한다. 이때 곁들어 내려막기처럼 양 팔을 회전하여 교차한다. 이어서 윗대는 오른쪽으로 회전하며 그 탄력을 살려 오른발로 돌개차기(째차기)를 한다. 아랫대는 좌품에서 우측을 향해 곁들어 내려막기를 한다. 이후부터 윗대는 지속적으로 회전을 하며 째차기를 돌개차기 형태로 차준다.

1-1	1-2	2

⑫ Gyeot-duhl-eoh Dui-roh Nae-ryo-mahk-kee

Kyeot-deul-uh Dui-roh Nae-ryo-mahk-kee is a variation of Kyeot-deul-uh Nae-ryo-mahk-kee. When Kyeot-deul-uh Nae-ryo-mahk-kee is performed in Woo-poom, you block your right side. While in Kyeot-deul-uh Dui-roh Nae-ryo-mahk-kee, you block your left side when it is performed in Woo-poom. This is to block strong kicks such as Dohl-gae-cha-kee from far away from your body. At the beginning, Wit-dae performs Jae-cha-kee with the left foot, while Ah-raet-dae blocks it with Kyeot-deul-uh Nae-ryo-mahk-kee in Woo-poom. Starting with the second time, Wit-dae performs Dohl-gae-cha-kee instead of Jae-cha-kee.

First, once Ah-raet-dae is ready, Wit-dae performs Jae-cha-kee with his/her left foot. At this time, Ah-raet-dae lowers his/her knees slightly and pulls his/her left foot back to make Woo-poom, and waits for the opponent's Jae-cha-kee with his/her both hands crossed in front of your face. Of the two hands, the left hand should be positioned outside to make the movement easy. Second, Ah-raet-dae springs up lightly from the slightly lowered Woo-poom, and rotates the body 90° to the left. Using the momentum, he/she performs Hwahl-gay Nae-ryo-mahk-kee with the left hand and does Gah-roh-mahk-kee with the right hand to block the opponent's Jae-cha-kee by bouncing it to the left. Third, when his/her Jae-cha-kee is blocked, Wit-dae takes a step forward with his/her left foot. Ah-raet-dae takes a step back with the right foot to form Jwa-poom and lowers his/her stance to prepare for the next defense. At this time, the arms are circling in front of the torso as if they were performing Kyeot-deul-uh Nae-ryo-mahk-kee then crossed. Wit-dae then spins to the right and performs Dohl-gae-cha-kee (Jae-cha-kee) with his/her right foot using the momentum. Ah-raet-dae performs Kyeot-deul-uh Nae-ryo-mahk-kee to the right from the stance of Jwa-poom. From then on, Wit-dae continuously spins and performs Dohl-gae-cha-kee.

3	next-1	next-2

돌개차기는 태권도의 뒤돌려차기(뒤후리기)와 같은 발차기로 몸의 회전을 이용하여 강하게 차는 발질을 말한다. 택견에서는 태권도와 비슷한 형태의 발차기와 더불어 째차기도 회전을 이용하여 돌개차기로 강하게 차주기도 한다. 내차기 역시 회전을 하며 비스듬히 갈기는 형태로 차기도 한다.

회전력이 실린 돌개질은 측면에서 자신의 몸을 향해 날아오게 되는데, 단순한 내려막기나 곁들어 내려막기로는 그 충격을 충분히 막아내지 못한다. 따라서 품을 반대로 하여 팔과 몸 사이의 공간을 키우고 몸을 발차기가 날아오는 방향으로 회전시키는 탄력까지 활용하여 상대의 돌개차기를 옆으로 튕겨내는 곁들어 뒤로 내려막기를 하게 된다. 즉 뒤로 내려막기라는 기술 이름과 달리 상대 발차기 공격을 내 몸의 뒤로 막는 것이 아니라 앞에서 옆으로 튕겨내며 막는 것이다. 이때 골반의 회전으로 막기에 탄력을 더해주어야 한다.

Dohl-gae-cha-kee refers to a strong kick using the rotation of the body, and is like a Dui-dohl-ryo-cha-kee (Dui-hoo-ri-kee) in Taekwondo. Taekgyeon uses a similar type of kick as Taekwondo, and Jae-cha-kee is also performed strongly using spinning, like Dohl-gae-cha-kee. Nae-cha-kee is also kicked in the form of a diagonal striking as it spins. Dohl-gae-jil with rotational force flies toward your body from the side, and you cant sufficiently prevent the shock with Nae-ryo-mahk-kee or Kyeot-deul-uh Nae-ryo-mahk-kee. Therefore, by reversing the arm position, the space between your arms and body is widened, and by using the elasticity to rotate your body in the direction of the kick, you perform Kyeot-deul-uh Dui-roh Nae-ryo-mahk-kee to bounce back the opponent's Dohl-gae-cha-kee to the side of your body. In other words, unlike the technical name of Dui-ro (backward) Nae-ryo-mahk-kee, it is not to block the opponent's kick from behind the body, but to block it by bouncing from the front to the side. At this point, the rotation of the pelvis should add to the momentum to the block.

2. 얼러 메기기

상대와 품밟기의 박자를 맞춰 움직이며 적절한 순간을 찾아 공격하는 연습 과정인 얼러 메기기는 혼자서 기본 움직임을 수련하는 얼름새와 상대와 공격 기술을 주고받는 얼러 메기기의 두 부분으로 구성된다.

'어르다'는 사전적 의미로 첫째, '몸을 움직여 주거나 또는 무엇을 보여 주거나 들려주어서, 어린아이를 달래거나 기쁘게 하여 주다.', 둘째, '사람이나 짐승을 놀리며 장난하다.', 셋째, '어떤 일을 하도록 사람을 구슬리다.' 등의 뜻을 갖고 있다. '어르다'의 부사형인 '얼러'와 '메기기'가 합쳐진 '얼러 메기기'는 상대가 편안히 품을 밟도록 놓아주고 거기에 자신의 품을 맞추어 상대 균형의 움직임을 좇아 공격기술을 사용한다. 따라서 얼러 메기기는'어르다'가 의미하는 두 번째와 세 번째의 뜻처럼 상대를 구슬려 기술을 먹이는 것을 의미한다고 볼 수 있다.

그 연장선에서 '얼름새'는 상대를 구슬리거나 놀리는 모양(얼름+새)으로 이해할 수 있을 것이다. 이를 증명하듯 얼름새의 넉장다리, 다가서기, 어리대기, 빗장걸이, 거리재고 키재기 등은 상대의 앞에서 여유롭게 자신을 드러내는 형태의 동작들이다.

막음새의 동작을 막음질에서 고스란히 사용하는 막음질과 달리 얼름새의 동작은 얼러 메기기에서 사용되지 않는다. 다만 '어르다'의 의미를 되새길 때, 자신을 드러내는 얼름새를 통해 상대에게 편안하게 움직일 수 있는 여지를 주고, 그 움직임을 파악하여 적절한 순간을 포착해 공격기술을 사용하는 것이 얼러 메기기인 것으로 둘 사이의 관계를 이해할 수 있을 것이다.

얼러 메기기는 상대와 품밟기의 박자를 맞추어 두세 번 품을 밟은 뒤, 상대의 발이 바닥에 닿기 직전이나 닿았다 떨어진 직후 등, 상대의 중심이 안정되지 않은 순간을 노려 공격한다. 또한 좌우 두 번의 연속 공격 뒤에는 다시금 품을 맞추어 상대가 공격할 수 있는 기회를 주게 된다. 마치 짝을 이루어 춤을 추듯이 서로 박자를 맞추어 공격을 주고받는 것이다.

2. Eol-luh Me-kee-kee

Eol-luh Me-kee-kee is a practice that moves with the beat of Poom-bahl-kee and attacks at the right moment. It consists of two parts: Eol-leum-sae, which makes you practice basic movements by yourself, and Eol-luh Me-kee-kee, which allows you to exchange attack techniques with your opponent.

The lexical meaning of 'Eo-reu-da' is first of all, to comfort or please a child by moving the body or showing or playing something. Second, to tease a person or animal. Thirdly, to coax a person to do something. Eol-luh Me-kee-kee is a combination of the word 'Eol-luh' which are adverbial to 'Eo-reu-da' and the word 'Me-kee-kee.' It is a move that you let the opponent step comfortably and adjust your steps to his/her steps while following the movement of the opponent's balance, then you use attack techniques. Therefore, 'Eol-luh Me-kee-kee' means using attack techniques by coaxing opponents as in the second and third meaning of 'Eo-reu-da.'

From that point of view, 'Eol-leum-sae(Eol-leom + sae)' may be understood as a situation where one coaxes or teases the opponent. As evidenced by this, the various movements of Eol-leom-sae such as Nuk-jang-da-ri, Da-gah-seo-kee, Eo-ri-dae-kee, Bit-jang-geo-ri, and Geo-ri-jae-go Ki-jae-kee are methods of openly displaying one's intentions to the opponent.

The movement of Mahk-eum-sae is used intact in Mahk-eum-jil, while the movement of Eol-leom-sae is not used in Eol-luh Me-kee-kee. However, when reflecting on the meaning of 'Eo-reu-da,' the relationship between the two will be understood as Eol-luh Me-kee-kee gives the opponent room to move comfortably through the Eol-leom-sae that opens oneself, and to grasp the movement and capture the appropriate moment and use an attack technique.

Eol-luh Me-kee-kee first steps two or three times to the beat of the opponent's Poom-bahl-kee, and then attacks at a moment when the opponent's balance is not stable, such as just before or after the opponent's foot touches the floor. In addition, after two consecutive attacks on the left and right, he/she gives the opponent a chance to attack by adjusting his/her steps again. As if they were dancing in pairs, they smoothly exchange attacks on the beat of the movements.

(1) 얼름새

막음새와 막음질의 수련과정이 방어기술을 익히는 과정이라면 얼름새와 얼러메기기는 공격기술을 익히는 과정이다. 하지만 얼름새의 동작들을 살펴보면 직접적인 공격기술로 보이는 기술들은 없다.

오히려 얼름새의 동작들은 실전에서 필요한 동작일까 하는 의구심이 생기는 동작들이 대부분이다. 왜냐하면 얼름새에서 익히는 것은 직접적인 공격기술이 아니라 공격하기 위한 준비자세 또는 공격을 위한 마음가짐을 가다듬는 자세들이기 때문이다.

하지만 얼름새의 자세들은 택견의 전 과정에서도 매우 중요한 자세이므로 각 기술의 세심한 부분까지 깊이 있게 수련하고 습득하는 것이 필요하다.

얼름새는 상대에게 당당하게 자신을 내보이는 개념의 '넉장다리', 상대에게 살짝 다가서서 여유 부리듯 가볍게 자세를 낮추며 자신의 허벅지를 툭 치는 '다가서기', 상대의 정면에서 자신의 방어를 열어 보이는 것 같은 '어리대기', 방어 자세를 취한 뒤 고고하게 일어서 상대를 내려다보며 여유를 부리는 것 같은 '빗장걸이', 어리대기와 빗장걸이를 연달아 선보이는 '어리대고 빗장걸이', 앞뒤로 길게 움직이며 손을 상대 쪽으로 뻗었다가 위로 들어 올렸다가 하며 서로의 위치를 재보는 듯 하는 '거리재고 키재기'의 여섯 동작으로 이루어진다.

이 얼름새를 연습할 때는 가능한 여유있게, 자신감 있게, 당당하게 동작을 취하는 것이 중요하다.

(1) Eol-leum-sae

If the training process of Mahk-eum-sae and Mahk-eum-jil is the process of learning defense techniques, Eol-leum-sae and Eol-luh Me-kee-kee are the process of learning attack techniques. However, if you look at the movements of Eol-leum-sae, there are no techniques that appear to be direct attack techniques. On the contrary, most of the movements of Eol-leum-sae are suspicious of whether they are necessary in a real fight. This is because what you learn from Eol-leum-sae is not direct attack techniques, but readiness postures for attack or a mindset for attack. However, since the posture of Eol-leum-sae is very important in the entire process of Taekkyeon training, it is necessary to train and learn in depth to the meticulous parts of each skill.

Eol-leom-sae is made up of six movements, as follows:

* Nuk-jang-da-ri with the concept of showing oneself confidently to the opponent,

* Da-gah-seo-kee with a slight move to the opponent, lightly lowering his/her posture and tapping his/her thighs,

* Eo-ri-dae-kee that seems to open up one's defense from the front of the opponent,

* Bit-jang-geo-ri which standing up right and relaxed, while looking down at the opponent after taking a defensive posture,

* Eo-ri-dae-go Bit-jang-geo-ri which presents Eo-ri-dae-kee and Bit-jang-geo-ri consecutively, and

* Geo-ri-jae-go Ki-jae-kee that moves back and forth while you stretch your hand to the opponent and raise it, as if you are measuring each other's position.

When practicing this Eol-leom-sae, it is important to be as relaxed, confident and dignified as possible.

① 넉장다리

넉장다리는 처음 익히기에서 배운 품, 즉 원품, 좌품, 우품을 낮은 활갯짓과 조화시켜 자신의 여유를 내보이는 동작이다.

넉장다리 원품의 경우, 첫째, 바로의 자세에서 원품으로 다리를 벌리며, 아랫배 앞에 포갰던 양 손을 허리 높이에서 앞으로 쭉 밀어준다. 둘째, 앞으로 밀어준 양 손을 가슴과 함께 활짝 열며 허리 높이에서 제치기 해준다(1-1~3 & side figure 1).

넉장다리 좌품의 경우, 첫째, 넉장다리 원품에서 양손을 왼손이 위로 가도록 당겨와 교차시키며 왼발을 원품의 중간지점으로 끌고 온다. 둘째, 좌품을 내딛으며 자세를 낮추고 양손으로 헤치기를 실시한다. 이때 자세를 보통의 좌품보다 낮게 취한다(2-1~3 & side figure 2).

넉장다리 우품은 첫째, 넉장다리 좌품에서 양손을 바로 자세로 모으며 내딛은 왼발을 원품의 중간으로 끌고 온다. 둘째, 넉장다리 원품 자세를 취한 다. 끝으로, 넉장다리 원품에서 오른발을 원품의 중간으로 끌고 오며 오른손이 위로 가도록 양손을 당겨와 교차시킨 후, 우품을 딛으며 양손 헤치기를 한다(3-1~4 & side figure 3).

① Nuk-jang-da-ri

Nuk-jang-da-ri is a movement in which you show your confidence by harmonizing Pooms such as Won-poom, Jwa-poom, and Woo-poom which you learned from Chuh-eum Ik-hee-gee with the low Hwahl-get-jit.

In the case of Nuk-jang-da-ri Won-poom, first, spread the legs apart in Won-poom from the position of Baro, and push the two hands of the lower abdomen all the way forward at waist level. Second, open both hands pushed forward with the chest and perform Jay-chee-kee at waist level (1-1 to 1-3 & side figure 1).

In the case of Nuk-jang-da-ri Jwa-poom, first, from Nuk-jang-da-ri Won-poom, bring back and cross your hands with your left hand going over the right one as you are dragging your left foot to the point of the middle of Won-poom. Second, lower your posture while you are stepping Jwa-poom, and then perform Hay-chee-Kee with both hands. At this time, take the position lower than original Jwa-poom(2-1 to 2-2 & side figure 2).

In the case of Nuk-jang-da-ri Woo-poom, first, bring back your hands as in the position of Baro as you are dragging your left foot to the point of the middle of Won-poom, and do Nuk-jang-da-ri Won-poom. Second, do same as Nuk-jang-da-ri Jwa-poom but with your right side from Nuk-jang-da-ri Won-poom(3-1~4 & side figure 3).

넉장다리를 할 때는 얼름새의 취지에 맞게 당당히 가슴을 열어 상대에게 자신의 기운을 보여준다는 느낌으로 실시한다.
넉장다리의 원품, 좌품과 우품을 연달아 실시할 때는 반드시 넉장다리 원품을 거쳐야 한다. 즉, 넉장다리 원품 → 넉장다리 좌품 → 넉장다리 원품 → 넉장다리 우품 의 형태로 이루어진다.
차후에 본때뵈기를 수련할 때, 넉장다리 가로 우품이 나오게 된다. 이것은 넉장다리 우품에서 뒤에 위치한 왼발을 보통의 우품보다 더 틀어지게, 즉, 45°보다 큰 각도로 디뎌준 자세를 의미한다. 즉, 우품보다 왼발을 더 바깥쪽으로 틀어 양 발사이의 각이 더 벌어진 넉장다리 우품이 바로 넉장다리 가로 우품이다.

1-1

1-2

1-3

2-1

2-2

3-1

When you perform Nuk-jang-da-ri, you proudly open your chest and show your energy to the opponent to suit the purpose of Eol-leum-sae.
If Nuk-jang-da-ri Won-poom, Jwa-poom and Woo-poom is carried out in succession, you must go through Nuk-jang-da-ri Won-poom. In other words, the performance consists of Nuk-jang-da-ri Won-poom → Nuk-jang-da-ri Jwa-poom → Nuk-jang-da-ri Won-poom → Nuk-jang-da-ri Woo-poom.
Later on, when you train Bohn-dae-bae-kee, you will see Nuk-jang-da-ri Gah-roh Woo-poom. This means that the left foot, which is located behind in Nuk-jang-da-ri Woo-poom, is tilted than the normal Woo-poom, that is, your left foot is stepped to an angle greater than 45°. In other words, Nuk-jang-da-ri Woo-poom which has more angles between the two feet by turning the left foot more outward than ordinary Woo-poom, is Nuk-jang-da-ri Gah-roh Woo-poom.

3-2

3-3

3-4

side figure 1

side figure 2

side figure 3

② 다가서기

다가서기는 상대를 향해 여유롭게 다가서는 모양을 취하는 것이다.

첫째, 원품에서 좌품을 취하며 양손을 가볍게 가슴 높이 정도로 들어올린다. 둘째, 좌품에서 자세를 조금 더 낮추며 양 손바닥으로 허벅지를 가볍게 내리치며 자세를 멈춘다. 셋째, 좌품 자세를 유지하며 가볍게 일어선다. 넷째, 품 내밟기로 우품을 내딛고, 양손을 가슴높이로 들어올린다. 우품에서 자세를 낮추며 양 허벅지를 툭 내리친 후, 우품을 유지하며 일어선다.

사진은 측면이 잘 보이는 좌품의 측면 모습을 추가한 대신, 정면사진은 우품으로 수록하였다.

> 다가서기는 이름 그대로 상대에게 당당히 다가서는 모양을 수련하는 과정이다. 그러나 기본 수련인 얼름새의 다가서기에서는 실제로 상대에게 다가가지 않고 제자리에서 실시한다. 간혹, 실제로 조금씩 전진하며 수련하는 경우가 있으니 얼름새 수련에서는 앞으로 나가지 않도록 주의해야 한다. 이를 실전에 응용할 경우에는 앞으로 내딛는 발을 품 내밟기보다 조금 더 멀리 내딛으며, 자세를 낮춤과 동시에 뒷발을 미끄러지듯이 끌어당겨 기본 품밟기 자세를 유지한다.

1-1

1-2

2

② Da-gah-seo-kee

Da-gah-seo-kee is to take the form of leisurely approaching one's opponent.

First, take a step of Jwa-poom from Won-poom and lift both hands lightly to chest level. Second, lower the posture a little more in Jwa-poom and stay by lightly hitting the thighs with both palms. Third, stand up lightly while maintaining the posture of Jwa-poom. Fourth, take a step of Woo-poom with Poom Nae-bahl-kee, and lift both hands at the chest level. In Woo-poom, lower the posture and hit both thighs again, then stand up while maintaining Woo-poom.

For the pictures, the side view of Jwa-poom was added to give a better view of the side, while the front picture was put in Woo-poom.

> As it's name implies, Da-gah-seo-kee (means getting closer) is the process of training to approach one's opponent confidently. However, in Da-gah-seo-kee of Eol-leum-sae, the basic training, it is performed in place without actually approaching the opponent. Sometimes, you actually go forward little by little while you are training, so you should be careful not to go forward in training of Eol-leum-sae. If this is applied in actual practice, take the step forward a little further than Poom Nae-bahl-kee, and at the same time as lowering the posture, you pull the back foot forward to maintain the basic Poom-bahl-kee position.

3

side figure 1

side figure 2

③ 어리대기

어리대기는 좌품(우품) 상태에서 왼팔(오른팔)을 이용해 상대에게 자신을 내보이는 자세이다.

첫째, 원품에서 좌품을 취하며 왼손을 오른쪽 골반뼈로 당겨온다. 둘째, 좌품에서 자세를 조금 더 낮추며 왼팔이 왼쪽 허벅지를 많이 벗어나지 않는 선에서 제치기한다. 이 제치기 동작이 어리대기이다. 이때 어리대기하는 팔과 앞쪽 허벅지의 수직 각도는 옆에서 봤을 때 동일해야 한다(side figure). 셋째, 어리대기가 끝난 후에는 왼손을 다시 오른쪽 골반뼈로 당겨온 후, 원품으로 되돌아가며 팔을 자연스레 풀어준다. 우품에서도 동일하게 실시한다(4~5).

어리대기를 할 때, 가장 주의할 점은 겨드랑이에 공간을 만들어주어야 한다는 것이다. 대개의 초보자들은 겨드랑이를 꽉 붙인 채, 팔만을 이용하여 어리대기를 하게 된다. 이 경우, 어깨가 위축되어 보이므로 얼름새의 본질적인 의미를 잃게 된다. 따라서 어리대기를 할 때에는 겨드랑이 속에 달걀이 하나 들어있다는 느낌으로 공간을 만들어주며 실시해야 자세가 크고 여유로워 보인다.
어리대기를 하며 팔을 굽히거나 손목을 틀어 손바닥이 하늘을 보지 않도록 주의해야 한다. 특히 손바닥은 바로 세워 전면을 향해 완전히 젖혀주어야 한다. 또한, 자신의 자세를 확인하느라 시선이 아래로 내려가는 경우가 있는데, 시선은 정면에 고정하고 허리를 반듯하게 펴 주어야 한다.

1	2	3

③ Eo-ri-dae-kee

Eo-ri-dae-kee is a posture in which you use your left (right) arm to open yourself to the opponent in Jwa-poom(Woo-poom).

First, pull your left hand to the right pelvic bone, taking Jwa-poom from Won-poom. Second, lower the position a little bit more in Jwa-poom and perform Jay-chee-kee with your left hand, while keeping the left arm not to deviate much from the left thigh. This Jay-chee-kee movement is Eo-ri-dae-kee. At this time, the vertical angles of the front thigh and the arm does Eo-ri-dae-kee should be same (side figure). Third, after you performed Eo-ri-dae-kee, pull the left hand back to the right pelvic bone, then return to Won-poom and release the arm naturally. Do the same in Woo-poom (4-5).

When you are performing Eo-ri-dae-kee, the most important thing to note is to make room under your armpits. Most beginners use only their arms, with their armpits tightly closed. In this case, the shoulders appear to be atrophied and thus lose the essential meaning of Eol-leum-sae. Therefore, when you perform Eo-ri-dae-kee, make a space in the sense of that there is an egg in your armpit and perform the movement to make it look big and relaxed.

You have to be careful not to bend your arms or twist your wrists for your palm to face the sky while you are performing Eo-ri-dae-kee. In particular, your hand should be bent backwards so your palm is facing forwards. Also, there are times when you might look down to check your posture, but you shouldn't. Your eyes must be fixed in the front and your back should be straightened.

4

5

side figure

④ 빗장걸이

빗장걸이는 문을 걸어 잠그는 빗장을 채운 것처럼 완전한 방어자세로 여유롭게 상대를 기다리는 동작이다.

첫째, 원품에서 왼 무릎을 우측 45°방향을 향하도록 들어올린다. 이때, 왼 발목은 오른 무릎 안쪽에 위치한다. 동시에 오른팔은 편 채로 옆으로 들어 올려 막음새의 치막기 형태로 머리 위에서 멈춰준다. 왼손은 왼쪽 허벅지에 가볍게 올려준다. 둘째, 왼다리로 방어자세를 취한 빗장걸이에서 반대편으로 옮겨 갈 때는 원품보다 1.5배가량 넓게 다리를 벌려 옆으로 째어 내딛는다. 품 째밟기의 동작이다. 그리고 치막기 한 오른팔은 자신의 몸통 앞으로 팔을 편 채 돌려준다. 셋째, 오른다리를 들어 올려 좌측 45°방향으로 고정시키며 왼 팔을 옆으로 들어 올려 치막기 한다. 몸통 앞으로 돌린 오른팔은 오른 허벅지에 올려준다. 다시 반대편 동작을 취할 때도 다리를 째며 내딛는다(4).

1	2	3

④ Bit-jang-geo-ri

Bit-jang-geo-ri is a move that waits for the opponent with full defense, as if it had been fastened with a latch(Bit-jang) to lock the door.

First, lift the left knee from Won-poom in a direction of 45° to the right. At this time, the left ankle is located inside the right knee. At the same time, the right arm is extended and lifted sideways, and stops above the head in the form of Chee-mahk-kee from Mahk-eum-sae. Your left hand is placed lightly on the left thigh. Second, when you switch from a defensive posture of Bit-jang-geo-ri with your left leg to the other side, step down about 1.5 times wider than Won-poom to the side. It is the movement of Poom Jae-bahl-kee. Then, the right arm which performed Chee-mahk-kee is rotated to the front of your body with the arm stretched out. Third, lift the right leg and fix it in a 45° direction to the left, and raise the left arm to the side to perform Chee-mahk-kee. Put your right arm, rotated to the front of your body, on your right thigh. When taking the action in the opposite side again, take a long step of Poom Jae-bahl-kee to the side(4).

4

side figure 1

side figure 2

빗장걸이의 첫 동작은 원품상태에서 그대로 실시하며 두 번 이상 반복하면서부터는 째밟기의 형태로 이동한다. 또한 초보자의 경우, 치막기 한 손을 몸통의 앞으로 회전시킨다는 점을 잊고 그냥 내리는 경우가 많으므로 항상 주의한다.
빗장걸이는 완전한 방어의 자세임에도 불구하고 막음새가 아닌 얼름새에서 배우게 되는데, 이는 방어 후에 공격으로 이어지는 자연스러운 움직임의 형태를 익힐 수 있도록 하기 위함이다. 방어의 기본은 상대의 공격을 째는(옆으로 길게 움직이는) 형태로 피하는 것이다. 그래야만 나에게 곧바로 공격의 기회가 생기기 때문이다. 이러한 이유에서 품 째밟기를 기본 움직임으로 하는 빗장걸이를 얼름새에서 익히게 되는 것이다.
빗장걸이는 한 다리로 서 있으므로 중심잡기가 어려운 경우가 많다. 이때 들어 올린 다리의 발목을 반대편 다리에 붙여주면 중심잡기가 수월해진다.

The first movement of Bit-jang-geo-ri is carried out in Won-poom, and after repeated more than once, you move in the form of Jae-bahl-kee. Also, for beginners, always be careful because they often forget to rotate the hand which performed Chee-mahk-kee in front of the body.
Although Biht-jang-guh-ree is a complete defense posture, it is learned in Eol-leum-sae, not in Mahk-eum-sae, because it is to learn the form of natural movement that leads to attack after defense. The basis of defense is to avoid attacks in the form of Jae-kee (long-moving sideways). That's because that's the only way you get an opportunity to attack right away. For this reason, you will learn Biht-jang-guh-ree, which is based on the movement of Poom Jae-bahl-kee, in Eol-leum-sae.
When you perform Bit-jang-geo-ri, it is often difficult to keep the balance because you stand on one leg. If you rest the ankle of the raised leg to the side of the other knee, it will be easier to balance.

⑤ 어리대고 빗장걸이

어리대고 빗장걸이는 어리대기와 빗장걸이를 연이어 하는 동작이다.

첫째, 원품에서 좌품으로 내딛으며 어리대기를 실시한다. 둘째, 좌품의 어리대기 상태에서 그대로 왼발을 들고 일어서며 빗장걸이를 실시한다. 셋째, 원품으로 왼발을 내딛는다. 이때 앞선 빗장걸이와 달리 째서 내딛지 않고 기본적인 원품의 폭으로 딛는다. 동시에 빗장걸이 할 때 올렸던 오른팔을 몸 앞으로 돌려준다. 넷째, 몸통 앞으로 돌린 오른팔의 손목이 왼편 허리에 왔을 때, 우품을 내딛으며 어리대기를 한다. 다섯째, 오른다리를 들어 올리며 빗장걸이를 실시한다.

> 어리대고 빗장걸이를 할 때에는 그냥 빗장걸이만 할 때와 달리 들어 올린 다리를 째서 내딛지 않는다.
> 어리대기와 빗장걸이가 이어질 때, 양팔의 움직임은 밖으로 들어 올려 안으로 내려오게 된다. 항상 치막기로 올라가는 손은 밖으로 회전시키고, 치막기 후 어리대기를 하는 손은 안으로 돌려 내려야 한다.

1	2	3

⑤ Eo-ri-dae-goh Bit-jang-geo-ri

Eo-ri-dae-goh Bit-jang-geo-ri is a sequence movement of Eo-ri-dae-kee and Bit-jang-geo-ri.

First, perform Eo-ri-dae-kee when you step into Jwa-poom from Won-poom. Second, from the position you performed Eo-ri-dae-kee in Jwa-poom, stand up with your left foot lifted and perform Bit-jang-geo-ri. Third, take a step with your left foot as Won-poom. At this time, unlike the previous Bit-jang-geo-ri, take a basic step of Won-poom rather than a long step. At the same time, rotate the right arm which lifted for Bit-jang-geo-ri to the front of your body. Fourth, when the wrist of the right arm, which is rotated to the front of your body, is near the left side of your waist, you perform Eo-ri-dae-kee while stepping Woo-poom. Fifth, raise your right leg and perform Bit-jang-geo-ri.

When you perform Eo-ri-dae-goh Bit-jang-geo-ri, you don't take a long step with the lifted leg unlike when you are performing just Bit-jang-geo-ri.
When Eo-ri-dae-kee and Bit-jang-geo-ri are performed in a row, the two arms are lifted outwards and brought down inwards. The hand that goes up to perform Chee-mahk-kee should be rotated outward, and the hand that perform Eo-ri-dae-kee after Chee-mahk-kee should be roated inside.

4-1

4-2

5

⑥ 거리재고 키재기

거리재고 키재기는 팔을 앞으로 뻗어 상대와 거리를 가늠해보는 거리재기와 팔을 위로 뻗어 상대의 키를 가늠해보는 키재기를 연이어 펼치는 동작이다. 거리재고 키재기는 품 길게 밟기와 맞추어 실시한다.

첫째, 원품에서 좌품으로 내딛으며 왼손과 팔꿈치를 반듯이 편 상태로 정면을 향해 왼팔을 어깨높이까지 수평으로 들어올린다. 이때, 손날을 수직으로 세워준다. 둘째, 들어 올린 왼 팔을 그대로 내리며 일어섬과 동시에 오른팔을 뒤쪽으로 쭉 뻗어 하늘을 향해 들어올린다. 이때, 오른손 엄지손가락이 정면을 향하게 비스듬히 올린다. 오른팔을 올릴 때는 자신의 몸통 옆으로 올려야 한다. 셋째, 오른팔을 올렸던 경로 그대로 내리며 품 길게 밟기의 형태에 맞춰 왼발을 뒤로 내딛는다. 넷째, 오른발을 틀어 우품을 디디며 뒤로 내린 오른팔을 그대로 들어 올려 거리재기 한다. 다섯째, 일어서며 오른팔을 내리고 왼팔을 뒤로 들어 올려 키재기 한다. 여섯째, 왼발을 길게 밟기에 맞춰 앞으로 내딛으며 반복한다. 품 길게 밟기와 마찬가지로 좌품에서 시작하는 거리재고 키재기를 연습한 후, 우품에서 시작하는 것도 연습한다.

> 옛 기록 영상에 보면 초대인간문화재인 신한승 선생께서 거리재고 키재기로 상대 앞에서 여유를 부리시며 실제로 거리를 조절하는 모습을 확인할 수 있다. 단순히 상대 앞에 자신감을 보이기 위한 용도이기도 하면서, 거리개념이 중요한 견주기 혹은 마주 메기기에서 실제로 사용되기도 하는 것이다.

1	2	3

⑥ Geo-ri-jae-go Ki-jae-kee

Geo-ri-jae-go Ki-jae-kee is a series of movements of Geo-ri-jae-kee measuring the distance from the opponent by extending the arm forward and Ki-jae-keei measuring the height of the opponent by extending the arm upwards. Geo-ri-jae-go Ki-jae-kee is carried out with Poom Keel-gay-bahl-kee.

First, raise your left arm horizontally to shoulder level towards the front with the left hand and elbow straight while you are taking a step of Jwa-poom from Won-poom. At this point, the knife edge of the hand should be vertical. Second, stand up as you put down your left arm, and at the same time stretch your right arm to the back and raise it toward the sky. At this point, the palm of your right hand must face diagonally forward with the thumb facing the front. When you raise your right arm, you have to raise it to the side of your body. Third, lower the right arm in the same path as it was raised and take the left foot back in the form of Poom Keel-gay-bahl-kee. Fourth, turn your right foot to step Woo-poom and raise your right arm forward to perform Geo-ri-jae-kee. Fifth, lower your right arm and raise your left arm to the back to perform Ki-jae-kee while standing up. Sixth, repeat from Jwa-poom. Just like Poom Keel-gay-bahl-kee, practice this starting with Woo-poom.

In the old video, you can see that GM Shin Han-seung, the first human cultural asset, was actually controlling the distance by taking his time in front of the opponent while he was performing Geo-ri-jae-go Ki-jae-kee. This is simply intended to show confidence in front of the opponent, and it is also used in Kyeon-joo-kee or Mah-joo Me-kee-kee in which the concept of distance is important.

4

5

6

(2) 얼러 메기기

얼러 메기기는 '바로-절-원품-서거라-섯다'의 구령에 따라 서로 마주 보는 상태에서 활개 두 손 옆으로 흔들며 품밟기를 하며 시작한다.

첫째, 상대와 마주보고 선 후, '바로', '절'의 구령에 맞추어 상대에게 예를 표한 후, '원품'의 구령에 따라 상대를 마주보고 원품으로 선다. 둘째, '서거라'의 구령에 따라 좌품 자세를 취한다. 이때, 서로의 거리는 좌품으로 내민 왼발 끝이 닿을 듯 말 듯한 거리를 유지한다. 셋째,'섯다'의 구령에 따라 좌품의 왼발을 들어 올려 상대와 호흡을 맞춘 후 동시에 좌품부터 활개 두 손 흔들며 품밟기를 시작한다. 이때 두 손 흔들기는 '두 손의 손등이 앞을 보며'의 형태로 한다.

1-1

1-2

1-3

(2) Eol-luh Me-kee-ke

Eol-luh Me-kee-keebegins with Hwahl-gay Doo-sohn Yeop-eu-roh Huhn-duhl-myuh Poom-bahl-kee while facing each other following the command of Baro, Jeol, Won-poom, Suh-guh-ra and Suht-da.

First, stand face to face with the opponent and show respect to the opponent in accordance with the command of Baro and Jeol, then face the opponent in Won-poom following the command of Won-poom. Second, take the posture of Jwa-poom according to the command of Suh-guh-ra. At this time, each other's distance is kept as close as the tips of their left feet touching. Third, lift the left foot of Jwa-poom to work with the opponent according to the command of Suht-da, and at the same time start Hwahl-gay Doo-sohn Yeop-eu-roh Huhn-duhl-myuh Poom-bahl-kee from Jwa-poom. At this time, the back of the two hands should be facing forward.

2	3-1	3-2

얼러 메기기는 품밟기의 박자에 맞춘 공격 동작들의 수련 과정이므로 항상 공격자가 중심이 되어 수련을 실시한다. 대개 먼저 공격을 시작하는 사람을 윗대로 정하고 나중에 공격을 시작하는 사람을 아랫대로 정해 번갈아 공격한다. 모든 동작은 윗대가 왼발로 공격 동작을 취하는 것으로 시작되며, 아랫대는 상대의 공격을 편안하게 받아주게 된다.
윗대가 두 번 연이어 공격한 후에는 다시 서로 왼발을 들어 올려 호흡을 맞춘 뒤, 좌품부터 품밟기를 시작한다. 좌품을 내딛을 때, 미끄러지듯이 움직여 서로 간에 처음 시작할 때의 적당한 거리를 유지하도록 한다.
얼러메기기에서는 중요한 두 가지 형태의 공격을 위한 품밟기를 배우는 것이 매우 중요하다. 첫 번째는 왼발로 공격 시 우품을 밟은 후 원품으로 돌아오지 않고 오른발을 걷기로 내디디며 공격하는 품의 형태이다. 두 번째는 왼발로 공격 시 우품을 밟지 않고 원품에서 곧바로 오른발을 걷기의 형태로 내디디며 공격하는 품의 형태이다. 참고로 첫 번째는 하나, 둘, '셋의 박자에서 공격을 하는 것'이라 부를 수 있고, 두 번째는 '하나의 박자에서 공격을 하는 것'이라 이름 붙일 수 있다.

Eol-luh Me-kee-kee is a training process for attack movements tailored to the beat of Poom-bahl-kee, so the training is always centered on attackers. Usually, a person who initiates an attack first is chosen as Wit-dae and a person who starts the attack later is chosen as Ah-raet-dae and alternately attacks. All movements start with the Wit-dae taking the offensive action with the left foot, and the Ah-raet-dae comfortably accepts the opponent's attack.
After two consecutive attacks by Wit-dae, they raise their left feet again to work together, and then start Poom-bahl-kee from Jwa-poom. When stepping on Jwa-poom move like slipping away, keep each other at a reasonable distance from the first start.
In Eol-luh Me-kee-kee, it is very important to learn Poom-bahl-kee for two important forms of attack. The first is to attack as you put down your right foot in Guht-kee instead of returning to Won-poom after you take a step of Woo-poom when you attack with the left foot. The second is to attack as you put down your right foot in Guht-kee directly from Won-poom instead of stepping Woo-poom when you attack with your left foot. For reference, the first can be called ‘attack on the third beat' and the second can be named ‘attack on the first beat'.

(2-1) 발질

① 발등걸이 및 무릎걸이

발등걸이 및 무릎걸이는 막음질의 발등걸이와 무릎걸이 동작을 공격으로 사용하는 동작이다. 발등걸이와 무릎걸이는 각각 따로 실시하지만 수련체계의 순서 상, 발등걸이 및 무릎걸이로 합쳐 칭한다.

첫째, 두 손 옆으로 흔들며 품밟기를 두세 번 한 후, 윗대는 우품을 내딛은 다음 오른 발을 원품자리로 놓지 않고 걷기의 형태로 상대에게 다가간다. 아랫대는 윗대의 움직임에 관계없이 지속적으로 품밟기를 한다. 둘째, 윗대는 아랫대의 왼발이 좌품으로 나오는 박자에 맞춰 상대의 왼발이 지면에 닿기 직전, 발등걸이로 상대의 왼쪽 정강이 중간 혹은 발목 부분을 찍어 누르듯 밀어낸다. 무릎걸이로 공격할 때에는 아랫대의 무릎이나 허벅지 중간부분을 공격한다. 이때, 아랫대는 발등걸이(무릎걸이)에 맞은 왼 다리를 자연스럽게 빼어 뒤로 한걸음 내딛고 멈춘다. 셋째, 윗대는 발등걸이(무릎걸이) 한 왼발을 걷기의 형태로 내려놓으며 아랫대를 좇아 들어가 오른발로 상대의 오른 다리에 발등걸이(무릎걸이)를 한다. 아랫대는 역시 오른발이 밀리는 대로 자연스럽게 뒤로 한걸음 내딛는다. 넷째, 윗대는 발등걸이 한 오른발을 바닥에 닿기 전에 뒤로 멀리 빼며 처음 시작의 위치로 돌아와 왼발을 들어올린다, 아랫대는 뒤로 내딛은 오른발에 체중을 이동한 후 왼발을 들어올린다. 다섯째, 서로 왼발을 들어 올린 상태에서 호흡을 맞춘 후, 좌품부터 내딛는다. 이후 아랫대는 품밟기를 하며 윗대를 향해 다가가서 처음의 위치로 돌아간다.

* 발등걸이

1-1	1-2	1-3

(2-1) Bahl-jil

① Bahl-deung-guh-ree & Moo-reup-guh-ree

Bahl-deung-guh-ree and Moo-reup-guh-ree are actions that use the movements of Bahl-deung-guh-ree and Moo-reup-guh-ree from Mahk-eum-jil as an attack. They are performed separately, but in the order of the training system, they are named while combined into Bahl-deung-guh-ree and Moo-reup-guh-ree.

First, after two or three Doo-sohn Yeop-eu-roh Huhn-duhl-myuh Foom-bahl-kee, Wit-dae steps out of Woo-poom and approaches the opponent in the form of Guht-kee instead of placing his right foot in Won-poom. Ah-raet-dae continues Poom-bahl-kee regardless of Wit-dae's movement. Second, Wit-dae pushes the opponent's left leg with Bahl-deung-guh-ree as if pressing down on the middle of the shin or ankle part of the opponent's left leg just before the opponent's left foot touches the ground in line with the beat of Ah-raet-dae's left foot moves forward in Jwa-poom. When attacking with Moo-reup-guh-ree, attack Ah-raet-dae's knee or the middle of the thigh. At this time, Ah-raet-dae naturally pulls back the left leg that is hit by Bahl-deung-guh-ree(Moo-reup-guh-ree) and steps one step back. Third, Wit-dae steps his/her left foot which performed Bahl-deung-guh-ree (Moo-reup-guh-ree) in the form of Guht-kee, chasing after Ah-raet-dae and performing Bahl-deung-guh-ree(Moo-reup-guh-ree) with his/her right foot in the opponents right leg. Ah-raet-dae naturally takes a step back as the right foot is pushed back. Fourth, Wit-dae brings his/her right foot which performed Bahl-deung-guh-ree far back before it touches the floor, returning to the beginning position and lifting his/her left foot. Ah-raet-dae moves his/her weight to the right foot that stepped back and lifts his/her left foot. Fifth, work with each other with their left feet raised, and then step into Jwa-poom. After that, Ah-raet-dae moves toward Wit-dae while performing Poom-bahl-kee, and returns to its original position.

* Bahl-deung-guh-ree

2 | 3-1 | 3-2

발등걸이(무릎걸이)의 공격이 끝나고 난 후에 윗대는 공격한 발을 딛지 않고 뒤로 뺀다. 이때 오른발을 뒤로 멀리 디뎌 가능한 처음 시작한 위치로 돌아간다. 그러고 나서 왼발을 들어 올려 아랫대를 기다린다. 반면 아랫대는 공격당한 오른발을 뒤로 내딛은 후 왼발을 들고 윗대가 왼발을 들어올리길 기다린다. 그러고 나서 서로 호흡을 맞춰 왼발을 내딛는다. 이후 아랫대는 품밟기를 하는 와중에 품 길게 밟기의 동작을 응용하여 윗대에게 다가간다. 처음의 위치로 돌아오면 양쪽 모두 앞에 내딛은 발의 끝이 닿을 듯 말 듯한 거리를 유지하며 품밟기를 한다.

윗대 혹은 아랫대의 한차례 공격이 마무리 된 후에는 동일한 방식으로 처음의 자리로 돌아가 거리를 조절한다. 그리고 모든 얼러 메기기는 한쪽의 공격이 마무리 되면 동일한 방식으로 각자의 위치와 거리를 유지한다. 이후의 설명에서는 특이한 상황이 있는 경우를 제외하고는 공격 후의 되돌아가기를 따로 설명하지 않을 것이다.

* 무릎걸이

1-1	1-2	1-3

공격 후 되돌아가기

4	5-1	5-2

After the attack of Bahl-deung-guh-ree(Moo-reup-guh-ree) is over, Wit-dae pulls the attacking foot back without stepping down. At this point, he/she pulls the right foot far back and returns to the first position where he/she started. Then he/she lifts his/her left foot and waits for Ah-raet-dae. At the same time, Ah-raet-dae puts his/her right foot back, raises his/her left foot, and waits for Wit-dae to lift his/her left foot. Then they work together to take a step with their left feet.

Ah-raet-dae then approaches Wit-dae by applying the movement of Poom Keel-gay-bahl-kee during the performance of Poom-bahl-kee. When you return to the starting position, both sides perform Poom-bahl-kee, while keeping the distance as if the tips of the feet were touching.

After one set of attacks of Wit-dae or Ah-raet-dae is completed, the distance is adjusted by returning to the first position in the same way. And all Eol-luh Me-kee-kee, maintains their position and distance in the same way when one side of the attack is completed. Subsequent explanations will not describe the return after an attack unless there are unusual circumstances.

* Moo-reup-guh-ree

2	3-1	3-2

Return after attacks

5-3	5-4	return to 1-1

② 발등걸며 무릎걸이

발등걸며 무릎걸이는 발등걸이와 무릎걸이를 한 번씩 순서대로 사용하여 상대를 공격하는 동작이다.

첫째, 두 손 옆으로 흔들며 품밟기를 두세 번 한 후, 윗대는 우품을 내딛은 다음 오른 발을 원품자리로 놓지 않고 걷기의 형태로 상대에게 다가간다. 아랫대는 윗대의 움직임에 관계없이 지속적으로 품밟기를 한다. 둘째, 윗대는 아랫대의 왼발이 좌품으로 나오는 박자에 맞춰 상대의 왼발이 지면에 닿기 직전, 발등걸이로 상대의 왼쪽 정강이 중간 혹은 발목 부분을 찍어 누르듯 밀어낸다. 이때, 아랫대는 발등걸이에 맞은 왼 다리를 자연스럽게 빼어 뒤로 한걸음 내딛고 멈춘다. 셋째, 윗대는 발등걸이 한 왼발을 걷기의 형태로 내려놓으며 아랫대를 좇아 들어가 오른발로 상대의 오른 무릎 혹은 그 윗부분에 무릎걸이를 한다. 아랫대는 역시 오른발이 밀리는 대로 자연스럽게 뒤로 한걸음 내딛는다. 넷째, 윗대는 무릎걸이 한 오른발을 바닥에 닿기 전에 뒤로 멀리 빼며 처음 시작의 위치로 돌아와 왼발을 들어올린다, 아랫대는 뒤로 내딛은 오른발에 체중을 이동한 후 왼발을 들어올린다. 이후 서로 호흡을 맞추어 품밟기를 하며 처음의 위치와 거리로 돌아간다.

1-1

1-2

1-3

② Bahl-deung-guhl-myuh Moo-reup-guh-ree

Bahl-deung-guhl-myuh Moo-reup-guh-ree is a movement in which Bahl-deung-guh-ree and Moo-reup-guh-ree are used in order to attack the opponent.

First, after two or three Doo-sohn Yeop-eu-roh Huhn-duhl-myuh Poom-bahl-kee, Wit-dae steps out of Woo-poom and approaches the opponent in the form of Guht-kee instead of placing his/her right foot in Won-poom. Ah-raet-dae continues his/her Poom-bahl-kee regardless of Wit-dae's movement. Second, Wit-dae pushes the opponent's left leg with Bahl-deung-guh-ree as if pressing down on the middle of the shin or ankle part of the opponent's left leg just before the opponent's left foot touches the ground in line with the beat of Ah-raet-dae's left foot moves forward from Jwa-poom. At this time, Ah-raet-dae naturally pulls back the left leg that is hit by Bahl-deung-guh-ree and steps one step back. Third, Wit-dae lowers his/her left foot which performed Bahl-deung-guh-ree in the form of Guht-kee, chasing after Ah-raet-dae and performing Moo-reup-guh-ree with his/her right foot to the opponent's right knee or upper part of it. Ah-raet-dae naturally takes a step back as the right foot is pushed back. Fourth, Wit-dae brings his/her right foot which performed Moo-reup-guh-ree far back before it touches the floor, returning to the position of the beginning and lifting his/her left foot. Ah-raet-dae moves his/her weight on the right foot that stepped back and lifts his/her left foot. After that, they return to their original location and distance while they are performing Poom-bahl-kee in harmony.

2

3-1

3-2

택견의 기술 중에는 양면성을 가지고 있는 기술들이 많이 있다. 같은 동작일지라도 상대의 공격에 대한 방어의 형태로 사용하는 경우와 상대의 공격 없이 내가 선제공격의 형태로 사용하는 경우가 있다. 즉 형태가 같은 동작이지만 상황에 따라 다르게 적용할 수 있는 것이다. 발등걸이와 무릎걸이도 이에 속한다.

막음질에서 상대의 발차기를 막는 동작이었던 발등걸이와 무릎걸이는 얼러 메기기에서는 공격동작으로 활용된다. 상대의 내딛는 발을 찍어 눌러 균형을 흩뜨리는 동시에 자신이 원하는 방향으로 움직여준다. 발등걸이 혹은 무릎걸이로는 상대를 넘어뜨리거나 얼굴 등을 때리기 어렵다. 단지 품밟기의 균형이나 상대의 움직임을 방해하여 자신의 의도대로 자세를 취하도록 하는 것에 그칠 뿐이다. 그러나 이를 통해 다른 공격을 이어갈 수 있는 기회를 만든다는 데 중점을 두고 수련하여야 한다.

발등걸이와 무릎걸이 그리고 발등걸며 무릎걸이를 비롯한 얼러 메기기의 공격 기술은 앞서 말한 바와 같이 두 번 연속으로 이어진다. 이때 초보자들은 아무 생각 없이, 그저 상대를 따라가며 기술을 사용한다. 그러나 보다 효과적으로 기술을 익히고 실전에 응용하기 위해서는 첫 공격에 밀려나는 상대의 움직임을 파악하고 다음 공격이 정확하고 쉽게 들어갈 수 있는 위치를 찾아서 두 번째 공격을 이어나가는 습관을 가져야 한다. 상대방의 성향이나 체형, 자신의 공격 방향이나 세기 등에 따라 첫 번째 공격 이후에 상대가 취하게 되는 자세나 발을 놓는 자리 혹은 중심의 위치 등이 항상 달라지기 때문이다. 연이은 공격의 순간에 상대의 반응을 읽고 그에 맞춰 공격을 이어가는 것 역시 얼러 메기기에서 수련해야할 내용인 것이다.

There are many multi-faceted techniques in Taekgyeon. Even if it is the same move, there are times when it is used as a defense against the opponent's attack and when you use it as a form of preemptive attack without the opponent's attack. In other words, it has the same form of motion, but can be applied differently depending on the situation. This includes Bahl-deung-guh-ree and Moo-reup-guh-ree.

Bahl-deung-guh-ree and Moo-reup-guh-ree, which used to block the opponent's kick in Mahk-eum-jil, are used as attack actions in Eol-luh Me-kee-kee. Press the opponent's foot to disperse the balance and move it in the direction you want at the same time. With Bahl-deung-guh-ree or Moo-reup-guh-ree, it is difficult to trip or hit the opponent's face. It only to break the balance of Poom-bahl-kee or interfere with the opponent's movements so that you can trick your opponent to take a certain position. However, the training should focus on creating opportunities to continue other attacks through this.

The attack techniques of Eol-luh Me-kee-kee, including Bahl-deung-guh-ree, Moo-reup-guh-ree, etc. continue twice in a row, as previously stated. At this time, beginners use their skills without thinking, just following the opponent. However, in order to learn the skills more effectively and apply them in practice, it is necessary to identify the opponent's movements pushed by the first attack and to have the habit of finding the correct and easy target for the next attack to continue the second attack. Depending on the opponent's tendency, body type, direction or strength of his or her attack, the stance, placement of foot, or position of balance that the opponent takes after the first attack always changes. Reading the opponent's response at the moment of an successive attack and continuing the attack accordingly is also something that needs to be trained in Eol-luh Me-kee-kee.

③ 딴죽 (앞 딴죽, 가로 딴죽)

얼러 메기기에서 딴죽은 서서 익히기의 비비기 동작으로 상대의 발목을 차내는 동작이다. 이때 상대의 발목 안쪽을 차내는 것을 앞 딴죽, 바깥쪽을 차내는 것을 가로 딴죽(뒷 딴죽)이라 부른다. 이 두 가지 딴죽을 시행하는 동작이 서로 차이가 있으므로 둘로 구분하여 설명한다.

ⓐ 앞 딴죽

첫째, 두 손 옆으로 흔들며 품밟기를 두세 번 한 후, 윗대는 우품을 내딛은 다음 오른 발을 원품자리로 놓지 않고 걷기의 형태로 상대에게 다가간다. 아랫대는 윗대의 움직임에 관계없이 지속적으로 품밟기를 한다. 둘째, 윗대는 아랫대의 왼발이 좌품으로 나오는 박자에 맞춰 상대의 왼발이 지면에 닿기 직전, 안쪽으로 꺾은 왼발의 발바닥을 이용하여 상대의 왼쪽 발목 안쪽 복사뼈를 밀어주듯이 차낸다. 이때 아랫대는 딴죽에 맞은 왼 다리를 자연스럽게 빼어 뒤로 한 걸음 내딛고 멈춘다. 셋째, 윗대는 딴죽을 친 왼발을 걷기의 형태로 내려놓으며 아랫대를 좇아 들어가 오른발로 상대의 오른 발목에 앞 딴죽을 친다. 아랫대는 역시 오른발이 밀리는 대로 자연스럽게 뒤로 한걸음 내딛는다. 넷째, 윗대는 딴죽을 친 오른발을 바닥에 닿기 전에 뒤로 멀리 빼며 처음 시작의 위치로 돌아와 왼발을 들어올린다. 아랫대는 뒤로 내딛은 오른발에 체중을 이동한 후 왼발을 들어올린다. 이후 서로 호흡을 맞추어 품밟기를 하며 처음의 위치와 거리로 돌아간다.

1-1	1-2	1-3

③ Dahn-jook (Ahp Dahn-jook, Gah-roh Dahn-jook)

In Eol-luh Me-kee-kee, Dahn-jook kicks off of the opponent's ankle with Bee-bee-kee of Suh-suh Ik-hee-kee. At this time, kicking the inside of the opponent's ankle is called Ahp Dahn-jook and kicking the outside is called Gah-roh Dahn-jook(Duit Dahn-jook). The behavior of implementing these two Dahn-jooks is different, so they are described separately.

ⓐ Ahp Dahn-jook

First, after two or three Doo-sohn Yeop-eu-roh Huhn-duhl-myuh Poom-bahl-kee, Wit-dae steps out of Woo-poom and approaches the opponent in the form of Guht-kee instead of placing his/her right foot in Won-poom. Ah-raet-dae continues Poom-bahl-kee regardless of Wit-dae's movement. Second, Wit-dae uses the sole of the left foot, which is turned inwards, to kick the opponent's left ankle, as if pushing the ankle bone inside the opponent's left ankle just before the opponent's left foot touches the ground in line with the beat of Ah-raet-dae's Jwa-poom stepping. At this time, Ah-raet-dae naturally pulls back the left leg that is hit by Dahn-jook and steps one step back. Third, Wit-dae lowers his/her left foot which perormed Dahn-jook in the form of Guht-kee, chasing after Ah-raet-dae and performing Ahp Dahn-jook with his/her right foot to the opponent's right ankle. Ah-raet-dae naturally takes a step back as the right foot is pushed back. Fourth, Wit-dae brings his/her right foot which performed Dahn-jook far back before it touches the floor, returning to the position at the beginning and lifting his/her left foot. Ah-raet-dae moves his/her weight on the right foot that stepped back and lifts his/her left foot. After that, they return to their original location and distance while they are performing Poom-bahl-kee in harmony.

2

3-1

3-2

③ 딴죽 (앞 딴죽, 가로 딴죽)

ⓑ 가로 딴죽 (뒷 딴죽)

첫째, 두 손 옆으로 흔들며 품밟기를 두세 번 한 후, 윗대는 좌품에서 원품을 거쳐 우품을 내딛을 순서에 오른발을 걷기의 형태로 디디며 상대에게 다가간다. 아랫대는 윗대의 움직임에 관계없이 지속적으로 품밟기를 한다. 둘째, 윗대는 아랫대의 오른발이 우품을 딛고 들리는 순간에 맞춰 안쪽으로 꺾은 왼발의 발바닥을 이용하여 상대의 오른쪽 발목 바깥쪽을 밀어주듯이 차낸다. 이때 아랫대는 딴죽에 맞은 오른 다리를 자연스럽게 빼어 뒤로 한걸음 내딛고 멈춘다. 셋째, 윗대는 딴죽을 친 왼발을 걷기의 형태로 내려놓으며 아랫대를 좇아 들어가 오른발로 상대의 왼쪽 발목에 가로 딴죽을 친다. 아랫대는 딴죽을 맞은 왼발을 자연스럽게 내려놓는다. 넷째, 윗대는 딴죽을 친 오른발을 바닥에 닿기 전에 뒤로 멀리 빼며 처음 시작의 위치로 돌아와 왼발을 들어올린다, 아랫대는 자연스럽게 내려놓았던 왼발을 들어올린다. 이후 서로 호흡을 맞추어 품밟기를 하며 처음의 위치와 거리로 돌아간다.

1-1	1-2	1-3

③ Dahn-jook (Ahp Dahn-jook, Gah-roh Dahn-jook)

ⓑ Gah-roh Dahn-jook (Duit Dahn-jook)

First, after two or three Doo-sohn Yeop-eu-roh Huhn-duhl-myuh Poom-bahl-kee, Wit-dae steps Jwa-poom & Won-poom, then readying Woo-poom, he/she approaches the opponent by stepping on his/her right foot in the form of Guht-kee. Ah-raet-dae continues Poom-bahl-kee regardless of Wit-dae's movement. Second, Wit-dae uses the sole of the left foot, which is turned inward, and kicks the outside of the opponent's right ankle as if he/she is pushing it at the moment of Ah-raet-dae's right foot was lifted after it stepped Woo-poom. At this time, Ah-raet-dae naturally pulls back the right leg that is hit by Dahn-jook and steps one step back. Third, Wit-dae is lowered his/her left foot which perormed Dahn-jook in the form of Guht-kee, chasing after Ah-raet-dae and performing Gah-roh Dahn-jook with his/her right foot in the opponent's left ankle. Ah-raet-dae naturally puts down the left foot that was hit by Dahn-jook. Fourth, Wit-dae brings his/her right foot which performed Dahn-jook far back before it touches the floor, returning to the position of the beginning and lifting his/her left foot. Ah-raet-dae lifts the left foot that was naturally lowered down. After that, they return to their original location and distance while they are performing Poom-bahl-kee in harmony.

1-4

2

3

앞 딴죽과 가로 딴죽의 차이는 발목의 안쪽을 노리는지 또는 바깥쪽을 노리는지 이다. 이로 인해 공격자의 왼발로 상대의 왼발을 노릴 것인지 오른발을 노릴 것인지가 달라진다. 왼발로 왼발을 노리는 것을 '엇'이라고 부르며 왼발로 오른발을 노리는 것을 '맞'이라고 부른다.

나아가며 익히기에서 왼다리에 왼손을 쓰는 경우를 '맞'이라고 설명하였다. 자신의 몸에서 같은 쪽은 사용하기 때문이다. 얼러 메기기에서도 같은 방향인지 다른 방향인지는 자신을 기준으로 판단한다. 따라서 나의 왼쪽은 상대의 오른쪽이 되며 이 경우가 '맞'이 된다.

'맞'과 '엇'은 공격을 하는 순간 내딛는 발에 차이가 생긴다. 얼러 메기기의 대부분을 차지하는 '엇'에서는 오른발을 우품으로 내딛었다가 원품으로 옮겨 딛는 타이밍에 걷기로 변화시킨다. 따라서 자신의 오른발을 내딛은 다음 박자가 상대의 왼발이 좌품을 딛기 위해 나오는 순간이 된다. 이때는 상대의 왼발이 완전히 디뎌지기 전이므로 상대의 균형이 가장 불안한 순간임과 동시에 왼발과 바닥의 마찰력이 전혀 없는 순간이 된다. 따라서 이때 왼발을 공격하는 것은 거의 아무런 저항 없이 자신의 공격을 성공시킬 수 있는 순간이다.

'맞'으로 공격을 하는 순간에는 우품을 딛어야 할 오른발을 걷기로 변화시켜 딛는다. 따라서 상대의 오른발이 바닥에 완전히 닿는 순간, 자신의 오른발도 바닥에 닿으며 이때 자신의 중심은 오른발 위에 안정적으로 서게 된다. 이후, 품밟기의 순서에 따라 상대의 오른발이 원품으로 되돌아가야 하는 순간이 자신의 왼발로 공격을 가할 수 있는 순간이 된다. 이때 상대는 오른발을 들어올리기 시작하여 오른발에 실린 체중과 마찰력이 없어지므로 공격하기 좋은 순간이 된다.

이처럼 얼러 메기기는 품밟기에 따른 상대의 체중과 균형 및 다리의 움직임을 읽어 최적의 순간을 잡아 공격하는 연습을 하는 수련과정이다. 앞서 발등걸며 무릎걸이에서 언급했던 상대의 움직임에 맞춰 좇아가는 연습 역시 놓쳐서는 안 된다.

The difference between Ahp Dahn-jook and Gah-roh Dahn-jook is whether you are aiming for the inside of the opponent's ankle or for the outside. This will change whether the attacker's left foot is aimed at the opponent's left foot or right foot. To aim for the left foot with the left foot is called 'Uht,' and to aim for the right foot with the left foot is called 'Maht.' The use of the left hand on the left leg in Nah-ah-gah-myuh Ik-hee-kee is described as 'Maht.' This is because he/she uses the same side of the body.

In Eol-luh Me-kee-kee, one judges whether it is in the same or different side based on one's own side. Therefore, my left side becomes my opponent's right side and this case becomes 'Maht.'

'Maht' and 'Uht' differ in the foot step at the moment of an attack. In 'Uht', which takes up most of Eol-luh Me-kee-kee, the right foot steps Woo-poom and then, at the moment of stepping Won-poom, change to Guht-kee. Therefore, the next beat after you put down your right foot is the moment when the opponent's left foot comes out to step Jwa-poom. Since this is before the opponent's left foot completely touches the ground, it is the moment when the opponent's balance is the most unstable, and at the same time, there is no friction between his/her left foot and the floor. Therefore, attacking his/her left foot at this time is a moment when you can make your attack successful with almost no resistance.

When you attack with 'Maht,' you change your right foot to Guht-kee instead of stepping Woo-poom. Therefore, as soon as the opponent's right foot touches the ground completely, your right foot touches the ground too and your balance is stable on the right foot. Afterwards, the moment when the opponent's right foot has to be returned to Won-poom in the order of Poom-bahl-kee becomes the moment when you can attack with your left foot. At this point, the opponent starts lifting his/her right foot and loses friction with the weight on his right foot, which is a good moment to attack.

As such, Eol-luh Me-kee-kee is a training course in which you practice attacking the best moment by reading the weight, balance, and leg movements of the opponent during Poom-bahl-kee. You should also not miss the practice of following the opponent's movements, which was mentioned earlier in the Bahl-deung-guhl-myuh Moo-reup-guh-ree.

앞 딴죽은 공격하는 발이 상대의 앞쪽 45도 방향으로 향하도록 공격한다. 공격의 각도는 보편적으로 45도 각도로 공격하는 것이 바람직한데 특히 딴죽의 경우가 그러하다. 또한 앞 딴죽은 엇의 형태로 공격하기 때문에 상대가 내디딘 발의 뒤쪽에 아무런 지지기반이 없으므로(균형의 중심이 내딛는 앞발에 쏠리는 중이므로 뒷발로 몸을 지지할 수 없다) 45도의 방향으로 힘차게 공격하고 나가면 된다.
가로 딴죽의 경우에는 다르게 적용되는데 맞의 형태로 공격하기 때문에 상대의 오른발을 내 왼발로 딴죽을 치게 된다. 이런 상황에서 45도 방향으로 딴죽을 하게 되면 상대방의 왼발이 뒤에서 지지기반이 되므로(앞발을 당기는 중이므로 균형의 중심이 뒷발에 쏠려있다) 효율적으로 기술이 걸리지 않게 된다. 그러므로 가로 딴죽은 용어 그대로 상대의 바깥쪽 복사뼈 부위를 가로 방향으로(직각 방향) 감듯이 공격했을 때 효과적인 공격이 될 수 있다.

When attacking in Ahp-dahn-jook, the attacking foot is directed 45 degrees forward of the opponent. The angle of attack is generally preferable to attack at a 45 degree angle, especially in the case of Dahn-jook. Also, Ahp-dahn-jook attacks in the form of 'Uht' so that there is no support base behind the foot that the opponent has taken (the center of balance is leaning on the front foot, so he/she can't support his/her body with the back foot), so you can attack vigorously at a 45 degree angle. In the case of Gah-roh-dahn-jook it applies differently. Because it attacks in the form of 'Maht,' you hit the opponent's right foot with your left foot. In this situation, if you perform Dahn-jook at a 45 degree angle, the opponent's left foot will be the base of support from the back (because the opponent is pulling the front foot, the center of the balance will be concentrated on the back foot), so the technique will not be efficient. Thus, Gah-roh-dahn-jook can be an effective attack when you attack the opponent's outer ankle bone horizontally (perpendicular) as if you wind it, as the term implies.

④ 발장다리

얼러 메기기의 발장다리는 맨나중 익히기의 발장다리를 상대에게 사용하는 연습이다.

첫째, 두 손 옆으로 흔들며 품밟기를 두세 번 한 후, 윗대는 우품을 내딛은 다음 오른 발을 원 품자리로 놓지 않고 걷기의 형태로 상대에게 다가간다. 아랫대는 윗대의 움직임에 관계없이 지속적으로 품밟기를 한다. 둘째, 윗대는 아랫대의 왼발이 좌품으로 나오는 박자에 맞춰 상대의 왼발이 지면에 닿기 직전, 오른발 쪽으로 끌어당긴 왼발의 발등을 이용하여 상대의 왼쪽 발목 바깥을 밀듯이 차준다. 이때 아랫대는 발장다리에 맞은 왼 다리를 자연스럽게 빼어 뒤로 한걸음 내딛고 멈춘다. 셋째, 윗대는 발장다리를 친 왼발을 걷기의 형태로 내려놓으며 아랫대를 좇아 들어가 오른발로 상대의 오른 발목에 앞 딴죽을 친다. 아랫대는 역시 오른발이 밀리는 대로 자연스럽게 뒤로 한걸음 내딛는다. 넷째, 윗대는 딴죽을 친 오른발을 바닥에 닿기 전에 뒤로 멀리 빼며 처음 시작의 위치로 돌아와 왼발을 들어올린다, 아랫대는 뒤로 내딛은 오른발에 체중을 이동한 후 왼발을 들어올린다. 이후 서로 호흡을 맞추어 품밟기를 하며 처음의 위치와 거리로 돌아간다.

1-1	1-2	1-3

④ Baht-jang-dah-ree

Baht-jang-dah-ree from Eol-luh Me-kee-kee is a practice in which you use Baht-jang-dah-ree from Maen-nah-joong Ik-hee-kee on your opponent.

First, after two or three Doo-sohn Yeop-eu-roh Huhn-duhl-myuh Poom-bahl-kee, Wit-dae steps out of Woo-poom and approaches the opponent in the form of Guht-kee instead of placing his right foot in Won-poom. Ah-raet-dae continues Poom-bahl-kee regardless of Wit-dae's movement. Second, Wit-dae uses the top of the left foot, which is pulled toward the right foot, to kick the outside of the opponent's left ankle, as if pushing the ankle just before his/her left foot touches the ground in line with the beat of Ah-raet-dae’s left foot comes forward as Jwa-poom. At this time, Ah-raet-dae naturally pulls out the left leg that is hit by Baht-jang-dah-ree and stops one step back. Third, Wit-dae lowers his/her left foot which performed Baht-jang-dah-ree in the form of Guht-kee, chasing after Ah-raet-dae and performing Ahp Dahn-jook with his/her right foot to the opponent’s right ankle. Ah-raet-dae naturally takes a step back as the right foot is pushed back. Fourth, Wit-dae brings his/her right foot which performed Dahn-jook far back before it touches the floor, returning to the starting point and lifting his/her left foot. Ah-raet-dae moves his/her weight on the right foot that stepped back and lifts his/her left foot. After that, they return to their original location and distance while they are performing Poom-bahl-kee in harmony.

2

3-1

3-2

밭장다리에서 가장 중요한 것은 왼발 공격 후, 좇아 들어가 오른발을 공격하는 과정에서 자신의 왼발을 놓는 위치이다. 앞서 말한 바와 같이 연속으로 공격하기 위해선 첫 번째 공격 이후, 상대의 움직임을 보고 따라가는 것이 중요하다. 특히 밭장다리에서는 자신의 왼발을 오른쪽 다리 앞까지 끌고 와 밭장다리를 하게 된다. 따라서 밭장다리를 친 후에 일반적인 걷기의 위치에 딛게 되면 다음 공격 대상인 상대의 오른발이 자신의 왼발보다 바깥쪽에 위치하게 된다. 이를 오른발 밭장다리로 공격하기 위해선 다시 한 번 발을 딛거나 몸을 심하게 틀어주어야 하며 힘이 잘 실리지 않게 된다. 따라서 왼발로 공격한 후, 상대의 오른발의 위치를 확인하고 밭장다리로 공격하기 적절한 위치를 찾아 왼발을 디뎌야 한다.

The most important part of Baht-jang-dah-ree is the position where you put your left foot in the process of attacking the right foot after the left foot attack. As mentioned earlier, it is important to watch and follow the opponent's movements after the first attack in order to attack continuously. In particular, in Baht-jang-dah-ree, you pull your left foot in front of the right leg and play Baht-jang-dah-ree. So if you perform Baht-jang-dah-reeand then step down into a normal Guht-kee position, the opponent's right foot, the next target of the attack, will be placed outside of your left foot. In order to attack it with your right foot Baht-jang-dah-ree, you have to take another step or twist your body severely, but you won't have much power. Therefore, after attacking with the left foot, you have to check the position of the opponent's right foot and find a suitable target to attack with Baht-jang-dah-ree and step down with your left foot.

⑤ 안짱다리

얼러 메기기의 안짱다리는 서서 익히기의 안짱걸이를 상대에게 사용하는 연습이다. 오른발을 걷기로 내딛은 후, 안쪽으로 꺾어 고정한 왼쪽 발목으로 상대방의 왼쪽 발목 뒤쪽을 걸어 당겨준다.

첫째, 두 손 옆으로 흔들며 품밟기를 두세 번 한 후, 윗대는 우품을 내딛은 다음 오른 발을 원 품자리로 놓지 않고 걷기의 형태로 상대에게 다가간다. 아랫대는 윗대의 움직임에 관계없이 지속적으로 품밟기를 한다. 둘째, 윗대는 아랫대의 왼발이 좌품으로 나오는 박자에 맞춰 상대의 왼발이 지면에 닿기 직전, 안쪽으로 꺽은 왼쪽 발목을 이용하여 상대의 왼쪽 발목 뒤쪽을 걸어 당겨준다. 이때 아랫대는 들렸던 왼 다리를 자연스럽게 빼어 뒤로 한걸음 내딛고 멈춘다. 셋째, 윗대는 안짱다리를 한 왼발을 걷기의 형태로 내려놓으며 아랫대를 좇아 들어가 오른발로 상대의 오른 발목에 안짱다리를 걸어준다. 아랫대는 역시 오른발이 밀리는 대로 자연스럽게 뒤로 한걸음 내딛는다. 넷째, 윗대는 안짱다리를 건 오른발을 바닥에 닿기 전에 뒤로 멀리 빼며 처음 시작의 위치로 돌아와 왼발을 들어올린다, 아랫대는 뒤로 내딛은 오른발에 체중을 이동한 후 왼발을 들어올린다. 이후 서로 호흡을 맞추어 품밟기를 하며 처음의 위치와 거리로 돌아간다.

1-1	1-2	2-1

⑤ Ahn-jang-dah-ree

Ahn-jang-dah-ree of Eol-luh Me-kee-kee is a practice in which you use Ahn-jang-guh-ree of Suh-suh Ik-hee-kee to your opponent. After taking the right foot down as Guht-kee, twist the left ankle inwards to pull your person's left ankle.

First, after two or three Doo-sohn Yeop-eu-roh Huhn-duhl-myuh Poom-bahl-kee, Wit-dae steps out of Woo-poom and approaches the opponent in the form of Guht-kee instead of placing his right foot in Won-poom. Ah-raet-dae continues Poom-bahl-kee regardless of Wit-dae's movement. Second, Wit-dae uses his/her left foot, which is turned inwards, to pull from the back of the opponent's left ankle, just before the opponent's left foot touches the ground in line with the beat of Ah-raet-dae's left foot moves forward from Jwa-poom. At this time, Ah-raet-dae naturally pulls out the left leg that was lifted by Wit-dae and steps one step back. Third, Wit-dae lowers his/her left foot which performed Ahn-jang-dah-ree in the form of Guht-kee, chasing after Ah-raet-dae and performing Ahn-jang-dah-ree with his/her right foot to the opponent's right ankle. Ah-raet-dae naturally takes a step back as the right foot is pushed back. Fourth, Wit-dae brings his/her right foot which performed Ahn-jang-dah-ree far back before it touches the floor, returning to the position at the beginning and lifting his/her left foot. Ah-raet-dae moves his/her weight on the right foot that stepped back and lifts his/her left foot. After that, they return to their original location and distance while they are performing Poom-bahl-kee in harmony.

2-2

3-1

3-2

서서 익히기의 안짱다리에서는 동작을 마칠 때까지 걸어주는 다리의 무릎은 굽히지 않고 축이 되는 다리의 무릎 탄력과 뒤쪽으로 가볍게 눕히는 체중의 이동만을 이용하여 상대의 다리를 걸게 된다. 그러나 얼러 메기기의 안짱다리에서는 상대의 발목을 건 후 무릎을 굽히며 들어 올려준다. 이는 기본자세와 응용동작의 차이 때문이라 말할 수도 있지만 안짱다리로 상대의 중심만 흩뜨릴 것인지 혹은 이어지는 동작으로 상대의 들린 다리를 잡아채거나 안으로 파고들 것인지의 목적이 다르기 때문이기도 하다. 즉, 얼러 메기기의 안짱다리는 기본동작과 달리 안짱다리 이후에 이어지는 연계 동작을 염두에 두었기 때문이라 할 수 있다.

When you perform Ahn-jang-dah-ree of Suh-suh Ik-hee-kee, you hook and pull the opponent's leg using only the knee elasticity of the supporting leg and the weight shifted to it without bending the knee of the leg that hooks and pulls until the movement is completed. However, when you perform Ahn-jang-dah-ree of Eol-luh Me-kee-kee, you lift the opponent's ankle by bending your knee after you hook the opponent's ankle. This may be said to be due to the difference in basic stance and applied movement, but it is also because the purpose of the movement is different whether to scatter the opponent's balance with Ahn-jang-dah-ree or grab the opponent's lifted leg or penetrate with a continuous movement. In other words, Ahn-jang-dah-ree of Eol-luh Me-kee-kee, is different from the basic movements, because the subsequent movement is more important.

⑥ 깎음다리

얼러 메기기의 깎음다리는 서서 익히기의 깎음다리를 상대에게 사용하는 연습이다.

첫째, 두 손 옆으로 흔들며 품밟기를 두세 번 한 후, 윗대는 우품을 내딛은 다음 오른 발을 원 품자리로 놓지 않고 걷기의 형태로 상대에게 다가간다. 아랫대는 윗대의 움직임에 관계없이 지속적으로 품밟기를 한다. 둘째, 윗대는 아랫대의 왼발이 좌품으로 나오는 박자에 맞춰 상대의 왼발이 지면에 닿는 순간, 왼발의 발장심으로 무릎에서 발등까지 훑어내리는 형태로 상대의 나오는 다리의 정강이 부위를 깎아내리듯 찍는다. 이때 아랫대는 깎음다리에 밀린 왼 다리를 자연스럽게 빼어 뒤로 한걸음 내딛고 멈춘다. 셋째, 윗대는 깎음다리를 한 왼발을 걷기의 형태로 내려놓으며 아랫대를 좇아 들어가 오른발로 상대의 오른 정강이에 깎음다리를 한다. 아랫대는 역시 오른발이 밀리는 대로 자연스럽게 뒤로 한걸음 내딛는다. 넷째, 윗대는 깎음다리 한 오른발을 바닥에 닿기 전에 뒤로 멀리 빼며 처음 시작의 위치로 돌아와 왼발을 들어올린다, 아랫대는 뒤로 내딛은 오른발에 체중을 이동한 후 왼발을 들어올린다. 이후 서로 호흡을 맞추어 품밟기를 하며 처음의 위치와 거리로 돌아간다.

1-1	1-2	2

⑥ Gahk-gum-dah-ree

Gahk-gum-dah-ree of Eol-luh Me-kee-kee is a practice of using Gahk-gum-dah-ree of Suh-suh Ik-hee-kee on the opponent.

First, after two or three Doo-sohn Yeop-eu-roh Huhn-duhl-myuh Poom-bahl-kee, Wit-dae steps out of Woo-poom and approaches the opponent in the form of Guht-kee instead of placing his/her right foot in Won-poom. Ah-raet-dae continues Poom-bahl-kee regardless of Wit-dae's movement. Second, Wit-dae uses the arch of the left foot to stamp on the opponent's approaching left shin as if you cut down at it at the moment that the opponent's left foot touches the ground in line with the beat of Ah-raet-dae's left foot moves forward for Jwa-poom. At this time, Ah-raet-dae naturally pulls back the left leg that is pushed by Gahk-gum-dah-ree and steps one step back. Third, Wit-dae lowers his/her left foot which performed Gahk-gum-dah-ree in the form of Guht-kee, chasing after Ah-raet-dae and performing Gahk-gum-dah-ree with his/her right foot to the opponent's right shin. Ah-raet-dae naturally takes a step back as the right foot is pushed back. Fourth, Wit-dae brings his/her right foot which performed Gahk-gum-dah-ree, far back before it touches the floor, returning to the position at the beginning and lifting his/her left foot. Ah-raet-dae moves his/her weight on the right foot that stepped back and lifts his/her left foot. After that, they return to their original location and distance while they are performing Poom-bahl-kee in harmony.

3	4-1	4-2

깎음다리에서 중요한 점은 깎음다리를 하는 자신의 다리를 충분히 높게 놀려야 한다는 것이다. 실제로 상대의 무릎 바로 아래부터 깎음다리를 하려면 그보다 윗부분을 노리고 들어가야 원하는 지점에 정확히 맞출 수 가 있다.
또한 깎음다리를 할 때는 세게 친다는 느낌보다는 문지른다는 느낌으로 해야 한다. 자신의 골반을 상대의 정강이 쪽으로 슬며시 밀며 발바닥에 체중을 실어 눌러주어야 한다. 그렇게 해야 상대의 다리가 튕겨나가지 않고 제자리에서 눌리며 주저앉도록 할 수 있다.

The important thing about Gahk-gum-dah-ree is that you have to raise your legs high enough when you perform it. In fact, if you want to perform Gahk-gum-dah-ree, from just below the opponent's knee, you have to aim for the thigh to get the exact spot you want. Also, when you perform Gahk-gum-dah-ree to your opponent, you should feel like you are rubbing rather than striking. You have to gently push your pelvis toward the opponent's shin and put your weight on the sole of your foot to press down. That way, the opponent's legs can be pushed down and collapsed without bouncing off.

⑦ 오금차기 및 중방걸이

ⓐ 오금차기

오금차기는 제치기로 상대의 목을 제치며 같은 쪽 다리로 무릎 뒤쪽에 후려차기를 해주는 동작이다. 이 동작은 상대를 넘어뜨리는 기술로 제치기와 후려차기가 순간적으로 이어져 연속으로 들어가게 되며, 제치기와 후려차기의 반복 없이 첫 번째에 상대방을 넘어뜨린다.

첫째, 두 손 옆으로 흔들며 품밟기를 두세 번 한 후, 윗대는 우품을 내딛을 순서에 걷기의 형태로 상대에게 다가간다. 아랫대는 윗대의 움직임에 관계없이 지속적으로 품밟기를 한다. 둘째, 윗대는 아랫대의 오른발이 우품을 딛고 들리는 박자에 맞춰 왼팔로 상대의 목에 제치기를 해준다. 셋째, 윗대는 제치기에 걸린 상대의 목을 자신의 왼쪽 뒤를 향해 더욱 밀어주며 동시에 왼 발목으로 상대의 오른 오금을 후려차서 아랫대를 넘어뜨린다. 아랫대는 윗대의 공격이 완전하게 들어오면 안전하게 넘어진다. 넷째, 아랫대가 넘어진 후, 윗대는 처음의 자리로 돌아가 좌품으로 기다린다. 아랫대는 일어나 시작 자리로 돌아와서 좌품으로 선다. 서로 왼발을 살짝 들어 올린 후, 호흡을 맞추어 품밟기를 하며 아랫대의 공격 순서를 시작한다.

1-1	1-2	2

⑦ Oh-gum-cha-kee & Joong-bang-guh-ree

ⓐ Oh-gum-cha-kee

Oh-gum-cha-kee is a movement in which you do Hoo-ryuh-cha-kee to the back of the opponen's knee with the same side leg, pushing away the opponent's neck with Jay-chee-kee. The move is a technique that throws down an opponent, with Jay-chee-kee and Hoo-ryuh-cha-kee. The two techniques are momentarily connected, and they throw the opponent down at once without repetition.

First, after two or three Doo-sohn Yeop-eu-roh Huhn-duhl-myuh Poom-bahl-kee, Wit-dae steps his/her right foot in the form of Guht-kee, and approaches the opponent instead of placing his/her right foot in Woo-poom. Ah-raet-dae continues Poom-bahl-kee regardless of Wit-dae's movement. Second, Wit-dae performs Jay-chee-kee to the opponent's neck with his/her left arm in line with the beat of Ah-raet-dae's right foot was lifted after it stepped Woo-poom. Third, Wit-dae pushes the opponent's neck further behind him/her while at the same time performing Hoo-ryuh-cha-kee to the opponent's back of the right knee with his/her left ankle and knocking him/her over. Ah-raet-dae falls safely when the attack of the Wit-dae is performed perfectly. Fourth, after Ah-raet-dae falls, Wit-dae returns to the first place and waits in the stance of Jwa-poom. Ah-raet-dae gets up, comes back to the starting position, and stands in Jwa-poom. Both raise their left feet slightly, then Ah-raet-dae starts his/her turn of attack while they are performing Poom-bahl-kee in harmony.

3

4-1

4-2

⑦ 오금차기 및 중방걸이

ⓑ 중방걸이

중방걸이는 덜미잽이로 상대의 목을 잡아채며 같은 쪽 다리의 발목으로 상대의 발목 뒤쪽을 걸어올리는 동작이다. 이 동작은 오금차기와 비슷하나 오금차기는 팔 동작이 제치기로서 손등으로 상대의 목을 걸어 수평으로 제친다. 중방걸이의 팔 동작은 덜미잽이로 상대의 목을 손바닥으로 감아 자신의 왼쪽 아래로 잡아채게 된다. 오금차기의 다리 동작은 접어서 차는 후려차기로 수평으로 상대의 무릎 뒤쪽을 차준다. 중방걸이의 다리 동작은 상대의 발목 뒤쪽을 노리며, 단지 차는 것에서 그치지 않고 자신의 발도으로 상대의 뒤쪽 발목을 채듯이 걸어준다. 그리고 이를 다리의 진행방향 위쪽으로 걷어 올린다. 기술을 사용하는 과정은 오금차기와 똑같으며, 단지 팔과 다리의 동작만이 차이가 있다.

하단의 사진은 중방걸이 기술이 잘 보이도록 오른쪽 다리로 공격하는 장면을 담았다. 본래 얼러 메기기는 왼발을 먼저 사용하고 오른발 방향의 기술을 반복한다. 그러나 걸이기술의 경우 한 번에 상대를 넘어뜨리게 되므로 좌우를 각각 연습할 필요가 있다. 따라서 이후의 설명에서는 이해를 돕기 위하여 동작이 잘 보이는 방향의 사진과 그 사진에 맞춘 설명을 사용하기로 한다.

1-1	1-2	1-3

⑦ Oh-gum-cha-kee & Joong-bang-guh-ree

ⓑ Joong-bang-guh-ree

Joong-bang-guh-ree is a movement in which you snatch the opponent's neck with Duhl-mee-jae-bee and hook the back of the opponent's ankle and pull up with your ankle on the same side. This movement is similar to Oh-gum-cha-kee, but its arm movement is Jay-chee-kee to grab the opponent's neck with the back of your hand and throw him/her back horizontally. The arm movement of Joong-bang-guh-ree uses Duhl-mee-jae-bee to wrap the opponent's neck with the palm of your hand and yank him/her down to your left. The leg movement of Oh-gum-cha-kee is Hoo-ryuh-cha-kee which folds up and kicks. It kicks the back of the opponent's knee horizontally. The leg movement of Joong-bang-guh-ree aims for the back of the opponent's ankle, not only just for kicking, but also for hooking like you are snatching the opponent's ankle with your own ankle. Then lift it upwards in the direction of the movement of the leg. The process of using the technique is the same as Oh-gum-cha-kee, and only the movements of the arms and legs are different.

The photos below show the attack performing with the right leg so that you can see the Joong-bang-guh-ree technique. Originally, Eol-luh Me-kee-kee uses the left foot first and the right foot repeats the technique. However, in the case of a trip over technique, it is necessary to practice left and right, as you have to throw the opponent over at once. Therefore, later explanations will use pictures of the side with the best motion and descriptions tailored to them to help understand.

2

3-1

3-2

한 손 제치기를 할 때, 손목은 힘이 빠진 상태에서 채찍처럼 움직여야 한다. 오금차기에서도 상대에게 제치기가 닿는 순간 손목이 젖혀지며 상대의 목을 걸어주어야 한다. 이를 위해서는 제치기를 하는 팔의 손목이 상대의 목에 닿도록 팔을 깊숙이 밀어주어야 한다.
오금차기에서 제치기를 하는 이유는 오금차기가 다리를 거는 것이 아닌 작게 후려차기 하는 기술로서, 신속하게 실행해주는 것이 중요하기 때문이다. 그러므로 덜미잽이처럼 잡고 넘기는 박자보다 빠르게, 제치기 형태로 상대의 목을 제쳐주면서 오금차기로 신속하게 제압해야 하는 것이다.
중방걸이는 오금차기와는 다르게 상대를 잡고 넘긴다는 기분으로 정확히 덜미잽이를 한 후, 그 다음 박자에서 중방걸이로 상대의 발목을 삽으로 퍼 올리듯 걸어 올려 상대를 제압해야 한다.
오금차기와 중방걸이는 실전에서 상대의 타이밍에 따라 두 기술 중, 한 가지를 선택할 수 있으며, 상대의 중심에 따라 다르게 걸 수도 있다. 즉 두 기술은 비슷하지만 전혀 다른 형태의 기술이기 때문에 함께 수련하도록 하는 것이다.
오금차기를 할 때는 후려차기 동작을 작고 빠르게 해주어야 한다. 제치기가 상대의 목에 닿을 거리에서는 자신의 다리를 쭉 뻗은 채로는 상대의 오금을 찰 수 없다. 따라서 다리를 접은 상태에서 반만 펴며 허리의 회전을 살려 상대의 오금이 정확히 자신의 발목에 걸리도록 차주어야 한다.
중방걸이의 팔 동작인 덜미잽이를 할 때에도 팔을 깊숙이 넣어 상대의 목을 내 손목과 손바닥 전체로 완전히 감을 수 있어야 한다. 또한 상대의 목을 감은 후에는 수평이 아닌 자신의 왼쪽 아래 바닥으로 잡아채야한다.
중방걸이의 다리 동작은 오금차기와 달리 마치 골프의 스윙처럼 U자형의 궤적을 그리며 상대의 발목을 채 올려야 한다. 이때, 딴죽이 아닌 비스듬한 후려차기의 형태로 다리를 차 주어야 한다. 또한 상대의 발목 뒤쪽에 자신의 발목이 닿는 순간, 발등을 몸 쪽으로 꺾어 올려 상대의 발목을 놓치지 않도록 감아주어야 한다.
얼러 메기기에서 오금차기와 같이 상대를 넘어뜨리는 기술을 수련할 때는 그 기술 전체를 두 번 반복하지 않고 첫 번째 공격에 상대를 넘어뜨린다. 그리고 공격 기술이 끝난 후, 넘어진 사람이 일어나면 처음의 시작 위치로 돌아와 왼발부터 호흡을 맞추어 품밟기를 시작하며 역할을 바꿔준다.

When you perform Han-sohn Jay-chee-kee, the wrist should move like a whip with no force. Even when you do Oh-gum-cha-kee, the wrist is bent as soon as the Jay-chee-kee touches the opponent and grab the opponent's neck. To do this, you have to push your arm deep so that the wrist that performing Jay-chee-kee can touch your opponent's neck.
The reason why you perform Jay-chee-kee in Oh-gum-cha-kee is because Oh-gum-cha-kee is not a technique for hooking a leg but a small version of Hoo-ryuh-cha-kee, which is important to implement quickly. Therefore, it is necessary to push aside the opponent's neck in the form of Jay-chee-kee faster than the beat of throwing down the opponent with Duhl-mee-jae-bee and to quickly overpower the opponent with Oh-gum-cha-kee. In Joong-bang-guh-ree, unlike Oh-gum-cha-kee, you should perform Duhl-mee-jae-bee accurately with the feeling of throwing down the opponent, and then hooking the opponent's ankle up with Joong-bang-guh-ree on the next beat to subdue the opponent. Oh-gum-cha-kee and Joong-bang-guh-ree can be chosen as one of the two skills depending on the opponent's timing in the real match, and can also be performed differently depending on the opponent's balance. In other words, the two techniques are similar but with completely different forms, so they are trained together.
When you do Oh-gum-cha-kee, you have to do Hoo-ryuh-cha-kee smaller and quicker. You can't kick the back of your opponent's knee with your legs stretched out from the same distance that Jay-chee-kee reaches the opponent's neck. Therefore, with your legs folded, you should stretch your leg only half way and use the rotation of your waist to make sure that the back of your opponent's knee is caught in your ankle.
Even when you do Duhl-mee-jae-bee, the arm movement of Joong-bang-guh-ree, you should be able to put your arm deep into it so that you can completely wrap your opponent's neck with your wrist and palm. Also, after you wrap around the opponent's neck, you must yank it downward to the left of your own body, not horizontally.
Unlike Oh-gum-cha-kee, the leg movement of Joong-bang-guh-ree has to draw a U-shaped trajectory like a swing in golf and lift the opponent's ankle. At this time, kick his/her leg in the form of a slanted Hoo-ryuh-cha-kee, not Dahn-jook. Also, the moment your ankle touches the back of your opponent's ankle, you should bend your foot toward your body and wrap it around so that you don't miss your opponent's ankle.
In Eol-luh Me-kee-kee, when you are training a technique that knocks the opponent down such as Oh-gum-cha-kee, you should not repeat the entire technique twice, but knock the opponent down at the first attack. After the attack technique is completed, the person who was knocked down gets up and both go back to the starting position and starts Poom-bahl-kee with their left foot in harmony to change the role.

⑧ 낚시걸이

낚시걸이는 나아가며 익히기의 낚시걸이를 실제로 상대방에게 사용하는 연습 과정이다. 상대의 다리를 바깥쪽에서 걸 경우 뒷낚 혹은 바깥낚이라고 부르고, 상대의 다리 안쪽에서 걸 경우 안낚이라고 나누어 부른다.

ⓐ 뒷낚 (뒷 낚시걸이)

첫째, 두 손 옆으로 흔들며 품밟기를 두세 번 한 후, 윗대는 좌품을 내딛은 다음 왼발을 원품자리로 놓지 않고 걷기의 형태로 상대에게 다가간다. 아랫대는 윗대의 움직임에 관계없이 지속적으로 품밟기를 한다. 둘째, 윗대는 아랫대의 오른발이 우품으로 나오는 박자에 맞춰 상대의 목을 오른손 덜미걸이로 감싸 잡아준다. 셋째, 윗대는 오른 다리를 상대의 오른 다리 밖으로 빼낸 후, 낚시걸이로 오금을 걸어 아랫대를 넘어뜨린다. 이때, 오른손은 상대의 목을 왼쪽 아래로 잡아챈다. 아랫대는 윗대의 공격이 완전하게 들어오면 안전하게 넘어진다. 넷째, 아랫대가 넘어진 후, 윗대는 처음의 자리로 돌아가 좌품으로 기다린다. 아랫대는 일어나 시작 자리로 돌아와서 좌품으로 선다. 서로 왼발을 살짝 들어 올린 후, 호흡을 맞추어 품밟기를 하며 아랫대의 공격 순서를 시작한다.

1-1	1-2	2-1

⑧ Nak-shee-guh-ree

Nak-shee-guh-ree is a practice that actually uses Nak-shee-guh-ree of Nah-ah-gah-myuh Ik-hee-kee to the opponent. If you hook your opponent's leg from the outside, you'll call it Duit-nak (back fishing) or Ba-gaht-nak (outside fishing). You hook from inside the opponent's leg, you'll call it Ahn-nak (inside fishing).

ⓐ Duit-nak (Duit Nak-shee-guh-ree)

First, after two or three Doo-sohn Yeop-eu-roh Huhn-duhl-myuh Poom-bahl-kee, Wit-dae steps out of Jwa-poom and approaches the opponent in the form of Guht-kee instead of placing his left foot, which stepped Jwa-poom, in Won-poom. Ah-raet-dae continues his Poom-bahl-kee regardless of Wit-dae's movement. Second, Wit-dae grabs the opponent's neck with right-hand Duhl-mee-guh-ree according to the beat of Ah-raet-dae's right foot comes out to step Woo-poom. Third, Wit-dae pulls his/her right leg to the outside of the opponent's right leg, then knocks Ah-raet-dae down by hooking his/her back of the knee with Nak-shee-guh-ree. At this point, the right hand grabs the opponent's neck and yanks it downward to the left. Ah-raet-dae falls safely when the attack of Wit-dae is completed. Fourth, after Ah-raet-dae falls, Wit-dae returns to the first place and waits in the stance of Jwa-poom. Ah-raet-dae gets up, comes back to the starting position, and stands in Jwa-poom. Both raise their left feet slightly, then Ah-raet-dae starts his/her turn to attack while they are performing Poom-bahl-kee in harmony.

2-2

3-1

3-2

⑧ 낚시걸이

ⓑ 안낚 (안 낚시걸이)

첫째, 두 손 옆으로 흔들며 품밟기를 두세 번 한 후, 윗대는 좌품을 내딛은 다음 왼발을 원품 자리로 놓지 않고 걷기의 형태로 상대에게 다가간다. 아랫대는 윗대의 움직임에 관계없이 지속적으로 품밟기를 한다. 둘째, 윗대는 아랫대의 오른발이 우품으로 나오는 박자에 맞춰 자신의 오른발을 상대의 다리 사이로 딛는다. 또한 오른손 덜미걸이로 상대의 목을 감싸 잡으며 동시에 왼손으로 오금을 걸어준다. 셋째, 윗대는 두발을 동시에 미끄러뜨려 상대의 다리 사이로 좀 더 파고든다. 이때, 왼발이 오른발 뒷꿈치를 지나쳐 두 다리가 교차 되도록 해야 더 깊숙이 파고들 수 있으며, 낚시걸이를 하는 순간에 디딤발의 힘을 더 잘 이용할 수 있다. 직후, 오른 다리로 상대의 왼다리를 낚시걸이하며, 동시에 오른다리를 걸어 잡은 왼손을 당겨 아랫대를 넘어뜨린다. 이때, 오른손은 상대의 목을 뒤로 밀며, 왼손은 오른다리를 들어 올린다. 아랫대는 윗대의 공격이 완전하게 들어오면 안전하게 넘어진다. 넷째, 아랫대가 넘어진 후, 윗대는 처음의 자리로 돌아가 좌품으로 기다린다. 아랫대는 일어나 시작 자리로 돌아와서 좌품으로 선다. 서로 왼발을 살짝 들어 올린 후, 호흡을 맞추어 품밟기를 하며 아랫대의 공격 순서를 시작한다.

1-1	1-2	2-1

⑧ Nak-shee-guh-ree

ⓑ Ahn-nak (Ahn Nak-shee-guh-ree)

First, after two or three Doo-sohn Yeop-eu-roh Huhn-duhl-myuh Poom-bahl-kee, Wit-dae steps out of Jwa-poom and approaches the opponent in the form of Guht-kee instead of placing his left foot, which stepped Jwa-poom, in Won-poom. Ah-raet-dae continues his Poom-bahl-kee regardless of Wit-dae's movement. Second, Wit-dae steps his/her right foot down between the opponent's legs according to the beat of Ah-raet-dae's right foot comes out to step Woo-poom. Wit-dae also grabs the opponent's neck with right-hand Duhl-mee-guh-ree, and at the same time holds the opponent's right knee with his/her left hand, Third, Wit-dae slides both feet at the same time and digs further between the opponent's legs. When moving through the legs, the left foot should pass by and cross the right heel for getting into deeper and allow more power from the stationary left leg.

Immediately after, he/she performs Nak-shee-guh-ree to the opponent's left leg with his/her right leg, and at the same time, he/she pulls his/her left hand, which holds the opponent's right leg and knock Ah-raet-dae over. At this point, the right hand pushes the opponent's neck down to the back, and the left hand lifts the opponent's right leg up. Ah-raet-dae falls safely when the attack of Wit-dae is done completely. Fourth, after Ah-raet-dae falls, Wit-dae returns to the first place and waits in the stance of Jwa-poom. Ah-raet-dae gets up, comes back to the starting position, and stands in Jwa-poom. Both raise their left feet slightly, then Ah-raet-dae starts his/her turn of attack while they are performing Poom-bahl-kee in harmony.

2-2 | 3-1 | 3-2

안낚과 뒷낚의 차이는 상대의 다리를 상대 몸 바깥에서 걸어주는지 아니면 상대의 다리 사이에서 걸어주는지에 있다. 뒷낚을 위해서는 걸고자 하는 상대의 다리보다 바깥에 서 있어야 하며, 안낚을 위해서는 상대의 두 다리 사이에 서 있어야 한다.
따라서 품밟기에서 걷기로 변화시켜 상대에게 다가갈 때, 뒷낚은 상대의 오른발이 디뎌질 위치보다 바깥쪽으로 자신의 왼발을 디뎌야 한다. 안낚은 상대 오른발보다 안쪽으로 디뎌야 한다.
특히, 안낚의 경우는 상대의 몸 안쪽으로 파고 들수록 기술이 정확하게 걸리게 되므로 왼발에 이어 오른발을 상대방 다리 사이에 디딘 후, 왼발에서 오른발로 이어지는 슬라이드 스텝을 이용하여 조금 더 안쪽으로 파고 들어야 한다. 그리고 슬라이드 스텝의 탄력까지 활용하여 상대의 몸을 밀치며 오른발로 상대의 왼다리를 걸어 올려야 한다.
뒷낚에서는 오른손으로 상대의 목을 잡아 자신의 왼쪽 아래로 잡아채며 내려준다. 안낚에서 오른손은 상대를 뒤쪽 아랫방향으로 밀어주어야 효과적이다. 안낚시걸이를 할 때, 상대의 키가 자신보다 많이 크다면 오른손 덜미걸이로 상대의 허리를 끌어안으며 낚시걸이를 사용할 수도 있다. 이때는 오른쪽 어깨를 상대의 복부에 밀착시키고 그 어깨로 상대를 밀어주는 것이 중요하다.
왼손은 안낚에서만 사용하게 된다. 안낚의 경우 오른다리로 상대의 왼다리를, 왼손으로 상대의 오른다리를 걸어 당겨 넘긴다는 사실을 명심하고 왼손으로 상대의 오금을 확실히 채주어야 한다. 다만, 왼손은 보조적 역할이므로 손에 신경 쓰느라 다리 움직임을 소홀히 해서는 안 된다.

The difference between Ahn-nak and Duit-nak is whether you hook the opponent's leg from outside the opponent's body or between the opponent's legs. For Duit-nak, you have to stand outside the opponent's leg that you want to hook, and for Ahn-nak, you have to stand between the opponent's two legs.
Therefore, when you change from Poom-bahl-kee to Guht-kee to approach your opponent, you have to step your left foot outwards rather than where your opponent's right foot will be in order to perform Duit-nak. For Ahn-nak, you have to step inwards than the opponent's right foot.
In particular, in the case of Ahn-nak, the more you dig into the opponent's body, the more accurate the technique gets, so you should step your right foot between the opponent's legs and then dig a little more inwards using a slide step from the left foot to the right foot. You should also use the elasticity of the slide step to push the opponent's body and hook the opponent's left leg upwards with your right foot.
In Duit-nak, you grab the opponent's neck with your right hand and yank it down to your left side. In Ahn-nak. the right hand should push down the opponent to the back to be more efficient. When doing Ahn-nak with a much taller opponent, you can grasp his(her) waist in your right arm with Duhl-mee-guh-ree. At this time, it is important to make your right shoulder to adhere to the opponent's stomach and push him(her).
The left hand will only be used for Ahn-nak. Keep in mind that if you perform Ahn-nak, you'll pull the opponent's left leg with your right leg and the opponent's right leg with your left hand, so you'll have to hold the opponent's back of the knee firmly with your left hand. However, the left hand acts as an assistant, so you should not neglect your leg movements while performing your hand technique.

⑨ 밭장다리치며 오금밟기 (오금걸이)

밭장다리치며 오금밟기는 밭장다리와, 깎음다리로 무릎 뒤를 밟아 내리는 오금밟기를 연이어 사용하는 기술이다.

첫째, 두 손 옆으로 흔들며 품밟기를 두세 번 한 후, 윗대는 좌품을 내딛은 다음 왼발을 원품자리로 놓지 않고 걷기의 형태로 상대에게 다가간다. 아랫대는 윗대의 움직임에 관계없이 지속적으로 품밟기를 한다. 둘째, 윗대는 아랫대의 오른발이 우품으로 나오는 박자에 맞춰 오른발로 밭장다리를 친다. 이때, 상대의 발을 가볍게 툭 치는 것이 아니라 발이 완전히 밀려 몸이 돌아가도록 밀어차야 한다. 셋째, 윗대는 밭장다리를 친 오른발을 상대를 향해 내려놓는다. 동시에 양손으로 상대의 어깨를 잡아준다. 이어서 왼발을 높이 올려 상대의 엉덩이 아랫부분부터 오금에 이르는 허벅지 뒷부분을 밀 듯이 내리밟아준다. 동시에 상대의 어깨는 잡아당겨 넘어뜨린다. 아랫대는 윗대의 공격이 완전하게 들어오면 안전하게 넘어진다. 넷째, 아랫대가 넘어진 후, 윗대는 처음의 자리로 돌아가 좌품으로 기다린다. 아랫대는 일어나 시작 자리로 돌아와서 좌품으로 선다. 서로 왼발을 살짝 들어 올린 후, 호흡을 맞추어 품밟기를 하며 아랫대의 공격 순서를 시작한다.

1-1 | 1-2 | 2

⑨ Baht-jang-dah-ree-chee-myuh Oh-gum-bahl-kee (Oh-gum-guh-ree)

Baht-jang-dah-ree-chee-myuh Oh-gum-bahl-kee is a technique that uses Baht-jang-dah-ree and Oh-gum-bahl-kee which steps down the back of the knee with Gahk-gum-dah-ree in succession.

First, after two or three Doo-sohn Yeop-eu-roh Huhn-duhl-myuh Poom-bahl-kee, Wit-dae steps out of Jwa-poom and approaches the opponent in the form of Guht-kee instead of placing his/her left foot in Won-poom. Ah-raet-dae continues his/her Poom-bahl-kee regardless of Wit-dae's movement. Second, Wit-dae performs Baht-jang-dah-ree with his/her right foot according to the beat of Ah-raet-dae's right foot comes out to step Woo-poom. At this time, you should not lightly tap the opponent's foot, but rather, push hard enough to turn the body around. Third, Wit-dae puts down his/her right foot which performed Baht-jang-dah-ree toward the opponent. At the same time, hold the opponent's shoulder with both hands. Then, raise your left foot high and press down the back of the opponent's thigh from the lower part of his/her hip to the back of the knee. At the same time, you pull the opponent's shoulder down. Ah-raet-dae falls safely when the attack of Wit-dae is done completely. Fourth, Both recover the start position, then Ah-raet-dae starts his/her turn to attack while they are performing Poom-bahl-kee in harmony.

3-1

3-2

3-2

깎음다리로 오금밟기를 할 때에는 상대의 허벅지 뒤쪽을 엉덩이 아래부터 오금까지 문지르는 느낌으로 밀 듯이 밟아주어야 한다. 이때 자신의 골반 역시 체중을 실어 다리 방향으로 같이 밀어준다. 만약 엉덩이 아래에서부터 밀어주는 느낌 없이 오금을 직접 밟으면 상대의 다리가 밀리지 않아 넘어지지 않고 밟힌 다리로 버틸 수 있다.

When you perform Oh-gum-bahl-kee with Gahk-gum-dah-ree on the back of your opponent's thigh, you should step on it as if you were rubbing it from the bottom of his/her butt to the back of his/her knee. At the same time, put your weight on your pelvis and push it in the direction of your kicking leg. If you step directly on the back of the opponent's knee without feeling pushing from the bottom of the opponent's butt, your opponent's leg will not be pushed and he/she can resist without falling.

⑩ 안짱걸며 덧걸이

안짱걸며 덧걸이는 얼러 메기기에서 연습한 안짱다리로 상대의 다리 위치와 중심을 원하는 위치로 끌고 온 후, 나아가며 익히기의 덧걸이를 실제로 사용하는 연습이다.

첫째, 두 손 옆으로 흔들며 품밟기를 두세 번 한 후, 윗대는 좌품을 내딛은 다음 왼발을 원품 자리로 놓지 않고 걷기의 형태로 상대에게 다가간다. 아랫대는 윗대의 움직임에 관계없이 지속적으로 품밟기를 한다. 둘째, 윗대는 아랫대의 오른발이 우품으로 나오는 박자에 맞춰 자신의 오른발로 상대의 오른발을 안짱걸이 한다. 셋째, 윗대는 안짱걸이 한 오른발을 상대의 두 발과 삼각형을 이루는 지점에 내려놓으며 오른손 덜미걸이로 상대의 목을 감싸 잡는다. 직후, 왼다리로 저기치기를 하며 상대의 왼쪽 오금을 걸어 넘긴다. 이때, 오른손은 상대의 목을 왼쪽 아래로 밀어 누른다. 아랫대는 윗대의 공격이 완전하게 들어오면 안전하게 넘어진다. 넷째, 아랫대가 넘어진 후, 윗대는 처음의 자리로 돌아가 좌품으로 기다린다. 아랫대는 일어나 시작 자리로 돌아와서 좌품으로 선다. 서로 왼발을 살짝 들어 올린 후, 호흡을 맞추어 품밟기를 하며 아랫대의 공격 순서를 시작한다.

1-1

1-2

2-1

⑩ Ahn-jang-guhl-myuh Duht-guh-ree

Ahn-jang-guhl-myuh Duht-guh-ree is an exercise in which you drag the opponent's leg and balance with Ahn-jang-dah-ree which is practiced in Eol-luh Me-kee-kee to the desired position and then use Duht-guh-ree of Nah-ah-gah-myuh Ik-hee-kee.

First, after two or three Doo-sohn Yeop-eu-roh Huhn-duhl-myuh Poom-bahl-kee, Wit-dae steps out of Jwa-poom and approaches the opponent in the form of Guht-kee instead of stepping Won-poom. Ah-raet-dae continues his Poom-bahl-kee regardless of Wit-dae's movement. Second, Wit-dae performs Ahn-jang-guh-ree to the opponent's right foot with his/her right foot according to the beat of Ah-raet-dae's right foot comes out to step Woo-poom. Third, Wit-dae puts down his/her right foot which performed Ahn-jang-guh-ree at the point where it forms a triangle with the opponent's two feet, and grabs the opponent's neck with right hand Duhl-mee-guh-ree. Immediately after, he/she performs Juh-kee-chee-kee with his/her left leg and trips over the back of the opponent's left knee. At this point, his/her right hand pushes the opponent's neck down to the left. Ah-rat-dae falls safely when the attack of Wit-dae is completed. Fourth, after Ah-raet-dae falls, Wit-dae returns to the first place and waits in the stance of Jwa-poom. Ah-raet-dae gets up, comes back to the starting position, and stands in Jwa-poom. Both raise their left feet slightly, then Ah-raet-dae starts his/her turn to attack while they are performing Poom-bahl-kee in harmony.

2-2

3-1

3-2

앞서 안짱걸이를 설명하며 목적에 따라 걸이를 하는 다리의 모양이 적절하게 변화된다고 설명한 바 있다. 안짱걸며 덧걸이에서의 안짱걸이는 상대의 다리를 덧걸이에 적절한 위치로 가볍게 끌고 오며 균형을 흩뜨리는 것이다. 따라서 끌고 오는 다리를 높이 들어 올릴 필요가 없다.
한편, 덧걸이를 상대에게 실제로 행할 때에는 자신의 몸을 지탱하는 서있는 다리와 걸어오는 다리가 서로 부딪히지 않도록 주의해야 한다. 그림에서는 상대의 다리를 건 상태에서 오른다리의 안쪽으로 끌고 옴으로써 충돌을 피하는 모습을 볼 수 있다.

Earlier, when Ahn-jang-guh-ree was explained, it is said that the shape of the leg that hooks changes according to the purpose. In Ahn-jang-guhl-myuh Duht-guh-ree, the Ahn-jang-guh-ree is to distract the opponent's balance by dragging his/her leg lightly to the appropriate position to perform Duht-guh-ree on it. Therefore, there is no need to raise the leg that drags the opponent's leg high.
On the other hand, when you actually perform Duht-guh-ree to the opponent, you should be careful not to bump the supporting leg and the hooking leg against each other. In the picture, you can see that the opponent's leg is hooked and dragged inside the right leg to avoid a collision.

⑪ 덧걸이 및 안우걸이

얼러 메기기의 덧걸이는 이 앞에 수련한 안짱걸며 덧걸이에서 상대의 다리를 끌어오는 안짱걸이를 뺀 것이다. 상대의 품을 읽어 예비동작 없이 바로 덧걸이를 사용하는 연습이다.

안우걸이는 '맞'으로 하는 덧걸이를 말한다. 덧걸이는 상대의 다리 바깥쪽을 저기치기로 걸며 반대편의 손으로 목을 밀어 넘어뜨린다. 반면 안우걸이는 상대의 다리 안쪽을 걸며 같은 쪽 손으로 상대를 밀어 넘어뜨린다.

ⓐ 덧걸이

첫째, 두 손 옆으로 흔들며 품밟기를 두세 번 한 후, 윗대는 우품을 내딛은 순서에 오른발을 상대의 몸 중심을 향해 내딛는다. 아랫대는 윗대의 움직임에 관계없이 지속적으로 품밟기를 한다. 둘째, 오른발을 내딛음과 동시에 윗대는 아랫대의 오른발이 우품으로 나오는 박자에 맞춰 상대의 목을 오른손 덜미걸이로 감싸 잡아준다. 셋째, 윗대는 오른 다리로 체중을 이동한 뒤, 왼발 저기치기로 오금을 걸어 아랫대를 넘어뜨린다. 이때, 오른손은 상대의 목을 왼쪽 아래로 밀어 내린다. 아랫대는 윗대의 공격이 완전하게 들어오면 안전하게 넘어진다. 넷째, 아랫대가 넘어진 후, 윗대는 처음의 자리로 돌아가 좌품으로 기다린다. 아랫대는 일어나 시작자리로 돌아와서 좌품으로 선다. 서로 왼발을 살짝 들어 올린 후, 호흡을 맞추어 품밟기를 하며 아랫대의 공격 순서를 시작한다.

1-1	1-2	2

⑪ Duht-guh-ree & Ahn-woo-guh-ree

Duht-guh-ree of Eol-luh Me-kee-kee is a technique that minuses Ahn-jang-guh-ree, which drags the opponent's leg, from the previous training of Ahn-jang-guhl-myuh Duht-guh-ree. It is a practice to read the steps of the opponent and use Duht-guh-ree without any preliminary action.

Ahn-woo-guh-ree refers to Duht-guh-ree performed with the same side of the hand and foot. Duht-guh-reeis a movement in which you hook the outside of the opponent's leg with Juh-kee-chee-kee and push his/her neck with the hand of the other side of the leg. On the other hand, Ahn-woo-guh-ree is a movement in which you hook the inside of the opponent's leg and push the opponent over with the same side of the hand.

ⓐ Duht-guh-ree

First, after two or three Doo-sohn Yeop-eu-roh Huhn-duhl-myuh Poom-bahl-kee, Wit-dae steps his/her right foot toward the center of the opponent instead of stepping Woo-poom. Ah-raet-dae continues his Poom-bahl-kee regardless of Wit-dae's movement. Second, as soon as the right foot is taken a step, Wit-dae grabs the opponent's neck with right-hand Duhl-mee-guh-ree according to the beat of Ah-raet-dae's right foot comes out to step Woo-poom. Third, Wit-dae moves his/her weight on his/her right leg and then hooks the back of the opponent's knee with left foot Juh-kee-chee-kee to knock down. At this point, the right hand pushes the opponent's neck down to the left. Ah-raet-dae falls safely when the attack of Wit-dae is completed. Fourth, after Ah-raet-dae falls, both return to the first place and then Ah-raet-dae starts his/her turn.

3-1

3-2

3-2

⑪ 덧걸이 및 안우걸이

ⓑ 안우걸이

첫째, 두 손 옆으로 흔들며 품밟기를 두세 번 한 후, 윗대는 좌품을 내딛은 다음 왼발을 원품 자리로 놓지 않고 걷기의 형태로 상대에게 다가간다. 아랫대는 윗대의 움직임에 관계없이 지속적으로 품밟기를 한다. 둘째, 윗대는 아랫대의 오른발이 우품으로 나오는 박자에 맞춰 오른손 덜미걸이로 상대의 목을 감싸 잡는다. 셋째, 윗대는 왼발로 체중을 이동하며 오른발 저기치기로 상대의 왼다리 오금을 안쪽에서 걸어당겨 넘어뜨린다. 이때 오른손은 상대의 목을 왼쪽 아래로 밀어 누른다. 아랫대는 윗대의 공격이 완전하게 들어오면 안전하게 넘어진다. 넷째, 아랫대가 넘어진 후, 윗대는 처음의 자리로 돌아가 좌품으로 기다린다. 아랫대는 일어나 시작 자리로 돌아와서 좌품으로 선다. 서로 왼발을 살짝 들어 올린 후, 호흡을 맞추어 품밟기를 하며 아랫대의 공격 순서를 시작한다.

1-1	1-2	1-3

⑪ Duht-guh-ree & Ahn-woo-guh-ree

ⓑ Ahn-woo-guh-ree

First, after two or three Doo-sohn Yeop-eu-roh Huhn-duhl-myuh Poom-bahl-kee, Wit-dae steps out of Jwa-poom and approaches the opponent in the form of Guht-kee instead of placing his left foot, which stepped Jwa-poom, in Wone-poom. Ah-raet-dae continues his Poom-bahl-kee regardless of Wit-dae's movement. Second, Wit-dae grabs the opponent's neck with right-hand Duhl-mee-guh-ree according to the beat of Ah-raet-dae's right foot comes out to step Woo-poom. Third, Wit-dae shifts his/her weight on his/her left foot, and at the same time, he hooks the back of the opponent's left knee from the inside with right foot Juh-kee-chee-kee and pulls it to knock down the opponent. The right hand pushes the opponent's neck down to the left. Ah-raet-dae falls safely when the attack of Wit-dae is completed. Fourth, after Ah-raet-dae falls, Wit-dae returns to the first place and waits in the stance of Jwa-poom. Ah-raet-dae gets up, comes back to the starting position, and stands in Jwa-poom. Both raise their left feet slightly, then Ah-raet-dae starts his/her turn to attack while they are performing Poom-bahl-kee in harmony.

2	3-1	3-2

자신을 기준으로 덧걸이와 안우걸이는 덧걸이가 엇, 안우걸이가 맞의 형태로 사용하는 손발의 방향이 서로 다르다. 얼러메기기에서 기술을 거는 상대의 좌우를 기준으로 볼 때도 덧걸이는 왼다리로 상대의 오른다리를 걸어주므로 맞, 안우걸이는 오른다리로 오른다리를 걸어주므로 엇이 된다.
두 기술의 이러한 차이는 품밟기에서 상대에게 다가가는 걸음에서도 차이가 나는데, 덧걸이는 맞의 공격을 하게 되므로 우(좌)품을 디뎌야 하는 순간에 앞으로 나아간다. 이런 모양을 '바로 짼다.'라고 표현한다. 안우걸이는 엇의 공격을 하게 되므로 왼(오른)발이 좌(우)품을 디딘 후, 원품으로 옮겨가는 순간에 앞으로 나아간다. 이를 '딛고 짼다.'라고 표현한다. 대부분의 얼러 메기기 기술은 엇의 공격을 하므로 '딛고 째는' 경우가 많다.'

The sides of the hands and feet used by the movements of Duht-guh-ree and Ahn-woo-guh-ree are different. Duht-guh-ree uses the hand and foot in the form of Uht (different side of foot and hand : left foot + right hand, etc.), and Ahn-woo-guh-ree uses them in the form of Maht (same side of foot and hand : left foot + left hand, etc.). Even in Eol-luh Me-kee-kee (in which you can check Maht or Uht by which side of opponent's leg you will hook,), Duht-guh-ree hooks the opponent's right leg with your left leg, so it makes Maht. And Ahn-woo-guh-ree hooks the opponent's right leg with your right leg, so it makes Uht.

This difference between the two techniques is also different in the way they approach the opponent in Poom-bahl-kee. As Duht-guh-ree attacks in the form of Maht, you move forward at the moment you have to step on Woo-poom (Jwa-poom). This shape of movement is described as 'Ba-ro Jaen-da' (step for attack directly after Won-poom).

Ahn-woo-guh-ree makes an attack in the form of Uht, so your left (right) foot steps Jwa (Woo)-poom, and moves forward at the moment it moves to Won-poom. This is described as 'Dit-go Jaen-da' (step for attack after Jwa (Woo)-poom). Since most Eol-luh Me-kee-kee techniques are Uht type of attack, so they are often, Dit-go Jaen-da.

* Jaen-da (Jae-kee) means stepping in the form of Guht-kee to take the proper position to attack.

⑫ 무릎걸며 좌우 발따귀

무릎걸며 좌우 발따귀는 무릎걸이로 상대의 균형을 흩뜨리고 이를 이용해 다가가며 상대의 얼굴을 발바닥으로 연달아 때리는 기술이다.

첫째, 두 손 옆으로 흔들며 품밟기를 두세 번 한 후, 윗대는 좌품을 내딛은 다음 왼발을 원품자리로 놓지 않고 걷기의 형태로 상대에게 다가간다. 아랫대는 윗대의 움직임에 관계없이 지속적으로 품밟기를 한다. 둘째, 윗대는 아랫대의 오른발이 우품으로 나오는 박자에 맞춰 오른발로 무릎걸이를 한다. 아랫대는 무릎걸이 당한 오른발을 자연스럽게 뒤로 한걸음 딛는다. 셋째, 윗대는 무릎걸이 한 오른발을 상대를 향해 디디며 왼발을 들어 올려 발바닥으로 상대의 우측 얼굴을 때려준다(발따귀). 그리고 발따귀를 한 왼발을 걷기로 내딛으며 오른발로 다시 발따귀를 한다. 아랫대는 윗대의 발따귀를 적절히 피하며 자연스럽게 물러선다. 넷째, 발따귀가 끝난 후, 처음의 자리로 돌아가 서로 왼발을 살짝 들어 올린 후, 호흡을 맞추어 품밟기를 하며 아랫대의 공격 순서를 시작한다.

1-1	1-2	1-3

⑫ Moo-reup-guhl-myuh Jwa-woo Bahl-dah-gui

Moo-reup-guhl-myuh Jwa-woo Bahl-dah-gui is a technique that disperses the opponent's balance with Moo-reup-guh-ree and uses it to approach and hit the opponent's face in succession with the sole of his or her feet.

First, after two or three Doo-sohn Yeop-eu-roh Huhn-duhl-myuh Poom-bahl-kee, Wit-dae steps out of Jwa-poom and approaches the opponent in the form of Guht-kee instead of placing his left foot in Won-poom. Ah-raet-dae continues his Poom-bahl-kee regardless of Wit-dae's movement. Second, Wit-dae performs Moo-reup-guh-ree with his/her right foot according to the beat of Ah-raet-dae's right foot comes out to step Woo-poom. Ah-raet-dae naturally takes a step back with his/her right foot that was performed Moo-reup-guh-ree by Wit-dae. Third, Wit-dae raises the left foot and hits the right side of the opponent's face with the sole of the foot (Bahl-dah-gui) as he/she steps down the right foot, which performed Moo-reup-guh-ree, toward the opponent. Then, he/she steps down the left foot, which performed Bahl-dah-gui, in the form of Guht-kee, and performs Bahl-dah-gui, again with his/her right foot. Ah-raet-dae naturally retreats, avoiding Bahl-dah-gui from Wit-dae. Fourth, after Bahl-dah-gui is completed, they return to the starting position and both raise their left feet slightly, then Ah-raet-dae starts his/her turn to attack while they are performing Poom-bahl-kee in harmony.

2	3-1	3-2

무릎을 접은 다리를 자신의 몸 바깥을 향해 들어 올린 후 안쪽으로 회전시키며 무릎을 펴 발바닥으로 상대의 얼굴을 찰싹 때리는 발차기를 발따귀라 한다. 혹은 무릎을 안으로 들어 바깥으로 돌리며 차기도 한다.
발따귀는 내차기와는 다른 형태의 발질이다. 손으로 따귀를 때리듯이 발로 따귀를 때리는듯 한 발질이므로 내차기와 달리 발이 무거워서는 안 되고 가볍고 경쾌하게 차야 한다. 발따귀를 할 때는 발을 상대 얼굴보다 높게 올리지 않고 같은 높이로 들어 올려 빠르게 옆으로 때린다는 느낌으로 한다. 또한 발의 모양은 발가락이 하늘이 아닌 상대의 얼굴을 향하도록 눕혀 주어야 한다.
얼러 메기기의 무릎걸며 좌우 발따귀에서는 왼발과 오른발로 연이어 차기도 하며, 왼발로만 혹은 오른발로만 차기도 한다. 한쪽 발만 쓰는 경우에는 무릎을 안으로, 밖으로 돌리며 발따귀를 찬다.

A kick that raises the leg that folds the knee towards the outside of the body and rotates it inward, stretches the knee and slaps the opponent's face with the sole of the foot is called Bahl-dah-gui. Or you can lift your knee towards inside and turn it outward and kick.
Bahl-dah-gui is different from Nae-cha-kee. It is a slapping kick on the opponent's cheek, so should be quick and nimble when kicking, differing from the heavy kicking of Nae-cha-kee. For Bahl-dah-gui, you need to lift your foot just at the height of the opponent's face, not too high, and swing it quick and horizontal. Also, the toes should head toward the opponent's face, not the sky, to make your kicking foot lay down properly.
In Moo-reup-guhl-myuh Jwa-woo Bahl-dah-gui of Eol-luh Me-kee-kee, you can perform Bahl-dah-gui with your left foot and right foot consecutively. You can also perform it only with left foot or with right foot. If only one foot is used, turn the knee inwards and outwards and kick Bahl-dah-gui.

⑬ 좌우로 딴죽치고 는질러차기

좌우로 딴죽치고 는질러차기는 얼러 메기기에서 연습한 딴죽을 연속으로 사용하여 상대의 다리 위치와 중심을 원하는 대로 흔들어 놓은 후, 상대의 복부를 향해 는질러차기를 하는 연습이다.

첫째, 두 손 옆으로 흔들며 품밟기를 두세 번 한 후, 윗대는 우품을 딛은 오른발을 걷기의 형태로 옮기며 상대에게 다가간다. 아랫대는 윗대의 움직임에 관계없이 지속적으로 품밟기를 한다. 둘째, 윗대는 아랫대의 왼발이 좌품으로 나오는 박자에 맞춰 자신의 왼발로 상대의 왼발에 딴죽을 친다. 그리고 왼발을 걷기로 디디며 따라가 오른발로 딴죽을 친다. 아랫대는 왼발과 오른발이 딴죽에 맞는 대로 자연스럽게 뒤로 내딛는다. 셋째, 윗대는 오른발로 딴죽을 친 후, 한걸음 더 따라 들어가 왼발 는질러차기로 상대를 힘껏 밀어 차 넘긴다. 아랫대는 다치지 않게 는질러차기를 적절히 방어하며 안전하게 넘어진다. 넷째, 아랫대가 넘어진 후, 윗대는 처음의 자리로 돌아가 좌품으로 기다린다. 아랫대는 일어나 시작 자리로 돌아와서 좌품으로 선다. 서로 왼발을 살짝 들어 올린 후, 호흡을 맞추어 품밟기를 하며 아랫대의 공격 순서를 시작한다.

좌우로 딴죽치고 는질러차기는 예비 공격을 통해 상대의 상태를 자신이 원하는 대로 만들어 놓고 마지막 공격으로 연결하는 동작을 연습하는 과정이다. 이는 앞선 무릎걸며 좌우 발따귀 역시 마찬가지이다. 마지막 공격까지의 연결동작은 신속하고 안정적인 움직임을 위하여 몸이 상하로 크게 흔들리지 않게 미끄러지듯 움직여야 한다.

1-1	1-2	2-1

⑬ Jwa-woo-ro Dahn-jook-Chi-go Neun-jil-luh-cha-kee

Jwa-woo-ro Dahn-jook-Chi-go Neun-jil-luh-cha-kee is a practice to use Dahn-jook you practiced in Eol-luh Me-kee-kee consecutively to shake the position of the opponent's leg and balance as desired, and then to kick Neun-jil-luh-cha-kee to the abdomen.

First, after two or three Doo-sohn Yeop-eu-roh Huhn-duhl-myuh Poom-bahl-kee, Wit-dae steps out of Woo-poom and approaches the opponent by moving his right foot, which stepped Woo-poom, in the form of Guht-kee. Ah-raet-dae continues Poom-bahl-kee regardless of Wit-dae's movement. Second, Wit-dae performs Dahn-jook to the opponent's left foot with his/her left foot in line with the beat of Ah-raet-dae's left foot moves forward from Jwa-poom. Then he/she steps down his/her left foot in the form of Guht-kee to chase the opponent, and then performs Dahn-jook with his right foot. Ah-raet-dae naturally steps back as his/her left and right feet get hit by Dahn-jook. Third, Wit-dae performs Dahn-jook with his/her right foot, then chase the opponent one step further and pushes him/her hard with left-foot Neun-jil-luh-cha-kee. Ah-raet-dae falls safely while he/she defends the attack properly. Fourth, after 'Ah-rat-dae' falls, both returns to the first place and then Ah-rat-dae starts his/her turn.

Jwa-woo-ro Dahn-jook-Chi-go Neun-jil-luh-cha-kee is a process to practice a connecting movement that making the opponent's condition as you wish through the preliminary attack then performing the last attack, as in the Moo-reup-guhl-myuh Jwa-woo Bahl-dah-gui described above. The connecting movement to the last attack must be smooth and slide so that the body does not move much up and down for quick and stable movement.

2-2	3-1	3-2

⑭ 두루치기

두루치기는 내차기를 두 번 연속 사용하여 상대를 공격하는 기술이다.

첫째, 두 손 옆으로 흔들며 품밟기를 두세 번 한 후, 윗대는 우품을 내딛은 다음 오른발을 원품자리로 놓지 않고 걷기의 형태로 상대에게 다가간다. 아랫대는 윗대의 움직임에 관계없이 지속적으로 품밟기를 한다. 둘째, 윗대는 아랫대의 왼발이 좌품으로 나오는 박자에 맞춰 왼발로 내차기를 한다. 아랫대는 자연스럽게 방어하며 뒤로 한걸음 딛는다. 셋째, 윗대는 내차기 한 왼발을 상대를 향해 디디며 오른발을 들어 올려 한 번 더 내차기를 한다. 아랫대는 윗대의 내차기를 적절히 피하며 자연스럽게 물러선다. 넷째, 내차기가 끝난 후, 처음의 자리로 돌아가 서로 왼발을 살짝 들어 올린 후, 호흡을 맞추어 품밟기를 하며 아랫대의 공격 순서를 시작한다.

두루치기를 할 때는 상대에게 내차기를 성공시키기 위한 박자와 거리가 중요하다. 상대의 왼발 혹은 오른발이 앞으로 나오는 순간은 중심이 이동 중이므로 동작을 갑작스럽게 바꾸기 어렵다. 이때가 내차기 등의 발차기 공격을 적중시키기 좋은 순간이다. 또한 두 번째 내차기를 위해 따라갈 때에도 첫 번째 내차기를 피하는 상대의 움직임을 확인한 후, 그 다음 동작이 이어지기 어려운 순간을 포착하여 들어가야 한다. 좇아 들어갈 때, 내차기를 위한 적절한 거리를 확보하는 것 또한 잊어서는 안 된다.

1-1

1-2

2-1

⑭ Doo-ruh-chee-kee

Doo-ruh-chee-kee is a technique of attacking an opponent by using 'Nae-cha-kee' twice in a row.

First, after two or three Doo-sohn Yeop-eu-roh Huhn-duhl-myuh Poom-bahl-kee, Wit-dae steps out of Woo-poom and approaches the opponent in the form of Guht-kee. Ah-raet-dae continues Poom-bahl-kee regardless of Wit-dae's movement. Second, Wit-dae performs Nae-cha-kee with his/her left foot in line with the beat of Ah-raet-dae's left foot moves forward for Jwa-poom. Ah-raet-dae naturally steps back as he/she defends the attack. Third, Wit-dae takes his/her left foot which performed Nae-cha-kee down toward the opponent and performs another Nae-cha-kee with his/her right foot, Ah-raet-dae naturally retreats avoiding the kick properly. Fourth, after the end of Nae-cha-kee, both return to the first position and raise their left feet slightly, then Ah-raet-dae starts his/her turn of attack while they are performing Poom-bahl-kee in harmony.

When you do Doo-ruh-chee-kee, the beat and distance to succeed your Nae-cha-kee on the opponent's are important. When the opponent's left or right foot comes forward, the balance is shifting, making it difficult to change the movement suddenly. This is a good moment to make a successful kick attack, such as Nae-cha-kee. Also, when chasing after the opponent for the second Nae-cha-kee, check his/her movement to avoid the first kick, and then capture the moment when his/her next move is difficult to continue. When chasing after for the second kick, you should also not forget to secure the proper distance for Nae-cha-kee.

2-2

3-1

3-2

⑮ 곧은 발질하며 오금차기

곧은 발질하며 오금차기는 곧은 발질로 상대의 허벅지를 차 물러나게 한 후, 좇아 들어가며 오금차기로 넘어뜨리는 기술이다.

첫째, 두 손 옆으로 흔들며 품밟기를 두세 번 한 후, 윗대는 원품에서 좌품을 디딜 왼발을 걷기의 형태로 옮기며 상대에게 다가간다. 아랫대는 윗대의 움직임에 관계없이 지속적으로 품밟기를 한다. 둘째, 윗대는 좌품을 디딘 아랫대의 왼다리 허벅지에 곧은 발질을 한다. 아랫대는 왼 허벅지에 곧은 발질을 맞은 후 자연스럽게 뒤로 내딛는다. 셋째, 윗대는 곧은 발질 한 오른발을 상대의 오른발 앞에 놓으며 따라 들어가 오금차기를 하여 넘어뜨린다. 아랫대는 공격이 완전하게 들어오면 안전하게 넘어진다. 넷째, 아랫대가 넘어진 후, 윗대는 처음의 자리로 돌아가 좌품으로 기다린다. 아랫대는 일어나 시작 자리로 돌아와서 좌품으로 선다. 서로 왼발을 살짝 들어 올린 후, 호흡을 맞추어 품밟기를 하며 아랫대의 공격 순서를 시작한다.

> 곧은 발질하며 오금차기 역시, 예비 공격을 통하여 상대의 자세를 원하는 대로 변화시킴으로써 본 공격이 원활히 성공할 수 있도록 하는 연속 공격을 수련하는 과정이다. 예비공격으로 곧은 발질을 하는 대신 얼굴에 걷어차기를 하며 연습할 때도 있다. 그 경우는 '걷어차기하며 오금차기'라고 부른다.
> 곧은 발질을 할 때는 왼발을 충분히 째서 밟아 상대의 정면이 아닌 대각선 방향에서 차야 한다(그림 2-1). 그래야 제대로 된 곧은 발질을 위한 거리와 각도를 만들 수 있기 때문이다.

1-1

1-2

2-1

⑮ Gohd-eun-bahl-jil-ha-myuh Oh-gum-cha-kee

Gohd-eun-bahl-jil-ha-myuh Oh-gum-cha-kee is a technique that kicks off the opponent's thigh with Gohd-eun-bahl-jil, then chases him/her in and knocks him/her down with Oh-gum-cha-kee.

First, after two or three Doo-sohn Yeop-eu-roh Huhn-duhl-myuh Poom-bahl-kee, Wit-dae steps his/her left foot in the form of Guht-kee and approaches the opponent, instead of stepping his/her left foot in Jwa-poom out of Won-poom. Ah-raet-dae continues Poom-bahl-kee regardless of Wit-dae's movement. Second, Wit-dae performs Gohd-eun-bahl-jil to the opponent's left thigh which stepped on Jwa-poom. Ah-raet-dae takes Gohd-eun-bahl-jil on the left thigh and naturally steps back. Third, Wit-dae puts the right foot, which performed Gohd-eun-bahl-jil, in front of the opponent's right foot and chases him in, and knocks him down with Oh-gum-cha-kee. Ah-raet-dae falls safely when the attack of Wit-dae is completed. Fourth, after Ah-raet-dae falls, both return to the first place and then start Ah-rat-dae's turn.

Gohd-eun-bahl-jil-ha-myuh Oh-gum-cha-kee is also a process of training consecutive attacks that allow the main attack to succeed smoothly by changing the opponent's posture as desired through the preliminary attack. There are times when they practice Guh-duh-cha-kee to their faces instead of Gohd-eun-bahl-jil as a preliminary attack. In that case, it is called Guh-duh-cha-kee-ha-myuh Oh-gum-cha-kee.
When using Gohd-eun-bahl-jil, you need to move in a diagonal direction towards the opponent with enough room to side step so as to ensure the proper distance (figure 2-1).

2-2	3-1	3-2

⑯ 곧은 발질 두발 낭상

곧은 발질 두발 낭상은 상대의 나오는 발의 허벅지를 곧은 발질로 밀어낸 후, 공중으로 뛰어올라 발차기로 공격하는 기술이다. 곧은 발질 두발 낭상에는 곧은 발질을 한 발을 땅에 구르며 반대쪽 발의 탄력을 얻어 뛰어올라 곧은 발질 했던 다리로 발차기를 하는 방법과 곧은 발질 한 다리를 그대로 공중에 띄운 채로 뛰어올라 반대 발로 발차기를 하는 방법의 두 가지가 있다.

ⓐ 곧은 발질 두발 낭상 - 1

첫째, 두 손 옆으로 흔들며 품밟기를 두세 번 한 후, 윗대는 원품에서 좌품을 디딜 왼발을 걷기의 형태로 옮기며 상대에게 다가간다. 아랫대는 윗대의 움직임에 관계없이 지속적으로 품밟기를 한다. 둘째, 윗대는 좌품을 디딘 아랫대의 왼다리 허벅지에 오른발로 곧은 발질을 한다. 아랫대는 왼 허벅지에 곧은 발질을 맞은 후 자연스럽게 뒤로 내딛는다. 셋째, 윗대는 곧은 발질 한 오른발을 상대의 오른발 앞에 놓으며 따라 들어가 왼 무릎을 접은 채로 튕겨 올리며 뛰어오른다. 이어서 공중에서 발을 바꾸는 탄력으로 오른발을 차올리며 상대를 공격한다. 아랫대는 적절하게 방어하며 물러선다. 넷째, 낭상 후, 윗대와 아랫대는 시작 자리로 돌아와 호흡을 맞추어 품밟기를 하며 아랫대의 공격 순서를 시작한다.

1-1	1-2	2

⑯ Gohd-eun-bahl-jil Doo-bahll Nahng-sahng

Gohd-eun-bahl-jil Doo-bahll Nahng-sahng is a technique wherein you push the opponent's thigh that comes out to step with Gohd-eun-bahl-jil and then jump into the air and attack with a kick. There are two types of Gohd-eun-bahl-jil Doo-bahll Nahng-sahng. One type is that you stamp the foot which performed Gohd-eun-bahl-jil on the ground and jump up with the elasticity of the other foot, then kick with the leg which performed Gohd-eun-bahl-jil. The other one is that you jump up with the leg which performed Gohd-eun-bahl-jil in the air, and kick with the other foot.

ⓐ Gohd-eun-bahl-jil Doo-bahll Nahng-sahng - 1

First, after two or three Doo-sohn Yeop-eu-roh Huhn-duhl-myuh Foom-bahl-kee, Wit-dae steps his/her left foot in the form of Guht-kee and approaches the opponent, instead of stepping his/her left foot in Jwa-poom. Second, Wit-dae performs Gohd-eun-bahl-jil with his/her right foot to the opponent's left thigh which stepped on Jwa-poom. Ah-raet-dae takes Gohd-eun-bahl-jil on the left thigh and naturally steps back. Third, Wit-dae puts the right foot, which performed Gohd-eun-bahl-jil, in front of the opponent's right foot and chases him in, then bounces off and jumps with his/her left knee folded. Subsequently, he/she kicks his/her right foot up with the elasticity of changing feet in the air and attacks his/her opponent. Ah-raet-dae retreats while he/she defends properly. Fourth, after Nahng-sahng, both return to the starting position then Ah-raet-dae starts his/her turn to attack.

3-1	3-2	3-3

⑯ 곧은 발질 두발 낭상

ⓑ 곧은 발질 두발 낭상 - 2

첫째, 두 손 옆으로 흔들며 품밟기를 두세 번 한 후, 윗대는 원품에서 우품을 디딜 오른발을 걷기의 형태로 옮기며 상대에게 다가간다. 아랫대는 윗대의 움직임에 관계없이 지속적으로 품밟기를 한다. 둘째, 윗대는 우품을 디딘 아랫대의 오른다리 허벅지에 왼발로 곧은 발질을 한다. 아랫대는 오른 허벅지에 곧은 발질을 맞은 후 자연스럽게 뒤로 내딛는다. 셋째, 윗대는 곧은 발질 한 왼다리의 무릎을 접은 채로 튕겨 올리며 뛰어오른다. 이어서 공중에서 발을 바꾸는 탄력으로 오른발을 차올리며 상대를 공격한다. 아랫대는 적절하게 방어하며 물러선다. 넷째, 낭상 후, 윗대와 아랫대는 시작 자리로 돌아와 호흡을 맞추어 품밟기를 하며 아랫대의 공격 순서를 시작한다.

1-1	1-2	2

⑯ Gohd-eun-bahl-jil Doo-bahll Nahng-sahng

ⓑ Gohd-eun-bahl-jil Doo-bahll Nahng-sahng - 2

First, after two or three Doo-sohn Yeop-eu-roh Huhn-duhl-myuh Poom-bahl-kee, Wit-dae steps his/her right foot in the form of Guht-kee and approaches the opponent, instead of stepping his/her right foot in Woo-poom. Ah-raet-dae continues Poom-bahl-kee regardless of Wit-dae's movement. Second, Wit-dae performs Gohd-eun-bahl-jil with his/her left foot to the opponent's right thigh which stepped on Woo-poom. Ah-raet-dae takes Gohd-eun-bahl-jil on the right thigh and naturally steps back. Third, Wit-dae bounces off and jumps with his/her left knee folded. Subsequently, he/she kicks his/her right foot up with the elasticity of changing feet in the air and attacks his/her opponent. Ah-raet-dae retreats while he/she defence properly. Fourth, after Nahng-sahng, both return to the starting position then Ah-raet-dae starts his/her turn to attack.

3-1

3-2

3-3

곧은 발질 두발 낭상을 연습할 때, 높이 뛰어오르려고만 노력하는 경우가 있다. 그러나 이를 실전에 적용하기 위해서는 거리를 조절하며 앞으로 멀리, 혹은 측면으로 뛰어오르는 것도 연습해야 한다.
공중에서 찰 때의 발차기는 대체로 걷어차기를 많이 활용한다. 그러나 상황이나 필요에 따라 후려차기, 째차기 등 여러 발질을 활용할 수 있다. 이때 중요한 점은 점프할 때와 발차기를 위해 다리를 끌어올릴 때 반드시 무릎을 굽혀주어야 한다는 것이다. 무릎을 펼친 채로 다리를 들어 올리는 것은 기다란 지렛대(펴진 다리)를 올리려고 짧은 쪽(몸통)을 누르는 것과 같이 과도한 힘이 들기 때문이다.
이는 혼자 익히기의 발질에서 다리를 접어서 발차기를 해야 하는 이유와 동일하다. 발차기 하는 다리의 무릎은 최종적으로 목표를 맞추는 순간에만 펴져야 한다.

When practicing Gohd-eun-bahl-jil Doo-bahll Nahng-sahng, there are cases that you only try to jump high. However, in order to apply this in practice, you should practice adjusting the distance and jumping forward or laterally.

When kicking in the air, Guh-duh-cha-kee is generally used a lot. However, depending on the situation or needs, a number of different kicks can be used, such as Hoo-ryuh-cha-kee,-Jae-cha-kee, and so on.

The important point here is that you must bend your knees when you jump and raise your legs for kicks. Raising the leg with the knee stretched out is as hard as pressing the short side (torso) to raise the long side of the lever (stretched out leg). This is the same reason why you have to fold your leg to kick in the footwork of Hone-jah Ik-hee-kee. The knee of the kicking leg should only be stretched at the moment it finally hits its target.

⑰ 곁치고 돌개치기

곁치고 돌개치기는 째차기를 이용하여 상대의 옆구리나 허벅지를 툭 쳐서(곁치기) 자신이 원하는 자세를 만든 뒤, 몸을 회전하는 탄력을 더하여 강한 마무리 발차기를 하는 공격기술이다. 곁치기를 하는 발차기로는 후려차기를 쓸 때도 있다.

첫째, 두 손 옆으로 흔들며 품밟기를 두세 번 한 후, 윗대는 우품을 디딘 오른발을 원품이 아닌 걷기로 내딛는다. 아랫대는 윗대의 움직임에 관계없이 지속적으로 품밟기를 한다. 둘째, 윗대는 좌품을 디딘 아랫대의 왼쪽 옆구리나 허벅지에 왼발로 째차기를 한다. 아랫대는 적절히 방어하며 째차기를 맞은 후 그대로 서 있는다. 셋째, 윗대는 째차기 한 왼발을 앞으로 디디며 그 탄력을 이용하여 회전한다. 그리고 회전력을 살려 돌개치기를 한다. 아랫대는 적절하게 방어하며 물러선다. 넷째, 윗대와 아랫대는 시작 자리로 돌아와 호흡을 맞추어 품밟기를 하며 아랫대의 공격 순서를 시작한다.

1-1	1-2	2

⑰ Gyeot-chee-goh Dohl-gae-chee-kee

Gyeot-chee-goh Dohl-gae-chee-kee is an attack technique that uses Jae-cha-kee to hit the opponent's side or thigh (Kyeot-chee-kee) to create the position you want, and then add the body's rotating elasticity to make a strong finishing kick. The kicking technique of Kyeot-chee-kee sometimes uses Hoo-ryuh-cha-kee, too.

First, after two or three Doo-sohn Yeop-eu-roh Huhn-duhl-myuh Poom-bahl-kee, Wit-dae steps his/her right foot, which was put down with a step of Woo-poom, in the form of Guht-kee instead of putting it back to One-poom. Ah-raet-dae continues Poom-bahl-kee regardless of Wit-dae's movement. Second, Wit-dae kicks Jae-cha-kee with his left foot on the left flank or thigh of Ah-raet-dae who took Jwa-poom. Ah-rat-dae defends properly and stands still after being kicked. Third, Wit-dae takes the left foot which performed Jae-cha-kee forward and uses its momentum to rotate. And he/she use the rotational force to perform Dohl-gae-chee-kee. Ah-rat-dae retreats with proper defense. Fourth, Wit-dae and Ah-raet-dae return to the starting position then Ah-raet-dae starts his/her turn to attack.

3-1	3-2	3-3

째차기를 이용한 곁치고 돌개치기에서는 딛고 째며 공격이 시작되지만 후려차기를 이용한 곁치고 돌개치기에서는 바로 째며 공격이 시작된다.
곁치고 돌개치기를 할 때에는 곁치기 동작을 통해 상대를 얼마나 움직이지 못하도록 만드느냐가 중요하다. 움직이는 상대를 회전하며 좇아가는 건 쉬운 일이 아니다. 따라서 상대의 움직임을 보며 좇아가던 다른 얼러 메기기 기술들에 비해 곁치고 돌개치기는 곁치기를 통해 상대의 움직임을 고정시켜주어야 하는 것이다.
아래 그림과 같이 공중으로 뛰어올라 돌개치기를 하는 것을 돌개질이라고 부른다.

*곁치고 돌개질

1-1	1-2	2

In Gyeot-chee-goh Dohl-gae-chee-kee with Jae-cha-kee, the attack begins with stepping and Jae-kee (Dit-go Jae-kee), but in Gyeot-chee-goh Dohl-gae-chee-kee with Hoo-ryuh-cha-kee, the attack begins right away with Jae-kee (Ba-ro Jae-kee).
When Gyeot-chee-goh Dohl-gae-chee-kee is being performed, it is important to prevent the opponent from moving through the Kyeot-chee-kee movement. It is not easy to track down a moving opponent while you are rotating. Therefore, when you perform Gyeot-chee-goh Dohl-gae-chee-kee, you have to fix the opponent's movements by Kyeot-chee-kee compared to other Eol-luh Me-kee-kee techniques that chase the opponent's movements.
Dohl-gae-jil is a technique that involves jumping into the air and performing Dohl-gae-chee-kee as shown in the picture below.

*Gyeot-chee-goh Dohl-gae-jil

3-1	3-2	3-3

⑱ 물구나무 쌍발차기

물구나무 쌍발차기는 양 손을 바닥에 짚고 도는 옆돌기를 활용한 발차기 기술이다. 특히 옆돌기의 회전력과 체중이 두 발에 실려 상당히 강한 힘을 자랑하는 큰 기술이다.

첫째, 두 손 옆으로 흔들며 품밟기를 두세 번 한 후, 윗대는 좌품에서 원품으로 이동한 후, 오른발을 우품으로 딛지 않고 바로 걷기의 형태로 상대에게 다가간다. 바로 째는 걸음이다. 아랫대는 윗대의 움직임에 관계없이 지속적으로 품밟기를 한다. 둘째, 윗대는 아랫대의 오른발이 우품으로 나오는 박자에 맞춰 왼발로 상대의 오른 허벅지에 곧은 발질을 하여 뒤로 밀어낸다. 아랫대는 곧은 발질을 맞은 오른발을 자연스럽게 뒤로 내딛는다. 셋째, 윗대는 곧은 발질을 한 왼발을 아랫대의 오른쪽 옆으로 비스듬히 내딛는다. 동시에 발을 딛는 탄력을 살려 양 손으로 바닥을 짚으며 옆돌기를 한다. 옆돌기를 할 때, 몸 전체가 바닥에 수직으로 서지 않고 발이 상대의 머리를 향하도록 비스듬히 돌아준다. 이때, 오른발, 왼발 순으로 상대의 머리를 타격한다. 아랫대는 적절히 방어하며 뒤로 물러난다. 넷째, 물구나무 쌍발차기가 끝난 후, 시작 자리로 돌아와 좌품으로 선다. 서로 왼발을 살짝 들어 올린 후, 호흡을 맞추어 품밟기를 하며 아랫대의 공격 순서를 시작한다.

1-1	1-2	2

⑱ Mool-goo-nah-moo Sahng-bahl-cha-kee

Mool-goo-nah-moo Sahng-bahl-cha-kee is a kick technique that uses a cartwheel with both hands on the floor. In particular, it is a large technique that boasts a very strong power since the rotational force and weight from the cartwheel with both feet.

First, after two or three Doo-sohn Yeop-eu-roh Huhn-duhl-myuh Poom-bahl-kee, Wit-dae moves from Jwa-poom to won-poom then approaches the opponent in the form of Guht-kee instead of placing his/her right foot in Woo-poom. This is a step of Ba-ro Jae-kee. Second, Wit-dae performs Gohd-eun-bahl-jil on the opponent's right thigh with his/her left foot to push back in line with the beat of Ah-raet-dae's right foot comes out to step Woo-poom. Ah-raet-dae naturally takes a step back with his/her right foot that was performed Gohd-eun-bahl-jil by Wit-dae. Third, Wit-dae slants the left foot which performed Gohd-eun-bahl-jil to the right side of Ah-raet-dae. At the same time, he/she puts both hands on the floor and does a cartwheel using the elasticity of the foot stepping on the floor. When performing the cartwheel, the entire body does not stand perpendicular to the floor, but turns obliquely so that the feet target the opponent's head. At this time, hit the opponent's head in order of the right foot then the left. Ah-raet-dae steps back while he/she defends the attack properly. Fourth, after Mool-goo-nah-moo Sahng-bahl-cha-kee is completed, they return to the starting position and stand in the stance of Jwa-poom. Both raise their left feet slightly, then Ah-raet-dae starts his/her turn to attack while they are performing Poom-bahl-kee in harmony.

3-1

3-1

3-2

물구나무 쌍발차기는 동작이 큰 만큼 위력이 강하긴 하지만 상대에게 적중시키기 어렵다. 따라서 상대가 다른 동작에 정신이 팔렸거나, 혼전 중에 예기치 못한 상황에서 사용해야 성공할 확률이 올라간다.
특히 상대가 물구나무 쌍발차기를 사전에 감지하면 숙여진 머리를 향해 쉽게 발차기로 반격할 수 있으므로 매우 주의해야 한다. 또한 상당한 반복 연습을 하지 않으면 목표지점에 발을 맞추기가 매우 어렵다. 따라서 빠르게, 최대한 간소한 동작으로 할 수 있도록 여러 번 반복해야 한다.
물구나무 쌍발차기를 할 때에는 차고자 하는 방향으로 곁치기(곧은 발질이나 후려차기 등)를 먼저 해서 상대의 발을 뒤로 물러나게 하고 그 길을 따라 물구나무 쌍발차기를 한다. 또한 물구나무 쌍발차기는 반듯하게 옆으로 도는 것이 아니라 발이 상대방 쪽으로 기울어지게 해서 돌아야 실제로 상대를 가격할 수 있다.

Mool-goo-nah-moo Sahng-bahl-cha-kee is powerful as it is a big move, but it is hard to hit the opponent. Therefore, the chances of success increase when the opponent is distracted by other movements or when he/she uses the technique in unexpected situations during the match.
In particular, if the opponent detects Mool-goo-nah-moo Sahng-bahl-cha-kee in advance, he/she can easily strike back at the lowered head with a kick, so be very careful. Also, it is very difficult to get your feet to the target point without considerable repetitive exercises. Therefore, it is necessary to practice it over and over again so that it can be done quickly and in as simple a motion as possible.
When you perform Mool-goo-nah-moo Sahng-bahl-cha-kee, you need to do Kyeot-chee-kee (like Gohd-eun-bahl-jil or Hoo-ryuh-cha-kee) first, towards where you will kick to make the opponent step back, and do kicks as you advance. Also, to really kick the opponent with Mool-goo-nah-moo Sahng-bahl-cha-kee, you need to keep your body leaning over a bit, not pefectly upright, with your feet pointed towards him(her) while rotating.

⑲ 걷어차고 후려차기

걷어차고 후려차기는 걷어차기를 한 후에 이를 막으며 피하는 상대를 좇아가 후려차기로 공격하는 기술이다. 공격 기술의 이름 순서대로 행하면 된다.

첫째, 두 손 옆으로 흔들며 품밟기를 두세 번 한 후, 윗대는 우품을 내딛은 다음 오른발을 원품자리로 놓지 않고 걷기의 형태로 상대에게 다가간다. 딛고 째는 동작이다. 아랫대는 윗대의 움직임에 관계없이 지속적으로 품밟기를 한다. 둘째, 윗대는 아랫대의 왼발이 좌품으로 나오는 박자에 맞춰 자신의 왼발로 상대의 얼굴을 향해 걷어차기 한다. 아랫대는 왼발을 좌품으로 디딘 직후이므로 적절히 방어하며 왼발을 뒤로 뺀다. 셋째, 윗대는 걷어차기 한 왼발을 적절한 위치에 내딛으며 그 탄력을 실어 오른발 후려차기를 한다. 아랫대는 윗대의 공격을 적절히 방어하며 물러난다. 넷째, 후려차기가 끝난 후, 시작 자리로 돌아와서 좌품으로 선다. 서로 왼발을 살짝 들어 올린 후, 호흡을 맞추어 품밟기를 하며 아랫대의 공격 순서를 시작한다.

1-1	1-2	1-3

⑲ Guh-duh-cha-goh Hoo-ryuh-cha-kee

Guh-duh-cha-goh Hoo-ryuh-cha-kee is a technique that attacks an opponent with Guh-duh-cha-kee and then follows the opponent who avoids it and attacks him/her with Hoo-ryuh-cha-kee. It can be done in order according to the name of the attack technique.

First, after two or three Doo-sohn Yeop-eu-roh Huhn-duhl-myuh Poom-bahl-kee, Wit-dae steps out of Woo-poom and approaches the opponent in the form of Guht-kee instead of Won-poom. This is a movement of Dit-go Jae-kee. Ah-raet-dae continues Poom-bahl-kee regardless of Wit-dae's movement. Second, Wit-dae performs Guh-duh-cha-kee at the opponent's face with his/her left foot in line with the beat of Ah-raet-dae's left foot moves forward to step Jwa-poom. Since Ah-raet-dae just stepped Jwa-poom with his/her left foot, he/she properly defends and pulls the left foot back. Third, Wit-dae puts his/her left foot which performed Guh-duh-cha-kee in a proper position and then performs Hoo-ryuh-cha-kee with his/her right foot using the momentum. Ah-raet-dae retreats defending against the attack properly. Fourth, after Hoo-ryuh-cha-kee is completed, they return to the starting position and then Ah-raet-dae starts his/her turn to attack.

2	3-1	3-2

걷어차고 후려차기는 연속 발질을 연습하기 위한 과정으로 걷어차기를 한 후에 상대 움직임을 빠르게 간파하는 것이 매우 중요하다. 때에 따라서는 걷어차기를 한 후에 발을 내딛는 곳을 다양하게 바꿔가며 후려차기로 연결하는 연습을 함께 해주기도 한다.
걷어차고 후려차기의 경우 실전에서 매우 효과적인 연속공격이다. 특히 상대를 향해 걷어차기를 한 다리를 바로 내려놓지 않고 균형을 유지하며 상대의 움직임을 기다리기에 적절한 기술이다. 이때 상대는 한 번의 움직임으로 피하거나 방어할 수 있는 시간밖에 갖지 못한다. 따라서 그 움직임을 좇아 상대를 관찰하며 걷어차기 한 발을 적절한 위치에 내딛으면 상대의 연속적인 움직임을 봉쇄한 채 후려차기 공격을 성공시킬 수 있다.

Guh-duh-cha-goh Hoo-ryuh-cha-kee is a good training method for continuous kicking, so it is very important to catch the opponent's movement after Guh-duh-cha-kee. Sometimes, the training for stepping down at various places after Guh-duh-cha-kee and connecting to Hoo-ryuh-cha-kee is reguired.
Guh-duh-cha-goh Hoo-ryuh-cha-kee is a very effective series of attacks for real fight. In particular, it is an appropriate technique to wait for the other's movement, keeping one's balance without putting the leg down, which performed Guh-duh-cha-kee at the opponent. At this time, the opponent only has time to avoid or defenc in one move. Therefore, observing the move and putting the foot on proper position which performed Guh-duh-cha-kee down, you can succeed in Hoo-ryuh-cha-kee attacks while blocking the opponent's successive moves.

(2-2) 손질

① 떼밀기 (복장밀기, 허구리밀기)

얼러 메기기의 떼밀기는 막음질의 떼밀기와 같다. 복장밀기는 칼재기 모양의 손으로 상대의 가슴 한복판을 밀어주는 것이며 허구리밀기는 상대의 갈비뼈를 밀어주는 것이다. 단, 막음질에서는 복장밀기와 허구리 밀기 모두 같은 쪽 손발을 사용하여 밀고 나갔지만, 얼러 메기기의 허구리 밀기는 엇의 형태로 서로 다른 쪽의 손과 발이 사용된다.

첫째, 두 손 옆으로 흔들며 품밟기를 두세 번 한 후, 윗대는 좌품을 내딛는 순서에 왼발을 앞으로 조금 더 길게 내딛는다. 아랫대는 윗대의 움직임에 관계없이 지속적으로 품밟기를 한다. 둘째, 왼발을 내딛음과 동시에 윗대는 아랫대의 가슴 한복판에 왼손을 대고 밀어준다. 이를 복장밀기라 하며 허구리밀기는 그림 3-2과 3-2처럼 오른손으로 옆구리를 밀어준다. 이때, 뒤에 있는 오른 다리를 쭉 펴는 힘으로 체중의 실어 밀어주어야 한다. 아랫대는 가볍게 저항하며 자연스럽게 밀려준다. 셋째, 윗대는 내딛었던 왼발을 당겨와 걷기로 디디고 오른발을 우품보다 길게 앞으로 내딛는다. 동시에 복장밀기나 허구리밀기를 해준다. 넷째, 윗대는 뒤로 길게 빠지며 처음의 자리로 돌아가 좌품으로 기다린다. 서로 왼발을 살짝 들어 올린 후, 호흡을 맞추어 품밟기를 하며 처음의 위치와 거리를 맞추어 아랫대의 공격을 준비한다.

1-1	1-2	2-1

(2-2) Sohn-jil

① Dde-mil-kee (Bohk-jang-mil-kee, Huh-goo-ree-mil-kee)

Dde-mil-kee in Eol-luh Me-kee-kee is the same as Dde-mil-kee in Mahk-eum-jil. Bohk-jang-mil-kee is a movement that pushes the center of the opponent's chest with Kahl-jae-kee, and Huh-goo-ree-mil-kee a movement that pushes against the opponent's ribs. However, while both Bohk-jang-mil-kee and Huh-goo-ree-mil-kee were pushed forward using the same sides of hand and foot in Mahk-eum-jil, the Huh-goo-ree-mil-kee in Eol-luh Me-kee-kee uses different sides of the hand and foot in the form of Uht.

First, after two or three Doo-sohn Yeop-eu-roh Huhn-duhl-myuhn Poom-bahl-kee, Wit-dae puts his/her left foot forward a little farther in the order in which he/she takes a step of Jwa-poom. Ah-raet-dae continues his Poom-bahl-kee regardless of Wit-dae's movement. Second, as soon as the left foot is stepped forward, Wit-dae pushes the left hand into the middle of the chest of the Ah-raet-dae. This is referred to as Bohk-jang-mil-kee, and Huh-goo-ree-mil-kee is a movement that pushes the side with the right hand as shown in figures 3-1 and 3-2. At this time you should push, putting your weight on it with the force of straightening your right leg, behind you. Ah-raet-dae is pushed naturally while he/she resists lightly. Third, Wit-dae pulls the left foot he/she has taken and takes a step of Guht-kee, then puts the right foot forward farther than Woo-poom. At the same time, he/she performs Bohk-jang-mil-kee or Huh-goo-ree-mil-kee. Fourth, Both return to starting position and then Ah-raet-dae prepares his/her turn to attack.

2-2

3-1

3-2

떼밀기 동작을 할 때는 허리를 반듯하게 세워주는 것이 좋다. 힘껏 밀겠다고 상체를 앞으로 숙이면 오히려 중심을 유지하기 어려워 정확하고 큰 힘을 낼 수 없다. 또한 상체를 숙이는 것이 몸에 익숙해질 경우, 실전에서 되치기를 허용할 확률이 매우 높아진다.
떼밀기의 경우에도 공격과 방어의 양면성을 가진 기술이다. 방어적 관점에서 체격이 큰 상대가 지속적으로 나에게 달려들 때, 상대를 떨어뜨리기 위해 사용하며, 공격적 관점에서는 직접적으로 내 공격의 활로를 찾기 위해 사용한다.

It's good to keep your back straight when you perform Dde-mil-kee. If you bend your upper body forward to push as hard as you can, it will be difficult to maintain your balance, so you can't exert exact and great strength. Also, if you get used to bending your upper body, you are very likely to allow a counterattack in an actual fight.
Dde-mil-kee can be used for attack or defense, too. In terms of defense, it is used to push away the bigger opponent from you to avoid him/ her overtaking you, and in terms of attack, it is used to set up my own attack.

② 덜미잽이

얼러 메기기의 덜미잽이도 떼밀기와 마찬가지로 막음질의 동작과 동일하게 실시한다. 다만, 상대의 품밟기 박자를 파악하여 기술을 사용한다는 점은 기억해야 한다.

첫째, 두 손 옆으로 흔들며 품밟기를 두세 번 한 후, 윗대는 좌품을 내딛는 순서에 왼발을 앞으로 조금 더 길게 내딛는다. 아랫대는 윗대의 움직임에 관계없이 지속적으로 품밟기를 한다. 둘째, 윗대는 왼발을 내딛음과 동시에 왼손으로 덜미잽이를 하며 상대의 목을 감싸 잡는다. 그리고 앞에 내딛었던 왼발로 바닥을 차며 왼쪽으로 몸을 틀고 발을 뒤로 내딛는다. 동시에 그 탄력을 이용하여 상대를 자신의 왼쪽 가슴아래 방향으로 잡아챈다. 아랫대는 가볍게 저항하며 자연스럽게 끌려온다. 셋째, 윗대는 왼손 덜미걸이가 끝난 상태 그대로 다리를 둔 채, 오른손으로 아랫대의 덜미를 잡는다. 그리고 오른발을 차는 탄력을 이용해 상대의 목을 오른 가슴 앞으로 끌고 온다. 넷째, 아랫대가 끌려왔으므로 뒤로 길게 빠지며 처음의 자리로 돌아가 좌품으로 기다린다. 서로 왼발을 살짝 들어 올린 후, 호흡을 맞추어 품밟기를 하며 처음의 위치와 거리를 맞추어 아랫대의 공격을 준비한다.

> 덜미잽이와 이어지는 덜미걸이는 얼러 메기기에서 뒤로 이동하며 하는 몇 안 되는 기술이다. 이를 반복 연습하여 상대를 끌고 올 때의 중심 이동이나 상대의 움직임을 익혀두면 실전에 유용하게 활용된다.

1-1

1-2

2-1

② Duhl-mee-jae-bee

Duhl-mee-jae-bee of Eol-luh Me-kee-kee is performed in the same way as the movement of Mahk-eum-jil, like how Dde-mil-kee is performed. However, it is important to remember that the opponent's Poom-bahl-kee beat should be identified when you perform the technique.

First, after two or three Doo-sohn Yeop-eu-roh Huhn-duhl-myuh Poom-bahl-kee, Wit-dae puts his/her left foot forward a little farther in the order in which he/she takes a step of Jwa-poom. Second, at the same time, Wit-dae performs Duhl-mee-jae-bee to hold the opponent's neck with his/her left hand. Then he/she kicks the floor with his/her left foot, twists the body to the left, and steps back. At the same time, he/she uses that momentum to yank the opponent down to his/her left chest. Ah-raet-dae is drawn naturally while he/she resists lightly. Third, Wit-dae holds the back of Ah-raet-dae's neck with his/her right hand while he/she keeps the same leg position as was used when Duhl-mee-guh-ree was performed with the left hand. Then, using the momentum of the right foot kick, he/she pulls the opponent's neck forward to his/her right chest. Fourth, both go back to the original position and then Ah-raet-dae prepares his/her turn to attack.

Duhl-mee-jae-bee and Duhl-mee-guh-ree in next are the few techniques that are performed by moving backward in Eol-luh Me-kee-kee. It will be useful in a real fight if you practice it repeatedly to learn the weight shift of the opponent or the movement of the opponent when you pull the opponent.

2-2

3-1

3-2

③ 덜미걸이

얼러 메기기의 덜미걸이도 덜미잽이와 마찬가지로 막음질의 동작과 동일하게 실시한다. 또한 손을 반대로 하여 덜미를 걸어오는 고개잽이도 있다.

첫째, 두 손 옆으로 흔들며 품밟기를 두세 번 한 후, 윗대는 좌품을 내딛는 순서에 왼발을 앞으로 조금 더 길게 내딛는다. 아랫대는 윗대의 움직임에 관계없이 지속적으로 품밟기를 한다. 둘째, 윗대는 왼발을 내딛음과 동시에 오른손으로 덜미걸이를 하며 상대의 목을 감싸 잡는다. 그리고 앞에 내딛었던 왼발로 바닥을 차며 왼쪽으로 몸을 틀고 발을 뒤로 내딛는다. 동시에 그 탄력을 이용하여 상대를 자신의 왼쪽 가슴아래 방향으로 밀어 내린다. 고개잽이는 이때 왼손으로 덜미를 걸어 끌어당긴다. 아랫대는 가볍게 저항하며 자연스럽게 끌려온다. 셋째, 반대쪽도 동일하게 실시한다.

고개잽이는 차후에 덜미를 건 반대 손으로 상대의 겨드랑이를 받쳐 올려 넘어뜨리는 고개잡고 재갈잽이 등의 기술로 연계되기도 한다.

1-1	1-2	2-1

③ Duhl-mee-jae-bee

Duhl-mee-guh-ree of Eol-luh Me-kee-kee is performed in the same way as the movement of Mahk-eum-jil. There is also Goh-gae-jae-bee that grabs the nape of the neck with the opposite hand.

First, after two or three Doo-sohn Yeop-eu-roh Huhn-duhl-myuh Poom-bahl-kee, Wit-dae puts his/her left foot forward a little farther in the order of Jwa-poom. Second, as soon as the left foot is stepped forward, Wit-dae performs Duhl-mee-guh-ree with his/her right hand to grab the opponent's neck. Then he/she kicks the floor with his/her left foot, twists the body to the left, and steps back. At the same time, he/she uses that momentum to push the opponent's neck down to his/her left chest. If you grab and pull with your left hand, it will be Goh-gae-jae-bee. Ah-raet-dae is naturally drawn with light resistance. Third, perform the same for the other side.

Goh-gae-jae-bee can be later linked to techniques such as Goh-gae-jahb-go Jae-gahl-jae-bee that holds up the opponent's armpit with the opposite hand of the hand that grabbed the neck and throw him/her down.

2-2	3-1	3-2

*고개잽이 Goh-gae-jae-bee

1-1	1-2	2-1

*고개잽이 Goh-gae-jae-bee

2-2	3-1	3-2

④ 가새질러막기

가새질러막기는 막음질의 두 손 내어막기의 응용이라 할 수 있다. 두 손 내어막기의 형태로 상대의 공격을 방어한 후, 상대의 다리를 비틀어 넘어뜨린다.

첫째, 두 손 옆으로 흔들며 품밟기를 두세 번 한 후, 아랫대가 오른발을 딛고 째며 왼발로 걷어차기를 한다. 이때 윗대는 왼발을 뒤로 빼며 두 손 내어막기를 한 후, 그대로 상대의 다리를 감아 잡는다. 아랫대는 다리를 잡힌 채로 중심을 잡고 선다. 둘째, 윗대는 오른손이 앞에 있을 경우, 오른손을 미끄러뜨려 올려 상대의 오금을 걸어준다. 동시에 왼팔을 안에서 밖으로 돌리며 상대의 종아리 부위를 아래에서 위로 감싸 안는다. 그리고 오른손을 아래로 잡아당기며 왼팔과 함께 상대의 무릎을 바깥으로 향하게 꺾어 돌려 상대를 넘어뜨린다(그림 2-1, 2-2). 왼손이 앞에 있을 경우, 왼손을 미끄러뜨려 상대의 오금을 걸어준다. 동시에 오른팔을 안에서 밖으로 돌리며 상대의 종아리 부위를 아래에서 위로 감싸 안는다. 그리고 왼손을 당기며 상대의 무릎을 접고 오른팔과 함께 상대의 무릎이 안쪽으로 향하도록 다리를 꺾어 돌려 넘어뜨린다(그림 3-1. 3-2). 이후, 아랫대가 일어나면 호흡을 맞춰 품밟기를 하며 아랫대의 순서를 준비한다.

1-1

1-2

2-1

④ Gah-sae-jil-luh-mahk-kee

Gah-sae-jil-luh-mahk-kee is an application of Doo-sohn Nae-eo-mahk-kee of Mahk-eum-jil. It defends the opponent's attack in the form of Doo-sohn Nae-eo-mahk-kee and then twists the opponent's leg and knocks him/her down.

First, after two or three Doo-sohn Yeop-eu-roh Huhn-duhl-myuh Poom-bahl-kee, Ah-raet-dae does Dit-go Jae-kee with the right foot and Guh-duh-cha-kee with the left foot. At this point, Wit-dae pulls his left foot back and performs Doo-sohn Nae-eo-mahk-kee at the same time. Right after, he/she holds the opponent's leg by twisting his/her hands. Ah-raet-dae stands keeping the balance with his/her leg held. Second, Wit-dae slides the right hand up and holds the crook of the opponent's knee if his/her right hand is closer to the opponent. At the same time, turn the left arm from the inside to the outside and hug the opponent's calf from the bottom up. Then pull down the right hand and turn the opponent's knee outward with the left arm to turn over the opponent (figure 2-1, 2-2). If the left hand is closer to the opponent, slides the left hand up and holds the crook of the opponent's knee. At the same time, turn the right arm from the inside to the outside and hug the opponent's calf from the bottom up. Then pull the left hand, fold the opponent's knee, and turn the opponent's knee inward with the right arm (figure 3-1 3-2). After that, when Ah-raet-dae picks himself/herself up, he/she prepares his/her turn to attack while they are performing Poom-bahl-kee in harmony.

2-2 | 3-1 | 3-2

가새질러막기는 상대의 무릎 아래 부분을 꺾어 잡고 이를 지렛대처럼 사용하여 상대를 넘어뜨리는 기술이다. 따라서 상대를 넘기기 위해서는 무릎에 가까운 손으로 상대의 오금을 걸어주고 앞으로 밀고 나가 상대의 무릎이 90°로 접히도록 만들어야 한다. 그리고 상대의 접힌 무릎을 중심으로 정강이 부분을 거대한 수도꼭지 돌리듯 돌려주어야 한다.

가새질러막기를 할 때, 상대를 넘기는 것에만 치중하게 되면 제대로 상대의 발질을 막거나 잡을 수 없다. 그러므로 첫째, 상대의 발질을 두손 내어막기로 정확히 막는 것과 둘째, 두 손이 벌어지지 않고 상대의 발질을 잡는 것에 먼저 집중해야 한다. 그 후에 상대를 넘어뜨려야 한다.

가새질러막기 후 상대를 넘어뜨릴 때는 정확한 다리 자세가 더욱 중요하다. 초보자들의 경우, 다리는 멈춰 있는 상태에서 팔로만 상대를 넘어뜨리려고 해서 기술이 제대로 안 되는 경우가 많다. 그림 1-2 → 2-1과 3-1 → 3-1처럼 상대를 밀며 한 걸음 나아가야 한다.

Gah-sae-jil-luh-mahk-kee is a technique in which you hold the opponent's lower knee by bending and using it as a lever to knock the opponent over. Therefore, in order to turn over the opponent, you must hold the crook of the opponent's knee with a hand close to the knee and push it forward so that the opponent's knee is folded at 90°. Also turn the shin around the opponent's folded knee like you are turning around a giant faucet.

When you do Gah-sae-jil-luh-mahk-kee, if you only concentrate on taking the opponent down, you cannot defend or grab his(her) kick properly. So, you need to think of blocking the opponent's kick with Do-sohn Nae-uh-mahk-kee, at first, then grabbing his(her) leg with gathered hands, afterwards. Knocking the opponent over is last.

To knock over the opponent with Gah-sae-jil-luh-mahk-kee, the leg position is the most important point. Some beginners usually use only their arms and fail. As shown in figures 1-2 → 2-1 & 3-1 → 3-1, you need to go one step forward when pushing the opponent.

⑤ 끼어잡기

끼어잡기는 방어를 연습하는 동작이다. 단, 끼어잡기를 하는 목적이 상대의 발차기를 잡아 그 다음의 공격으로 이어가기 위한 것임을 기억해야 한다.

첫째, 두 손 옆으로 흔들며 품밟기를 두세 번 한 후, 아랫대가 왼발을 딛고 째며 앞으로 한발 나온다. 이때 윗대는 좌품에서 원품으로 돌아간 후, 다시 우품을 내딛는 박자가 된다. 둘째, 아랫대가 오른발 후려차기를 하면 윗대는 발차기를 피해 우품을 딛지 않고 오른발을 우측 45°방향으로 길게 내딛는다. 동시에 오른손 손바닥으로 상대 후려차기의 정강이나 무릎을 막으며 왼팔을 크게 휘돌려 다리를 감아 옆구리에 단단히 끼운다. 셋째, 윗대가 다리를 놓아주면 아랫대는 그 다리를 원품으로 내딛으며 왼발 후려차기를 한다. 윗대는 왼쪽으로 발을 내딛어 피하며 동시에 왼손으로 상대의 후려차기 무릎을 막아주고 오른팔을 휘돌려 상대의 종아리부위를 감아 옆구리에 끼운다. 이후, 다리를 놓아주면 제자리로 돌아가 호흡을 맞춰 품밟기를 하며 아랫대의 순서를 준비한다.

1-1	1-2	1-3

⑤ Kee-eo-jahb-kee

Kee-eo-jahb-kee is an exercise in defense. However, it should be remembered that the purpose of Kee-eo-jahb-kee is to catch the opponent's kick and then continue on to the next attack.

First, after two or three Doo-sohn Yeop-eu-roh Huhn-duhl-myuh Poom-bahl-kee, Ah-rate-dae does Dit-go Jae-kee with the left foot to take a step forward. At this time, Wit-dae returns from Jwa-poom to won-poom, then it becomes the beat for him/her to take Woo-poom again. Second, when Ah-raet-dae performs Hoo-ryuh-cha-kee with his/her right foot, Wit-dae takes a long step with his/her right foot 45° to the right instead of stepping Woo-poom to avoid the kick. At the same time, he/she uses the right palm to block the knee or shin of the opponent's performing Hoo-ryuh-cha-kee and turns the left arm wide to wind the opponent's leg tightly around the side. Third, when Wit-dae lets go of the leg, Ah-raet-dae takes a step of won-poom with the leg and performs Hoo-ryuh-cha-kee with his/her left foot. Wit-dae steps to the left and avoids the kick. At the same time, he/she uses the left hand to block the knee of the opponent's performing Hoo-ryuh-cha-kee and turns the right arm wide to wind the opponent's leg tightly around the side. After that, when the leg is let go, they return to their positions and Ah-raet-dae prepares his/her turn to attack while they are performing Poom-bahl-kee in harmony.

1-4	2-1	2-2

끼어잡기는 옆구리에 상대의 다리를 끼우기 때문에 곁통 끼어잡기라고도 부른다. 기술 이름에 잡기가 들어가지만 실제로는 잡는다기보다 옆구리에 끼우는 느낌으로 해야 한다. 끼어잡기에서 날아오는 발차기를 피해 상대의 옆으로 발을 내딛을 때는 상대에게서 너무 멀리 떨어지지 않도록 몸통 바로 옆을 보며 나아가야 한다.
그 다음 기억할 것은 후려차기의 무릎이나 정강이를 막아주는 것이다. 발을 비스듬히 옆으로 내딛어 발차기를 피하더라도 상대가 조금만 몸을 틀면 옆구리에 맞을 수 있다. 따라서 반드시 무릎이나 정강이를 막아야 한다. 이때 무릎이나 그보다 윗부분을 막아주는 것이 힘이 덜 들며 충격이 덜하다.
끝으로 기억할 것은 상대의 다리를 감아주는 팔의 모양이다. 크게 휘돌리지 않으며 상대의 다리를 충분히 감지 못해 잡아챌 수 없다. 그러므로 활갯짓 치돌리기의 형태로 팔을 크게 휘감아주어야 한다. 이때 손은 쭉 편 채로 손가락을 모아주어야 부상을 막아준다.

Kee-eo-jahb-kee is also called Kyeot-tong-kee-eo-jahb-kee because it puts the opponent's leg in the side. When you step aside to avoid a kick that flies from the opponent, you have to look right next to the opponent's body so that you don't get too far from him/her.
The next thing to remember is to block the knee or shin of Hoo-ryuh-cha-kee. Even if you avoid a kick by slanting your foot on the side, you can get hit on the side if the opponent turns a little. Therefore, you must block the knee or shin, and it is less difficult and less shocking to block the knee or upper part of the knee.
The last thing to remember is the shape of the arm that wraps around the opponent's leg. If you don't swing your arms wide, you won't be able to wind your opponent's leg enough to hold. Therefore, it is necessary to wrap your arms around it in the form of Hwahl-get-jit Chee-dohl-lee-kee. At this point, you need to outstretch your hand with your fingers together to prevent finger injuries.

⑥ 오금잽이 및 무릎잽이

오금잽이와 모릎잽이는 상대의 무릎을 잡아채서 들어 올리는 동작이다. 상대의 다리 한쪽을 자신의 제어 아래에 둠으로써 넘어뜨리기 쉽게 된다. 상대 다리의 바깥쪽에서 오금을 잡아채는 동작을 오금잽이, 다리 사이에서 잡아채는 동작을 무릎잽이라 한다.

첫째, 두 손 옆으로 흔들며 품밟기를 두세 번 한 후, 윗대는 좌품을 내딛는 순서에 왼발을 앞으로 조금 더 길게 내딛는다. 아랫대는 윗대의 움직임에 관계없이 지속적으로 품밟기를 한다. 둘째, 윗대는 왼발을 내딛음과 동시에 자세를 낮추어 오른팔로 좌품을 디딘 상대의 오금을 밖에서 안으로 감싸 잡는다. 그리고 상대의 무릎을 단단히 고정한 상태로 일어난다. 이것이 오금잽이다(그림 2-1, 2-2). 이때 왼팔로 상대의 오금을 감싸 잡아 일어나면 무릎잽이가 된다(그림 3-1, 3-2). 즉 오금잽이는 엇, 무릎잽이는 맞의 동작이 된다. 셋째, 들어 올린 왼다리를 상대의 뒤쪽으로 밀어 놓아준 후, 오른발을 내딛으며 앞으로 나가 서있는 상대의 오른쪽 다리에도 오금잽이(무릎잽이)를 한다. 넷째, 처음 자리로 돌아가 서로 품을 맞추어 아랫대의 순서를 준비한다.

1-1	1-2	2-1

⑥ Oh-gum-jae-bee & Moo-reup-jae-bee

Oh-gum-jae-bee and Moo-reup-jae-bee are the moves that grab and lift the opponent's knee. It is a move that makes it easier to knock the opponent down by placing one of the opponent's legs under your control. The movement to grab the crook of the knee from the outside of the opponent's leg is called Oh-gum-jae-bee, and the movement to grab it between the legs is called Moo-reup-jae-bee.

First, after two or three Doo-sohn Yeop-eu-roh Huhn-duhl-myuh Poom-bahl-kee, Wit-dae puts his/her left foot forward a little farther in the order in which he/she takes a step of Jwa-poom. Second, Wit-dae lowers the position at the same time as he/she takes a step with his/her left foot, and wraps and holds the opponent's crock of the knee, which stepped Jwa-poom, from outside to inside with his/her right arm. Then he/she stands up with the opponent's knee firmly fixed. This is Oh-gum-jae-bee (figure2-1, 2-2). At this point, the left arm wraps and holds the opponent's crook of the knee and rises to become Moo-reup-jae-bee (figure 3-1, 3-2). Third, push the raised left leg to the back of the opponent, and then step forward with the right foot, and do Oh-gum-jae-bee (Moo-reup-jae-bee) on the opponent's right leg. Fourth, return to the first place and Ah-raet-dae prepares his/her turn while they are performing Poom-bahl-kee in harmony.

2-2

3-1

3-2

오금잽이와 무릎잽이를 할 때 가장 많이 하는 실수는 팔이 아닌 손을 이용해 상대의 다리를 잡으려 하다는 것이다. 그러나 다리는 매우 굵고 무거워 한 손으로는 잡아 올리기가 매우 어렵다. 따라서 팔꿈치 부분까지 상대의 무릎 뒤로 집어넣어 팔 전체로 감아올리도록 한다. 또한, 잡고 올리는 것이 아닌 잡아채는 동작이 되도록 한다.
또 한 가지 실수는 상대의 다리를 잡은 후 뒤로 일어나려 한다는 것이다. 그러면 허리에 무리가 갈 뿐 아니라 상대가 끌려오며 들린 다리로 체중이 실려 상대의 다리가 더 무거워지게 된다. 따라서 다리를 들어 올릴 때에는 상대방에게 다가가는 느낌으로, 아랫배를 앞으로 살짝 밀어주며 일어나야 한다.

The most common mistake when performing Oh-gum-jae-bee and Moo-reup-jae-bee is that they try to grab the opponent's leg using their hand, not their arm. However, the legs are very thick and heavy, making it very difficult to grab and lift them with one hand. Therefore, put it behind the opponent's knee up to the elbow and wrap it around the leg with the whole arm to lift it up. Also, the movement should be snatching upwards, not grabbing and lifting

Another mistake is that after grabbing the opponent's leg, they tries to get back up. This not only causes a strain on the waist, but also puts more weight on the leg that is lifted as the opponent is pulled in, making the opponent's leg heavier. Therefore, when you lift the leg, you have to stand up with a slight push in the lower abdomen, as if you are approaching the opponent.

⑦ 발회목잡고 칼잽이

발회목잡고 칼잽이는 막음질의 활개 발회목잡기를 공격으로 응용한 기술이다. 상대의 발목을 잡은 후, 칼잽이로 상대의 목을 밀어 넘어뜨린다. 칼잽이가 아닌 가로밀기를 이용해 어깨잽이를 하기도 한다.

첫째, 두 손 옆으로 흔들며 품밟기를 두세 번 한 후, 아랫대는 우품을 디딘 오른발을 딛고 째기로 앞으로 내려놓으며 왼발 는질러차기를 한다. 둘째, 윗대는 왼발을 뒤로 빼며 오른손으로 활개 발회목잡기를 한다. 셋째, 윗대는 잡아챈 발목을 자신의 몸 바깥으로 뺀다. 그리고 왼발을 앞으로 내딛으며 왼손 칼잽이로 상대의 목을 밀어 넘어뜨린다. 이때 오른손은 상대의 다리를 들어올린다. 아랫대는 윗대의 공격이 완전하게 들어오면 안전하게 넘어진다. 넷째, 윗대와 아랫대는 시작 자리로 돌아와 호흡을 맞추어 품밟기를 하며 아랫대의 공격 순서를 시작한다.

상대의 는질러차기를 안쪽에서 잡았을 때는 어깨잽이 그림처럼 상대의 다리를 자신의 바깥으로 빼낸 후, 가로밀기를 해서 넘어뜨린다.

1-1	1-2	1-3

*칼잽이 Kahl-jae-bee

2	3-1	3-2

⑦ Bahl-hoe-mohk-jahb-goh Kahl-jae-bee

Bahl-hoe-mohk-jahb-goh Kahl-jae-bee is a technique that uses Hwahl-gay Bahl-hoe-mohk-jahp-kee from Mahk-eum-jil as an attack. After grabbing the opponent's ankle, you push the opponent's neck with Kahl-jae-bee. You can sometimes use Gah-roh-mil-kee to do Uh-kae-jae-bee instead of Kahl-jae-bee.

First, after two or three Doo-sohn Yeop-eu-roh Huhn-duhl-myuh Poom-bahl-kee, Ah-raet-dae puts his/her right foot forward as Dit-go Jae-kee from Woo-poom, and performs Neun-jil-luh-cha-kee with his/her left foot. Second, Wit-dae performs Hwahl-gay Bahl-hoe-mohk-jahp-kee with his/her right hand while pulling his/her left foot back. Third, Wit-dae pulls the ankle which he/she grabbed out of his/her body. Then, with his/her left foot step forward, he/she pushes the opponent's neck down with his/her left hand Kahl-jae-bee. The right hand lifts the opponent's leg. Ah-raet-dae falls safely when the attack of Wit-dae is done completely.

Fourth, Wit-dae and Ah-raet-dae return to the starting position and Ah-raet-dae starts his/her turn to attack.

When you catch the opponent's Neun-jil-luh-cha-kee from the inside, you pull the opponent's leg out of your body, as shown in the figure of Uh-kae-jae-bee, and then push the opponent over with Gah-roh-mil-kee.

*어깨잽이 Uh-kae-jae-bee

1	2	3

3. 마주차기

마주차기는 상대와 마주 선채로 발질(공격)과 활갯짓(방어)을 번갈아 주고받는 수련과정이다. '바로-절-원품-서거라-거리재고-섯다'의 구령에 따라 윗대가 먼저 발차기를, 아랫대가 그에 대응하는 방어를 하며 시작된다.

첫째, '바로-절-원품'의 구령에 맞추어 인사를 주고받은 후, 상대를 마주보고 원품으로 선다. 둘째, '서거라'의 구령에 따라 좌품 자세를 취한다. 셋째,'거리재고'의 구령에 따라 왼발을 걷기로 내딛은 후, 오른발로 우품을 딛는다. 동시에 오른팔을 앞으로 들어 올려 서로 상대의 오른 어깨 안쪽에 자신의 오른쪽 손바닥을 댄다. 이때, 편안하게 일어서며 서로 팔을 편하게 뻗을 수 있는 거리가 되도록 자연스럽게 조절한다. 넷째, '섯다'의 구령에 따라 윗대가 오른손으로 맞닿은 상대의 팔을 가볍게 밀친다. 그리고 앞에 있는 오른발로 후려차기 한 후, 원품으로 딛는다. 다섯째, 아랫대는 내려막기 등을 이용하여 후려차기를 막는 즉시, 앞에 있는 오른발로 후려차기 한다. 이어서 윗대와 아랫대는 순서를 번갈아가며 자신이 원하는 발질로 공격하고 이를 방어한다.

1-1

1-2

1-3

3. Mah-joo-cha-kee

Mah-joo-cha-kee is a training course in which you and your opponent exchange Bahl-jil (attack) and Hwahl-get-jit (defense) alternately while facing each other. It starts with Wit-dae performing kicking in line with the phrase 'Baro → Jeol → Won-poom → Suh-guh-ra → Guh-ri-jae-go → Suht-da' and Ah-raet-dae defenses responding to it.

First, after exchanging greetings in accordance with the phrase of 'Baro → Jeol → Won-poom', they face each other and stand in Won-poom. Second, assume the stance of Jwa-poom following the command of 'Suh-guh-ra.' Third, take a step with your left foot as Guht-kee according to the command of 'Guh-ri-jae-go', then take a step of Woo-poom with your right foot. At the same time, raise your right arm forward and reach out with your fingertips so they almost touch the front of each other's right shoulder. Stand up comfortably and adjust the distance naturally so that the arms can be stretched out comfortably. Fourth, following the command of 'Suht-da', Wit-dae lightly pushes the arm of the opponent with the right hand. Then he/she performs Hoo-ryuh-cha-kee with his/her right foot, then takes a step of Won-poom. Fifth, as soon as Ah-raet-dae blocks the Hoo-ryuh-cha-kee using Nae-ryo-mahk-kee, he/she performs Hoo-ryuh-cha-kee with his/her right foot in front of him/her. In succession, Wit-dae and Ah-raet-dae take turns to attack with any Bahl-jil they want to perform and defend against it.

2	3-1	3-2

4-1

4-2

5

마주차기의 본질적인 수련목적은 첫째, 신속한 공방의 연결, 둘째, 정확한 부위에 대한 다양한 발질 공격, 셋째, 발질에 대한 정확한 방어 형태 습득이다.
마주차기에서 발차기 공격과 활갯짓을 통한 방어를 원활하게 잘 주고받기 위해서는 자신의 중심을 안정감 있게 유지하는 것이 중요하다. 예를 들면, 방어를 하며 오른쪽으로 체중을 이동하면, 이어지는 발차기는 몸의 균형과 빠른 연결을 위해 왼쪽 다리를 사용하는 것이다. 즉, 단순히 차고 막는 것이 아니라, 자연스런 체중의 이동과 조화되는 발차기와 방어가 몸에 배도록 신경 써야 한다.
마주차기를 할 때는 가능한 한 곁들어 내려막기 형태를 유지하면서 방어를 하는 것이 중요하다. 필요에 따라 가로막기나 세워막기도 사용하지만, 이때에도 한 손은 얼굴 부위를 막아, 항상 두 손으로 방어하는 것을 연습해야 한다.
또한 마주차기의 발차기는 상대를 실제로 때리기보다는 상대의 몸통 바로 직전에 멈출 수 있도록 한다. 부상을 방지하고, 발차기를 정확히 조정하는 동시에, 지속적인 공방의 흐름을 깨뜨리지 않기 위해서이다.
마주차기 수련을 할 때에는 일정한 공방이 이어진 후에 '그만'의 구령에 따라 마주차기를 멈춘다. 잠시 휴식 후에 연습을 이어갈 때는 인사나 서거라 등의 과정 없이, '거리재고'가 아닌 '품 바꿔서'라는 구령을 사용한다. 이때는 좌품 상태에서 서로 왼팔을 뻗어 마주 대며, 아랫대가 먼저 공격을 시작한다. 아랫대는 왼손으로 팔을 밀고 앞에 나와 있는 왼발로 후려차기를 하는 것이 첫 번째 공격이 되어야 하며, 윗대 역시 방어 후에, 앞에 있는 왼발 후려차기로 첫 공격을 시작한다. 마주차기에서 공격을 시작할 때, 윗대 아랫대를 막론하고 앞에 있는 발로 후려차기를 하는 것은 시작을 알리는 일종의 약속이다.

6	7	8

The basic purposes of Mah-joo-cha-kee training are first, quick connection of attack and defense, second, various kicks on exact target points, and third, correct defensive actions against kicking attacks.

It is important to keep your balance in order to smoothly exchange kick attacks and defend using Hwahl-get-jit in Mah-joo-cha-kee. For example, if you move your weight to the right while defending, the ensuing kick uses your left leg for balance and allows for a fast connection to the next technique. In other words, not just kick and block, but care must be taken to ensure that kicks and defenses are in harmony with natural weight movements.

When doing Mah-joo-cha-kee, it is important to defend with Gyeot-deul-uh Nae-ryo-mahk-kee as much as possible. Sometimes, Chi-mahk-kee or Gah-roh-mahk-kee can be used, but even in these cases you have to defend your face with the other hand and get used to blocking with both hands.

Also, the kick should stop just before you kick the opponent's torso, rather than actually hitting the opponent. This is to prevent injury, to accurately control the kick, and not to break the constant flow of the attack and defense.

When training Mah-joo-cha-kee, it is stopped according to the command of 'Geu-mahn' after sets of attacks and defenses. When continuing the practice after a short break, use the command 'Poom Ba-gwuh-suh' instead of 'Guh-ri-jae-go,' without any need for Jeol or Suh-guh-ra. At this time, the left arms stretch out to each other in Jwa-poom, and Ah-raet-dae starts the attack first. The first attack should be Ah-raet-dae pushing the arm with the left hand and performing Hoo-ryuh-cha-kee with the left foot, and Wit-dae also starting his/her first attack with a left Hoo-ryuh-cha-kee after defense. When starting an attack in Mah-joo-cha-kee, performing Hoo-ryuh-cha-kee with the front foot, regardless of Wit-dae or Ah-raet-dae, is a kind of telegraphed attack to mark the start.

(1) 본뜨기

① 그냥차기

- 우 허벅치기(곧은발질) -좌 후려차기- 우 후려차기 -좌 걷어차기
- 우 곁차기(후려차기낮게) - 좌 곁차기 - 우 후려차기 - 좌 걷어차기
- 좌 째차기 - 우 곁차기 - 좌 후려차기 - 우 후려차기
- 우 곧은발질 - 좌 째차기 - 우 곧은발질 - 좌 옆발질 및 좌 는질러차기

② 솟쳐차기

- 좌 째차기 - 우 허벅치기 - 좌 후려차기 및 좌 무릎걸이 - 우내차기 - 갈기기 및 발따귀(안, 밖으로)
- 우 곁차기 - 좌 후려차기 - 우 허벅치기 - 우 두발낭상(좌, 우로) 및 겅중치기(솟구치기)

③ 가미

- 좌 째차기 - 우 곧은발질 - 좌 곁치기(째차기를 낮게) - 돌개치기 및 꼭두질

본뜨기는 마주차기를 위한 연속적인 공격의 예시이다. 이는 마주차기 수련을 위한 표본인 동시에, 실전에서도 활용 가능한 일종의 콤비네이션(연계) 공격이라 할 수 있다. 그러나 실제로 마주차기를 할 때는, 원활한 진행을 위해 곧은 발질이나 내차기 등의 공격을 자제하기도 한다. 원품 상태에서 지속적으로 주고받는 마주차기의 흐름이 상대의 내차기나 곧은 발질을 방어하기 위해 뒤로 물러서는 순간, 깨질 수 있기 때문이다.
솟쳐차기는 줄넘기처럼 제자리에서 점프를 하며 마주차기를 하는 것이다. 점프에 맞춰 한발씩 앞으로 차는 줄넘기 동작처럼, 제자리 점프의 박자에 맞춰 차고 막기를 번갈아 한다.

(1) Bohn-deu-kee (Sampling)

① Geu-nyang-cha-kee

- Woo Huh-buhk-chee-kee (Gohd-eun-bahl-jil) → Jwa Hoo-ryuh-cha-kee → Woo Hoo-ryuh-cha-kee → Jwa Guh-duh-cha-kee
- Woo Kyeot-cha-kee (low Hoo-ryuh-cha-kee) → Jwa Kyeot-cha-kee → Woo Hoo-ryuh-cha-kee → Jwa Guh-duh-cha-kee
- Jwa Jae-cha-kee → Woo Kyeot-cha-kee → Jwa Hoo-ryuh-cha-kee → Woo Hoo-ryuh-cha-kee
- Woo Gohd-eun-bahl-jil → Jwa Jae-cha-kee → Woo Gohd-eun-bahl-jil → Jwa Yeop-bahl-jil and Jwa Neun-jil-luh-cha-kee

② Soht-chuh-cha-kee

- Jwa Jae-cha-kee → Woo Huh-buhk-chee-kee → Jwa Hoo-ryuh-cha-kee and Jwa Moo-re-up-guh-ree → Woo Nae-cha-kee → Gahl-kee-kee and Bahl-dah-gui (inwards, outwards)
- Woo Kyeot-cha-kee → Jwa Hoo-ryuh-cha-kee → Woo Huh-buhk-chee-kee → Woo Doo-bahl-Nahng-sahng (to the left, to the right) and Guhng-joong-chee-kee (Soht-goo-chee-kee)

③ Gah-mee

- Jwa Jae-cha-kee → Woo Gohd-eun-bahl-jil → Jwa Kyeot-chi-kee (low Jae-cha-kee) → Dohl-gae-chee-kee and Gohk-doo-jil

Bohn-deu-kee is an example of a series of attacks for Mah-joo-cha-kee. This is a kind of combination attack that can be used in actual fight as well as a sample of sorts for Mah-joo-cha-kee training. However, when you actually perform Mah-joo-cha-kee, you may refrain from attacking with certain kicks, such as Gohd-eun-bahl-jil or Nae-cha-kee, to allow for a smooth progression. This is because the flow of Mah-joo-cha-kee, which is continuously exchanged in Won-poom, can be broken when you step back to defend the opponent's Gohd-eun-bahl-jil or Nae-cha-kee.
Soht-chuh-cha-kee is jumping in place and performing Mah-joo-cha-kee like jumping rope with alternating feet. The kicks and blocks are performed alternately to the beat of the jump in place.

4. 마주걸이

마주걸이는 상대와 무릎을 맞대고 선 상태에서 여러 가지 걸이기술을 실제로 주고받는 연습을 하는 수련과정이다. '바로-절-원품-서거라-무릎대고'의 구령에 따라 기본자세를 취한 뒤, 윗대와 아랫대가 번갈아 기술을 연습한다.

첫째, '바로-절-원품'의 구령에 맞추어 인사를 주고받은 후, 상대를 마주보고 원품으로 선다. 둘째, '서거라'의 구령에 따라 좌품 자세를 취한다. 셋째,'무릎대고'의 구령에 따라 왼발을 걷기로 내딛은 후, 우품을 내딛어 서로 교차한다. 이때, 상대의 우품과 발은 안쪽 면이, 무릎은 바깥쪽 면이 닿도록 정강이를 엇갈려 마주 댄다. 이후, 필요에 따라 뒷발(왼발)을 조금씩 조정하여 정확한 우품을 유지한다. 넷째, 윗대와 아랫대가 번갈아가면 서로 무릎을 밀고 밀리고를 반복하며 걸이 기술의 시작을 기다린다.

1-1	1-2	2

4. Mah-joo-guh-ree

Mah-joo-guh-ree is a training course in which you practice performing a variety of Guh-ree techniques while standing knee to knee with the opponent. After taking the basic postures following the command of 'Baro → Jeol → Won-poom → Suh-guh-ra → Moo-reup-dae-go,' Wit-dae and Ah-raet-dae alternately practice their skills.

First, after exchanging greetings in accordance with the command of 'Baro → Jeol → Won-poom,' you and the opponent face each other and stand in Won-poom. Second, take a stance of Jwa-poom following the command of 'Suh-guh-ra'. Third, take a step with your left foot as Guht-kee following the command of 'Moo-reup-dae-go', then take a step of Woo-poom to cross the opponent's shin with yours. At this time, your foot shall be placed in contact with the inner side of the opponent's Woo-poom and foot, and your shin should be crossed against the opponent's shin so that the outer side of your knee shall be in contact with the outer side of the opponent's knee. Then, adjust the back foot (left foot) little by little as necessary to maintain the correct Woo-poom. Fourth, Wit-dae and Ah-raet-dae wait for the start of the Guh-ree technique, taking turns pushing each other's knees.

3-1	3-2	4

마주걸이의 수련목적은 첫째, 정확한 걸이기술 습득, 둘째, 걸이기술의 동작 순서와 정확한 위치 숙지, 셋째, 넘길 때의 탄력과 힘쓰는 포인트 습득이다. 이를 위해 서로 기술을 정확히 익힐 수 있도록 움직이지 않고 받아주는 것이다.
마주걸이에서 서로 무릎을 밀고 밀리는 동작을 하는 이유는 실제 기술을 사용할 때, 상대의 체중 이동을 파악해 활용하기 위해서이다. 내가 무릎을 밀게 되면, 상대는 무릎이 밀리면서 동시에 체중이 뒷발로 옮겨 가게 된다. 따라서 나는 상대의 앞다리를 체중의 부하 없이 움직일 수 있게 된다. 그리고 이 앞다리를 내가 원하는 곳으로 옮겨놓으면, 뒷발로 쏠렸던 상대의 체중은 다시 옮겨진 앞발로 이동하게 된다. 그리고 이 순간이 -얼러 메기기에서 상대가 품을 내딛기 직전에 기술을 거는 것처럼- 상대의 체중 이동을 이용해 쉽게 기술을 성공시킬 수 있는 순간이 된다. 따라서 마주걸이에서는 서로 무릎을 밀고 밀리며 상대의 체중이동을 지속적으로 파악하는 연습을 해야 한다.

The purposes of Mah-joo-guh-ree are first, getting used to the correct skills, second, knowing the correct position and movement procedure of Guh-ree (take down) skills, third, learning the momentum and exact point for using power. For that, the partner should wait for the other's skill without any defense.
The reason why we push each other's knees in Mah-joo-guh-ree is because to identify and utilize the shift of the opponent's weight when we use an actual technique. When I push my knee, the opponent's knee is pushed back and at the same time his/her weight moves to the back foot. Therefore, I can move my opponent's front legs effortlessly. When I move this front leg to where I want it, the weight of the opponent who was leaning on the back foot, shifts weight back to the front foot. This is the moment when you can easily succeed your technique using your opponent's change in weight distribution (as you try your technique just before the opponent steps down a Poom in Eol-luh Me-kee-kee). Therefore, in Mah-joo-guh-ree, you should practice continuously identifying the other's changes in weight distribution while you are pushing each other's knees.

(1) 기본수

① 우 안짱다리하고 우 앞딴죽

마주걸이는 상대의 중심을 불안정하게 만들거나 상대의 다리를 걸기 좋은 위치로 이동시키기 위한 동작과 실제 넘어뜨리는 동작으로 구성된다. 우 안짱다리하고 우 앞딴죽은 안짱다리로 상대의 앞다리를 끌어오고, 그 발목 안쪽에 딴죽을 치게 된다.

첫째, 서로 번갈아 무릎을 밀다가, '섯다'의 구령에 맞추어 오른 무릎을 좀 더 깊게 밀어 상대의 체중을 뒤로 이동시킨다. 둘째, 자신의 왼발을 뒤쪽으로 약 반 뼘 정도 옮겨 디디며, 그 반동을 이용하여 상대의 오른발을 오른발 안짱다리로 역시 반 뼘 정도 끌어온다. 셋째, 안짱다리 한 오른발을 원품으로 내려놓고, 왼발을 상대의 오른발 앞에 내려놓으며 오른손으로 덜미잽이를 한다. 이때 왼발의 위치는 오른발 딴죽을 치기에 좋은 위치를 찾아 딛어야 한다. 넷째, 오른발 바닥으로 상대의 오른 발목 안쪽을 밀어 찬다. 이때, 오른손은 덜미잽이 한 상대의 목을 자신의 뒤쪽 바닥을 향해 끝까지 당겨 뿌려준다. 아랫대가 안전하게 넘어진 후에는 원래 자리로 돌아와 무릎을 번갈아 밀며 아랫대의 순서를 시작한다.

1

2-1

2-2

(1) Kee-bon-soo (Basic Skills)

① Woo Ahn-jang-dah-ree-ha-goh Woo Ahp-dahn-jook

Mah-joo-guh-ree consists of actions to destabilize the opponent's balance or to move the opponent's leg to a position that is good to hook, and an action to actually throw him/her to the ground. Woo Ahn-jang-dah-ree-ha-goh Woo Ahp-dahn-jook is a series of movements that brings the opponent's front leg with Ahn-jang-dah-ree, and performs Dahn-jook to the inside of the ankle.

First, push each other's knees in turn, then push the right knee a little deeper at the command of 'Suht-da' to move the opponent's weight back. Second, move your left foot back about half a handspan, and use the rebound to draw the opponent's right foot about half a handspan with your right foot Ahn-jang-dah-ree. Third, put down the right foot which performed Ahn-jang-dah-ree in Won-poom and perform Duhl-mee-jae-bee with the right hand while you put down your left foot in front of the opponent's right foot. At this point, your left foot should be placed in a position that is good for performing a right Dahn-jook. Fourth, perform a push kick to the inside of the opponent's right ankle with the bottom of your right foot. At this time, your right hand pulls down the opponent's neck, which you grabbed by Duhl-mee-jae-bee, down to the ground behind you. After Ah-raet-dae falls safely, return to the original position and alternate pushing each other's knees to start Ah-raet-dae's turn.

3

4-1

4-2

실제로 딴죽을 사용할 때 가장 적절한 순간은 상대가 품을 밟는 동안 발이 지면에 닿기 직전이나 지면에서 떨어진 직후이다. 하지만 마주걸이에서는 이 타이밍에 대한 연습보다는 정확한 자세와 발을 놓는 위치를 배우는 것이 중요하다. 또한 딴죽은 거는 것이 아니라 상대의 복사뼈를 빠르고 가볍게 친다는 기분으로 연습해야 한다.
오른발로 앞딴죽을 칠 때는 상대 오른쪽 발목의 안쪽에 90°로 맞도록 하는 것이 가장 효과적이다. 그리고 이를 위하여 원품에서 딴죽(비비기)를 연습하던 자세 그대로 상대의 발목을 칠 수 있도록 왼발의 위치를 잘 골라 디뎌 주어야한다. 상대의 발을 기준으로 너무 멀리 디디면 자신의 오른발이 잘 닿지 않아 힘 있게 치기 힘들다, 너무 가까우면 자신의 다리가 방해가 되어 힘 있게 칠 수 없다. 상대의 발보다 너무 바깥쪽을 디디면, 딴죽에 힘을 얻기 위해 휘두를 공간이 적어진다. 너무 안쪽에 디디면 자신의 허벅지 안쪽이 방해가 되어 상대의 발목을 제대로 칠 수 없다.
중요한 것을 가장 기본적인 자세에서 딴죽을 칠 때, 가장 적절한 효과를 얻을 수 있으며, 이를 위해서는 자신의 몸을 움직여 적절한 자세를 만들어 내야 한다는 것이다. 한쪽 다리만 끌고 온 상대방이 자신이 원하는 자세나 위치가 되길 바라기보다는 언제든 마음대로 움직일 수 있는 자신의 몸을 움직이는 것이 당연히 더 쉽기 때문이다.

In a real altercation, the best time to use Dahn-jook is at the very moment when the opponent's foot is landing on or lifting off the ground while doing Poom-bahl-kee. But in Mah-joo-guh-ree, learning the stepping position and correct motion for Dahn-jook is more important. Also, Dahan-jook movement actually should be done with the idea of not hooking, but rather, hitting the targeted ankle.

When you perform Ahp-dahn-jook with your right foot, it is most effective to hit the inside of your opponent's right ankle at 90°. For this purpose, the position of the left foot should be carefully positioned so that it can hit the opponent's ankle from the same position as you practice Dahn-jook (Bee-bee-kee) in Won-poom. If you step too far from your opponent's foot, it's hard to hit it with power because your right foot barely touches it, and if you're too close, your own leg become a hindrance resulting in not being able to hit it with power. If you step too far outward from your opponent's foot, you will have less space to swing to gain momentum in Dahn-jook. If you step too far inward, you can't hit your opponent's ankles properly because the inside of your thigh gets in the way.

What's important is that when you perform Dahn-jook in the most basic position, you can get the most appropriate effect, and to do this, you have to position your body to ensure the right posture. This is because it is easier to position your body as opposed to maneuvering your opponent to a fixed position.

② 우 안짱다리하고 좌 덧걸이

우 안짱다리하고 좌 덧걸이는 안짱다리로 상대의 앞다리를 끌어오고, 그 다리의 오금을 왼발 저기치기로 걸어 넘기게 된다.

첫째, 서로 번갈아 무릎을 밀다가, '섯다'의 구령에 맞추어 오른 무릎을 좀 더 깊게 밀어 상대의 체중을 뒤로 이동시킨다. 둘째, 자신의 왼발을 뒤쪽으로 약 반 뼘 정도 옮겨 디디며, 그 반동을 이용하여 상대의 오른발을 오른발 안짱다리로 역시 반 뼘 정도 끌어온다. 셋째, 안짱다리 한 오른발을 상대의 중심선에 내려놓고 오른손으로 상대의 목을 덜미걸이 한다. 넷째, 왼다리로 상대의 오른 무릎 뒷부분을 걸어 당긴다. 이때, 오른손은 덜미걸이 한 상대의 목을 상대의 오른쪽 뒤 방향 바닥을 향해 끝까지 밀어준다. 아랫대가 안전하게 넘어진 후에는 원래 자리로 돌아와 무릎을 번갈아 밀며 아랫대의 순서를 시작한다. 그림 4-2는 덧걸이를 하는 순간의 모습을 다른 각도에서 촬영한 것이다.

1	2-1	2-2

② Woo Ahn-jang-dah-ree-ha-goh Jwa Duht-guh-ree

Woo Ahn-jang-dah-ree-ha-goh Jwa Duht-guh-ree is a movement in which you pull the opponent's front leg with Ahn-jang-dah-ree, then hook the back of the knee with a left foot Juh-kee-chee-kee and throw him/her down.

First, push each other's knees in turn, then push the right knee a little deeper at the command of 'Suht-da' to move the opponent's weight back. Second, move your left foot back about half a handspan, and use the rebound to draw the opponent's right foot about half a handspan with a right foot Ahn-jang-dah-ree. Third, put down the right foot, which performed Ahn-jang-dah-ree, between the opponent's feet and perform Duhl-mee-guh-ree to the opponent's neck with your right hand. Fourth, hook the back of the opponent's right knee and pull with your left leg. At this time, your right hand pushes the opponent's neck towards the floor behind his/her right side. After Ah-raet-dae falls safely, return to the original position and alternate pushing each other's knees to start Ah-raet-dae's turn. Figure 4-2 shows a different angle of the moment of Duht-guh-ree.

3	4-1	4-2

덧걸이를 할 때는 저기치기로 다리를 걸기 직전에 축이 되는 오른 다리의 무릎을 살짝 굽혀주어야 한다. 그리고 상대의 다리를 거는 순간, 굽혔던 다리를 펴는 탄력을 더해준다(처음 익히기의 저기치기 방법과 같다). 이를 통해 상대의 다리를 걸어 당기는 힘을 더할 수 있을 뿐만 아니라, 자신의 몸이 튕겨 올라가는 만큼 상대의 다리를 튕겨 올릴 수 있다. 즉, 상대의 발이 지면에서 떨어지도록 하여 마찰력에 의한 저항을 줄일 수 있는 것이다.
상대의 목을 밀어주는 방향은 상대의 다리를 끌어오는 정 반대방향이 되어야 한다. 저기치기로 걸려온 다리가 있던 자리로 상대의 몸을 밀어주어야 지지할 다리가 없어진 상대가 쉽게 넘어지기 때문이다. 엉뚱한 방향으로 밀게 되면 상대는 남아있는 왼다리로 버텨 넘어지지 않을 수 있다.

When you perform Duht-guh-ree, you should bend your right knee slightly, which becomes the axis just before you hook the opponent's leg with Juh-kee-chee-kee. At the moment you hook the opponent's leg, straighten your bent leg and add momentum (same as Juh-kee-chee-kee from Chuh-eum Ik-hee-gee). Not only can this add to the strength of pulling the opponent's leg, but it can also pull the opponent's leg up as much as your body bounces up. In other words, the opponent's feet can be removed from the ground to reduce the resistance caused by friction.

The direction of pushing the opponent's neck should be in the opposite direction of pulling the opponent's leg. This is because the opponent who has no leg to support himself/herself easily falls down when you push his/her body to the position where his/her leg, which you pulled with Juh-kee-chee-kee, was. If you push your opponent in the wrong direction, the opponent may keep his/her balance and not fall.

③ 우 안짱다리하고 좌 중방걸이

우 안짱다리하고 우 중방걸이는 안짱다리로 상대의 앞다리를 끌어오고, 그 다리의 발목 뒷부분을 자신의 왼 발목으로 걸어 올려 넘기게 된다.

첫째, 서로 번갈아 무릎을 밀다가, '섯다'의 구령에 맞추어 오른 무릎을 좀 더 깊게 밀어 상대의 체중을 뒤로 이동시킨다. 둘째, 자신의 왼발을 뒤쪽으로 약 반 뼘 정도 옮겨 디디며, 그 반동을 이용하여 상대의 오른발을 오른발 안짱다리로 역시 반 뼘 정도 끌어온다. 셋째, 안짱다리 한 오른발을 반대로 틀어 발의 안쪽 면이 상대의 오른발을 향하도록 내려놓고 왼손으로 상대의 목을 덜미걸이 한다. 이때 오른발의 위치는 상대의 오른발 한 뼘 정도 앞에 놓는다. 넷째, 왼발을 뒤로 올렸다가 왼 발목으로 상대의 오른 발목 뒷부분을 걸어 차올린다. 이때, 왼손은 덜미걸이 한 상대의 목을 자신의 왼쪽 뒤 방향 바닥을 향해 끝까지 잡아당겨 뿌려준다. 아랫대가 안전하게 넘어진 후에는 원래 자리로 돌아와 무릎을 번갈아 밀며 아랫대의 순서를 시작한다. 그림 4-2는 중방걸이를 하는 순간의 모습을 다른 각도에서 촬영한 것이다.

1	2-1	2-2

③ Woo Ahn-jang-dah-ree-ha-goh Jwa Joong-bang-guh-ree

Woo Ahn-jang-dah-ree-ha-goh Jwa Joong-bang-guh-ree is a movement in which you pull the opponent's front leg with Ahn-jang-dah-ree, then hook the back of the ankle of the leg with your left ankle and throw him/her down.

First, push each other's knees in turn, then push the right knee a little deeper at the command of 'Suht-da' to move the opponent's weight back. Second, move your left foot back about half a handspan, and use the rebound to draw the opponent's right foot about half a handspan with a right foot Ahn-jang-dah-ree. Third, twist your right foot which performed Ahn-jang-dah-ree the other way and place the inside of your foot facing your opponent's right foot, then perform Duhl-mee-guh-ree to the opponent's neck with the left hand. At this time, your right foot should be placed about a span away from the opponent's right foot. Fourth, raise your left foot backwards and then use your left ankle to hook and kick the opponent's right ankle to the side and upwards, simultaneously. At this time, your left hand pulls down the opponent's neck, which you performed Duhl-mee-guh-ree to, towards the floor behind your left side. After Ah-raet-dae falls safely, return to the original position and alternate pushing each other's knees to start Ah-raet-dae's turn. Figure 4-2 shows a different angle of the moment of Joong-bang-guh-ree.

3	4-1	4-2

앞딴죽을 비롯하여 덧걸이, 중방걸이를 막론하고 모든 마주걸이 기술을 연습할 때에는 자신의 균형을 잘 유지하여야 한다. 자신의 몸이 안정적이지 못한 상태에서 상대를 넘기게 되면, 걸이기술을 위한 힘을 효과적으로 전달하지 못하거나 끌려가서 넘어지게 된다. 나무에 매달린 매미는 나무를 넘길 수 없다. 자신의 몸이 독립적으로 서 있을 수 있어야만 상대를 안정적으로 넘어뜨릴 수 있는 것이다.
중방걸이에서 중요한 것은 상대의 목을 덜미걸이로 당겨주는 손의 반향이다. 상대의 발목을 걸어 올리는 정 반대방향으로 상대의 목을 당겨주어야 상대를 원활하게 넘어뜨릴 수 있다. 쉽게 설명하자면, 상대를 넘어뜨린다는 것은 상대의 머리와 발의 위치를, 막대기를 돌리듯이 바꾸어주는 것을 말한다. 그리고 이를 위해서는 회전하는 막대기 끝이 원을 그리듯이, 머리는 오른쪽(왼쪽) 아래로, 발은 왼쪽(오른쪽) 위로 돌려주어야 하는 것이다.

You should keep your balance when practicing all Mah-joo-guh-ree techniques, such as Ahp-dahn-jook, Duht-guh-ree, Joong-bang-guh-ree, etc. If you try to throw down your opponent while your body is not stable, you will not be able to effectively deliver the power for Guh-ree technique or you will be dragged and knocked over. Cicadas attached to trees cannot knock down trees. Only when your body is able to stand independently you can safely knock down your opponent.

What is important in Joong-bang-guh-ree is the direction of the hand that pulls the opponent's neck with Duhl-mee-guh-ree. You have to pull your opponent's neck in the opposite direction of lifting the opponent's ankle so that you can tip the opponent over smoothly. To put it simply, knocking down an opponent means changing the position of the opponent's head and feet, like turning a stick. To do this, you have to turn your opponent's head down to the right (left) side and the foot up to the left (right) side just like the end of a rod if you rotate it into a circle.

④ 우 밭장다리하고 좌 오금밟기 (오금걸이)

우 밭장다리하고 좌 오금밟기는 오른발 밭장다리로 상대의 앞다리를 자신의 우측으로 밀어낸 후, 상대의 왼다리 뒷무릎 부분을 자신의 왼발 깎음다리로 밟아 넘긴다. 오금밟기는 오금걸이라고도 부른다.

첫째, 서로 번갈아 무릎을 밀다가, '섯다'의 구령에 맞추어 오른 무릎을 좀 더 깊게 밀어 상대의 체중을 뒤로 이동시킨다. 둘째, 오른발 밭장다리로 상대의 오른발 발목을 쳐서 자신의 우측방향으로 옮겨 놓는다. 밭장다리를 치기 전에, 동작을 편하게 하기 위해, 자신의 왼발을 상대의 오른발 바깥쪽으로 조금 내딛는 경우도 있다. 셋째, 밭장다리 한 오른발을 상대의 두 발 사이에 내려놓고 양손으로 상대의 어깨를 잡는다. 이 때, 오른발의 위치는 상대의 오른발 쪽으로 좀 더 치우치게 밟아주는 것이 다음 동작이 편하다. 넷째, 왼발을 들어 올려 깎음다리로 상대의 왼쪽 뒷무릎을 밟아 밀어 누른다. 이때, 상대의 어깨를 잡은 양손은 상대를 뒤로 당겨 내리누른다. 아랫대가 안전하게 넘어진 후에는 원래 자리로 돌아와 무릎을 번갈아 밀며 아랫대의 순서를 시작한다.

1	2-1	2-2

④ Woo Baht-jang-dah-ree-ha-goh Jwa Oh-gum-bahl-kee (Oh-gum-guh-ree)

Woo Baht-jang-dah-ree-ha-goh Jwa Oh-gum-bahl-kee is a movement in which you push the opponent's front leg to the right with your right foot Baht-jang-dah-ree, then step on the back of the opponent's left knee with your left foot Gahk-gum-dah-ree. Oh-gum-bahl-kee is also called Oh-gum-guh-ree.

First, push each other's knees in turn, then push the right knee a little deeper at the command of 'Suht-da' to move the opponent's weight back. Second, you hit the opponent's right ankle with your right foot Baht-jang-dah-ree and move it to your right. Before performing Baht-jang-dah-ree, you may step a little outside the opponent's right foot to make the movement easier. Third, put the right foot, which performed Baht-jang-dah-ree, between the opponent's two feet and hold the opponent's shoulder with both hands. At this point, the position of the right foot makes the next move easier by stepping closer to the opponent's right foot. Fourth, lift up your left foot and press down on the back of the opponent's left knee with Gahk-gum-dah-ree. At this time, both hands, holding the opponent's shoulder, pull the opponent back and press him/her down. After Ah-raet-dae falls safely, return to the original position and alternates pushing each other's knees to start Ah-raet-dae's turn.

3

4-1

4-2

오금밟기를 하면서 상대의 뒷무릎을 밟아 누를 때는 단순히 뒷무릎만 밟아서는 안 된다. 상대가 버틸 경우, 무릎이 꺾이지 않기 때문이다. 따라서 상대 엉덩이 바로 아래의 뒷 허벅지 윗부분부터 밀듯이 깎아내려 밟아야 한다.
또한 밭장다리를 할 때에는 가능한 상대의 아킬레스건 부위를 칠 수 있도록 해야 한다. 그래야 상대의 아킬레스건이 받는 충격의 반동으로 상대의 발목이 잘 튕겨나가기 때문이다. 이를 위해 밭장다리를 치는 순간, 자신의 발목을 위로 꺾어 올리는 발목 스냅을 사용하기도 한다.

When you step down on the back of the opponent's knee while performing Oh-gum-bahl-kee, you should not just step on the back of the knee. This is because if the opponent holds out, the knee will not bend. Therefore, you have to scrape it downwards starting at the top of the opponent's back thigh.
Also, when you are performing Baht-jang-dah-ree, you should strive to kick the opponent's Achilles tendon as directly as possible. That way, the opponent's ankle bounces off easily due to the reaction of the shock on the opponent's Achilles tendon. For this purpose, the moment you hit with Baht-jang-dah-ree, you can use a snap as you pull your ankle upwards.

⑤ 우 밭장다리하고 우 낚시걸이

우 밭장다리하고 우 낚시걸이는 오른발 밭장다리로 상대의 앞다리를 자신의 우측으로 밀어 낸 후, 상대의 오른 뒷무릎 부분을 자신의 오른다리 낚시걸이로 걸어 넘기는 것이다.

첫째, 서로 번갈아 무릎을 밀다가, '섯다'의 구령에 맞추어 오른 무릎을 좀 더 깊게 밀어 상대의 체중을 뒤로 이동시킨다. 둘째, 오른발 밭장다리로 상대의 오른발 발목을 쳐서 자신의 우측방향으로 옮겨 놓는다. 밭장다리 한 오른발은 상대와 반대방향을 향하도록 살짝 안으로 돌려 상대의 오른발 근처에 내려놓는다. 셋째, 왼발을 상대의 오른발 옆으로 당겨 놓으며, 오른손으로 상대의 목을 덜미걸이 한다. 이때, 왼발의 위치는 상대의 오른발과 나란히, 옆으로 한 뼘 정도 떨어진 위치에 놓는 것이 좋다. 넷째, 오른 발을 앞으로 들며 살짝 자세를 낮추었다가, 튕겨 일어나는 탄력을 더하여 오른다리로 상대의 오른 뒷무릎을 걸어 올린다. 이때, 덜미걸이 한 오른손으로 상대의 목을 당겨, 자신의 좌측 아래로 밀어 누른다. 아랫대가 안전하게 넘어진 후에는 원래 자리로 돌아와 무릎을 번갈아 밀며 아랫대의 순서를 시작한다. 그림 4-2는 낚시걸이 순간의 다른 각도 모습이다.

1	2-1	2-2

⑤ Woo Baht-jang-dah-ree-ha-goh Woo Nak-shee-guh-ree

Woo Baht-jang-dah-ree-ha-goh Woo Nak-shee-guh-ree is a movement in which you push the opponent's front leg to the right with your right foot Baht-jang-dah-ree, then hook the back of the opponent's right knee with your right foot Nak-shee-guh-ree and throw him/her down.

First, push each other's knees in turn, then push the right knee a little deeper at the command of 'Suht-da' to move the opponent's weight back. Second, you hit the opponent's right ankle with your right foot Baht-jang-dah-ree and move it to your right. Turn the right foot, which performed Baht-jang-dah-ree, slightly inward and place it near the opponent's right foot. Third, pull your left foot to the side of the opponent's right foot, and perform Duhl-mee-guh-ree to the opponent's neck with your right hand. At this time, it is recommended that the left foot be placed next to the opponent's right foot, about a handspan away from the side. Fourth, lift your right foot forward while you slightly lower your posture, then bounce up and add momentum to hook and pull up the back of the opponent's right knee with your right leg. At this point, push the opponent's neck down to the left with your right hand which performed Duhl-mee-guh-ree. After Ah-raet-dae falls safely, return to the original position and alternate pushing each other's knees to start Ah-raet-dae's turn. Figure 4-2 shows a different angle of the moment of Nak-shee-guh-ree.

3

4-1

4-2

낚시걸이는 덧걸이와 더불어 실제 견주기에서 가장 많이 활용되는 기술이다. 동시에 일상생활에서 호신용으로 배우기도 쉬우며 사용하기도 쉽다. 중요한 점은 덧걸이와 마찬가지로 상대의 다리를 거는 순간, 자세를 낮추었다가 튕겨 일어나는 탄력을 이용하는 것이다.
한편, 낚시걸이에서 가장 많이 나타나는 실수는 상대를 넘기기 위해 목을 덜미걸이로 당기는 순간에 자신의 몸을 먼저 돌리는 것이다. 팔로 상대의 목을 감아 당기며 힘을 주기 위해 자신의 몸을 먼저 돌리고 매달리듯이 팔을 나중에 당기게 되는 것이다. 이 경우, 가슴이 열리고 어깨가 뒤로 빠지게 되어 상대에게 제대로 힘을 전달하지 못하게 된다. 따라서 항상 상대에게 시선을 고정하여 '자신의 가슴 안에 상대를 두고' 덜미걸이로 당겨오는 습관을 만들어야 한다.
낚시걸이는 상대를 회전시키며 넘기게 되는데 이 회전의 폭이 최대한 작고 간결해야 한다. 덜미걸이를 커다란 동작으로 하게 될 경우, 되치기를 당할 위험이 커지기 때문이다. 그러므로 덜미걸이를 할 때는 팔의 하박을 상대에게 정확히 밀착시키고 최대한 내 몸쪽으로 당겨서 회전 반경을 가능한 한 작게 해야 한다.

Nak-shee-guh-ree is the most commonly used technique in actual Kyeon-joo-kee, along with Duht-guh-ree. At the same time, it is easy to learn and use as a self-defense technique. The important point is to use the momentum from when you bounce up after you lowered your posture as you hooked your opponent's leg just like when in performing Duht-guh-ree.

Meanwhile, the most common mistake during performing Nak-shee-guh-ree is to turn your body first at the moment you pull the opponent's neck with Duhl-mee-guh-ree to throw the opponent over. When you wind your arm around your opponent's neck and pull down, you turn your body first to give strength and then pull your arm later, as if you were hanging. In this case, the chest will open and the arm will be fall back so that you will not be able to deliver the power properly to the opponent. Therefore, you should always keep your eyes fixed on the opponent and make a habit of 'putting the opponent into your chest' and pulling him/her with Duhl-mee-guh-ree.

When using Nak-shee-guh-ree, you should rotate the opponent to throw down. The size of the rotation should be as small as possible. Because if Duhl-mee-guh-ree is done with bigger motions, the opponent can counter-attack easier. Thus, when doing Duhl-mee-guh-ree for Nak-shee-guh-ree, you need to make your forearm adhere to the opponent's chest and pull him as close as you can to ensure the actual throw is as small as possible.

⑥ 우 밭장다리하고 좌 가로딴죽

우 밭장다리하고 좌 가로딴죽은 오른발 밭장다리로 상대의 앞다리를 자신의 우측으로 밀어낸 후, 앞딴죽과 반대로, 상대의 발목 바깥부분에 왼발로 딴죽을 치는 것이다.

첫째, 서로 번갈아 무릎을 밀다가, '섯다'의 구령에 맞추어 오른 무릎을 좀 더 깊게 밀어 상대의 체중을 뒤로 이동시킨다. 둘째, 오른발 밭장다리로 상대의 오른발 발목을 쳐서 자신의 우측방향으로 옮겨 놓는다. 셋째, 밭장다리 한 오른발을 상대의 오른발 한 뼘 정도 앞에 내려놓으며, 왼손으로 상대의 목을 덜미잽이 한다. 이때, 오른발은 상대의 오른발을 딴죽으로 치기 좋은 위치와 각도를 찾아 내려놓아야 한다. 넷째, 왼발 바닥으로 상대의 오른 발목 바깥 부위를 밀어 찬다. 이때, 덜미걸이 한 왼손은 상대의 목을 자신의 왼쪽 아래로 잡아당겨 뿌려준다. 아랫대가 안전하게 넘어진 후에는 원래 자리로 돌아와 무릎을 번갈아 밀며 아랫대의 순서를 시작한다.

1	2-1	2-2

⑥ Woo Baht-jang-dah-ree-ha-goh Jwa Gah-roh-dahn-jook

Woo Baht-jang-dah-ree-ha-goh Jwa Gah-roh-dahn-jook is a movement in which you push the opponent's front leg to the right with your right foot Baht-jang-dah-ree, then, as opposed to Ahp-dahn-jook, perform Dahn-jook on the outside of the opponent's ankle with your left foot.

First, push each other's knees in turns, then push the right knee a little deeper at the command of 'Suht-da' to move the opponent's weight back. Second, you hit the opponent's right ankle with your right foot Baht-jang-dah-ree and move it to your right. Third, place your right foot which performed Baht-jang-dah-ree about a handspan away from the opponent's right foot, then perform Duhl-mee-jae-bee to the opponent's neck with your left hand. At this time, your right foot should be placed down in a position and angle that is good for hitting the opponent's right foot with Dahn-jook. Fourth, perform a push kick to the outside of the opponent's right ankle with the bottom of your left foot. At this time, the left hand, which performed Duhl-mee-guh-ree, pulls the opponent's neck down to the left. After Ah-raet-dae falls safely, return to the original position and alternate pushing each other's knees to start Ah-raet-dae's turn.

3

4-1

4-2

앞딴죽이든 가로딴죽이든 딴죽을 할 때는 같은 쪽 손으로 상대의 목을 덜미잽이하여 잡아챈다. 이때 중요한 것은 손이 아닌 팔꿈치가 먼저 움직여야 한다는 것이다. 다시 말해, 상대의 목을 잡은 손으로 상대를 당겨오는 것이 아니라, 팔꿈치를 먼저 당겨오면 그 움직임에 내 손이 끌려오고, 그다음에 거기에 걸린 상대의 목이 끌려오는 것이다. 팔꿈치의 움직임에 손이 끌려오면, 감긴 채찍을 당기듯이 손목에 상대의 목이 휘감겨 돌아가는 효과가 나타난다. 그리고 이로 인해 상대는 목이 옆으로 휘감겨 틀어지며 더욱 쉽게 제압된다. 단, 이를 위해서는 덜미잽이를 깊숙이 하여 상대의 목이 자신의 손바닥이 아닌 손목에 걸리도록 해야 한다.

When you're performing Dahn-jook, whether it's Ahp dahn-jook or Gah-roh dahn-jook, you perform Duhl-mee-jae-bee to the opponent's neck with the same side hand and snatch. At this time, the important thing is that the elbow, not the hand, should move first. In other words, not pulling the opponent with the hand that grabs the opponent s neck, but pulling the elbow first, then your hand will be drawn in the movement, and then your opponent's neck will be drawn in it. When the hand is drawn to the movement of the elbow, it has the effect of twisting the opponent's neck around the wrist like pulling a wound whip. And because of this, the opponent is more easily overpowered by his/her neck twisting to the side. However, for this purpose, Duhl-mee-jae-bee should be performed further forward so that the opponent's neck is not on your palm, but on your wrist.

⑦ 우 앞딴죽하고 우 안낚걸이

우 앞딴죽하고 우 안낚걸이는 오른발 앞딴죽으로 상대의 다리 간격을 벌린 후, 파고들어 다리 사이에서 낚시걸이를 하는 기술이다. 안낚걸이는 안낚시걸이라고도 부른다.

첫째, 서로 번갈아 무릎을 밀다가, '섯다'의 구령에 맞추어 오른 무릎을 좀 더 깊게 밀어 상대의 체중을 뒤로 이동시킨다. 둘째, 오른발 앞딴죽으로 상대의 오른발 발목 안쪽을 쳐서 바깥쪽으로 벌어지게 한다. 셋째, 앞딴죽 친 오른발을 상대의 다리 사이에 내려놓으며, 오른손으로는 상대의 목을 덜미걸이하고 왼손으로는 상대의 오금을 감아 잡는다. 동시에 슬라이드 스탭으로 미끄러지듯이 왼발을 끌고 들어오며 자세를 낮추고 오른다리를 가볍게 낚시걸이 자세로 들어올린다. 넷째, 낮아진 자세에서 앞쪽을 튕겨 일어나며, 오른 다리로 상대의 왼 무릎을 걸어 올린다. 이때, 왼손으로는 상대의 오른 다리 오금을 잡아챈다. 동시에 오른 손으로는 상대의 목을 뒤쪽 아래로 밀어준다. 아랫대가 안전하게 넘어진 후에는 원래 자리로 돌아와 무릎을 번갈아 밀며 아랫대의 순서를 시작한다. 그림 4-2는 안낚걸이 순간의 다른 각도 모습이다.

1	2	3

⑦ Woo Ahp-dahn-jook-ha-goh Woo Ahn—nak-guh-ree

Woo Ahp-dahn-jook-ha-goh Woo Ahn-nak-guh-ree is a movement in which you spread the gap between the opponent's legs with a right foot Ahp-dahn-jook, then digging in and performing Nak-shee-guh-ree between the legs. Ahn—nak-guh-ree is also called Ahn-nak-shee-guh-ree.

First, push each other's knees in turn, then push the right knee a little deeper at the command of 'Suht-da' to move the opponent's weight back. Second, hit the inside of the opponent's right foot ankle with the right foot Ahp-dahn-jook to spread it outward. Third, put your right foot, which performed Ahp-dahn-jook, down between the opponent's legs, and perform Duhl-mee-guh-ree to the opponent's neck with your right hand and grab the opponent's back of the knee with your left hand. At the same time, slide your left foot in, lower your posture, and lift your right leg lightly as the form of performing Nak-shee-guh-ree. Fourth, bounce up from a lowered position, and hook the opponent's left knee with your right leg. At this time, your left hand snatches the opponent's right popliteal fossa. At the same time, with the right hand, push the opponent's neck down to backward. After Ah-raet-dae falls safely, return to the original position and alternate pushing each other's knees to start Ah-raet-dae's turn. Figure 4-2 shows a different angle of the moment of Ahn-nak-guh-ree.

3 (the other side)	4-1	4-2

안낚걸이에서 앞딴죽을 하고 난 후, 상대는 두 다리가 살짝 넓어진 상대로 반듯하게 서있게 된다. 이때, 상대 중심은 그냥 서있을 때보다 낮아지는 동시에 딴죽에 움직인 앞발로 쏠리게 된다. 중심이 낮게 앞으로 쏠린 상대의 품에 파고들어 낚시걸이를 성공시키기는 쉽지 않다. 따라서 안낚걸이를 성공시키기 위해 중요한 것은 상대의 몸을 뒤로 밀어주는 것이 된다. 상대의 몸이 뒤로 밀려야 중심이 흐트러지고 상대의 다리를 손과 발로 걸어 올릴 수 있기 때문이다.
이를 위해, 슬라이드 스텝으로 파고들 때 어깨로 상대방에게 충돌하며 상대의 중심을 흐트러뜨려 주어야 한다. 그리고 오른 다리를 낚시걸이로 걸고 왼손으로 상대의 오금을 당기는 순간에는 덜미걸이 한 오른팔로 상대의 목을 탄력 있게 밀어 쳐주어야 한다.

After you perform Ahp-dahn-jook during Ahn-nak-guh-ree, the opponent stands upright with his/her feet slightly apart. At this time, the opponent's center of gravity is lower than when he/she simply stands upright, and at the same time, is tilted to the front foot that is moved by Dahn-jook. It is not easy to make Nak-shee-guh-ree successful by slipping under the opponent's arms, when he/she is leaning forward. Therefore, the important thing to succeed in Ahn-nak-guh-ree is to push the opponent's body back. If the opponent's body is pushed back, the balance opponent's body can be disturbed and the opponent's legs can be raised with your hands and feet.

When digging past or slipping under the opponent's arms with a sliding step, you should disturb the opponent's balance by hitting him/her with your shoulder. When you hook your opponent's right leg with Nak-shee-guh-ree and pull the opponent's back of the knee with your left hand, you have to push the opponent's neck with your right arm which performed Duhl-mee-guh-ree.

(2) 가외수

가외수는 기본적인 수련과정에 택견꾼들이 자주 사용하는 응용기술을 더한 것을 말한다.

① 우 안짱다리하고 좌 엉덩잽이

우 안짱다리하고 좌 엉덩잽이는 안짱다리로 상대의 앞다리를 끌어오고, 두 다리 사이로 파고들어 허리 움직임을 이용하여 상대를 넘긴다.

첫째, 서로 번갈아 무릎을 밀다가, '섯다'의 구령에 맞추어 오른 무릎을 좀 더 깊게 밀어 상대의 체중을 뒤로 이동시킨다. 둘째, 자신의 왼발을 뒤쪽으로 약 반 뼘 정도 옮겨 디디며, 그 반동을 이용하여 상대의 오른발을 오른발 안짱다리로 역시 반 뼘 정도 끌어온다. 셋째, 안짱다리 한 오른발을 상대의 두 발 사이에 내려놓고 자세를 낮추며 왼발을 오른발 바로 옆으로 끌고 온다. 상대의 몸에 자신의 몸을 밀착시키는 동시에 오른손 덜미걸이로 상대의 목을 끌어안고 왼손으로 상대의 오른쪽 뒷허벅지를 당겨 붙인다. 이어서 골반을 이용하여 상대의 몸을 밀어 올린다. 넷째, 오른발을 바깥으로 돌려 빼며 양발의 위치를 신속하게 바꾸고 그 반동으로 자신의 허리를 틀어준다. 동시에 상대의 목을 오른손으로 아래로 잡아당기고 왼손에 잡힌 허벅지를 들어 올려준다. 그리고 허리를 숙이며, 허리 위에 얹혀있는 상대를 바닥으로 돌려 넘어뜨린다. 아랫대가 안전하게 넘어진 후에는 원래 자리로 돌아와 무릎을 번갈아 밀며 아랫대의 순서를 시작한다.

1	2	3-1

(2) Gah-woe-soo (Extra Skills)

Gah-woe-soo refers to the addition of applied techniques, frequently used by Taek-gyeon practitioners, to the basic training process.

① Woo Ahn-jang-dah-ree-ha-goh Jwa Uhng—dung-jae-bee

Woo Ahn-jang-dah-ree-ha-goh Jwa Uhng-dung-jae-bee is a movement in which you pull the opponent's front leg with Ahn-jang-dah-ree, burrow between the opponent's legs, and uses the waist movement to turn the opponent over.

First, push each other's knees in turn, then push the right knee a little deeper at the command of 'Suht-da' to move the opponent's weight back. Second, move your left foot back about half a handspan, and use the rebound to draw the opponent's right foot about half a handspan with a right foot Ahn-jang-dah-ree. Third, put down the right foot which performed Ahn-jang-dah-ree between the opponent's two feet, lower your position, and drag your left foot right next to your right foot. Get closer to your opponent's body, while simultaneously holding the opponent's neck with your right hand and pulling the opponent's right thigh with your left hand. Then use the pelvis to push up the opponent's body. Fourth, quickly change the positions of your two feet while turning, then pull out your right foot and turn your waist with the rebound. At the same time, pull the opponent's neck down with your right hand and lift up the thigh held in your left hand. Then bend down at the waist, and throw your opponent to the floor. After Ah-raet-dae falls safely, return to the original position and alternate pushing each other's knees to start Ah-raet-dae's turn.

3-2

4-1

4-2

엉덩잽이는 씨름의 들배지기와 상당히 유사한 기술이다. 상대를 자기 허리 위에 얹어서 자신의 몸을 회전시키는 탄력으로 넘기는 기술이다. 특히 엉덩잽이는 사람마다 약간씩 다르게 기술을 구사한다. 어떤 사람은 완전히 상대를 들어 올린 후, 거꾸로 돌려 넘기기도 한다. 어떤 사람은 상대를 들어 올리지 않고 자신의 몸을 회전하는 힘으로 끌어당겨 허리를 지렛대의 받침 삼아 넘기기도 한다. 또 어떤 사람은 상대를 들어 올린 후, 자신의 허벅지 위에 걸쳐서 돌려 넘기기도 한다. 중요한 것은 상대의 중심이 되는 허리가 자신의 허리 위에 오도록 한 뒤, 자신의 허리를 받침대 삼아 상대를 거꾸러뜨린다는 것이다.

Uhng-dung-jae-bee is a technique that is quite similar to a body-twist throw seen in Korean wrestling art of Ssireum. It's a technique in which the opponent is placed on your waist and turned over using the elasticity of your body rotates. In particular, Uhng-dung-jae-bee is performed slightly differently by each person. Some raise their opponents completely, and then turn them upside down. Some people do not lift the opponents, but instead pull the opponent with the power of rotating their bodies and throwing them over using their waists as leverage. Others lift their opponents and turn them over their thighs. The important thing is that the waist, the center of the opponent, is to be placed on your waist, and then you use your waist as a support to knock the opponent down.

② 우 안짱다리하고 우 무릎빗대기

우 안짱다리하고 우 무릎빗대기는 안짱다리로 상대의 오른 다리를 끌고 온 후, 그대로 자신의 정강이로 상대의 정강이를 눌러 넘기는 동작이다.

첫째, 서로 번갈아 무릎을 밀다가, '섯다'의 구령에 맞추어 오른 무릎을 좀 더 깊게 밀어 상대의 체중을 뒤로 이동시킨다. 둘째, 자신의 왼발을 뒤쪽으로 약 반 뼘 정도 옮겨 디디며, 그 반동을 이용하여 상대의 오른발을 오른발 안짱다리로 역시 반 뼘 정도 끌어온다. 셋째, 안짱다리 한 오른발을 풀지 않고 바닥에 내려놓은 그대로, 좌측 45°방향으로 무릎을 밀어준다. 동시에 자세를 낮추며 자신의 정강이로 상대의 정강이를 지그시 눌러준다. 이때, 상대의 정강이 넓은 면에 자기 정강이의 좁은 정면 부위가 닿도록 눌러야 한다. 넷째, 상대가 완전히 넘어질 때까지 정강이를 지그시 밀어준다. 아랫대가 안전하게 넘어진 후에는 원래 자리로 돌아와 무릎을 번갈아 밀며 아랫대의 순서를 시작한다.

1	2-1	2-2

② Woo Ahn-jang-dah-ree-ha-goh Woo Moo—reup-bit-dae-kee

Woo Ahn-jang-dah-ree-ha-goh Woo Moo-reup-bit-dae-kee is a movement in which you pull the opponent's right leg with Ahn-jang-dah-ree, and then press down the opponent's shin with your own shin and knock him/her down.

First, push each other's knees in turn, then push the right knee a little deeper at the command of 'Suht-da' to move the opponent's weight back. Second, move your left foot back about half a handspan, and use the rebound to draw the opponent's right foot about half a handspan with a right foot Ahn-jang-dah-ree. Third, put your right foot, which performed Ahn-jang-dah-ree, down on the floor, then push the knee 45° to the left, while holding right Ahn-jang-dah-ree motion. At the same time, lower your posture and gently press your opponent's shin with your shin. The opponent's shin should be pressed so that the narrow front part of your shin touches the wide side of the opponent's shin. Fourth, gently push the shin until the opponent falls completely. After Ah-raet-dae falls safely, return to the original position and alternate pushing each other's knees to start Ah-raet-dae's turn.

3-1

3-2

4

무릎빗대기를 할 때에는 안짱다리를 할 때 걸었던 상대의 발목을 놓치지 않도록 주의해야 한다. 상대의 발목을 조여 주는 동작이 느슨해지면, 무릎빗대기가 진행되는 동안 상대의 발목이 뒤로 미끄러져 빠질 수 있다.
또한 무릎을 밀어주는 각도는 대개 45°라고 설명은 하지만, 상대의 자세를 보고 적절하게 변경해주어야 한다. 중요한 것은 상대의 정강이 측면 넓은 곳에 자신의 정강이의 좁은 정면이 닿도록 해야 하는 것이다. 또한, 상대의 정강이가 바깥쪽으로 밀려나도록 방향을 잡아주어야 한다.
무릎빗대기는 상대에 따라 또는 상대의 중심에 따라 기술을 거는 부위가 달라질 수 있다. 그러므로 많이 연습해야 하며 보편적으로 슬개골 바로 아래 부위를 누르는 게 효과적이다.

When you perform Moo-reup-bit-dae-kee, be careful not to miss the opponent's ankle that you hooked with Ahn-jang-dah-ree. If the action of tightening around the opponent's ankle is loosened, the opponent's ankle may slip back while you are performing Moo-reup-bit-dae-kee.
It is also explained that the angle that you are pushing your knee forward is usually 45°, but should be adjusted accordingly to the opponent's position. The important thing is to make sure that the front of your shin touches the side of your opponent's shin. Also, the opponent's shin should be positioned so that it is pushed outward.
The target point of Moo-reup-bit-dae-kee would differ based on the balance or size of the opponent. So, exhaustive practice is very important. As a general rule, just under the kneecap is an effective target point to push.

③ 우 안짱다리하고 안아잽이

우 안짱다리하고 안아잽이는 안짱다리로 상대의 오른 다리를 끌고 온 후, 두 손으로 상대의 양쪽 오금을 끌어안듯이 잡아채며 어깨로 밀어 넘기는 동작이다.

첫째, 서로 번갈아 무릎을 밀다가, '섯다'의 구령에 맞추어 오른 무릎을 좀 더 깊게 밀어 상대의 체중을 뒤로 이동시킨다. 둘째, 자신의 왼발을 뒤쪽으로 약 반 뼘 정도 옮겨 디디며, 그 반동을 이용하여 상대의 오른발을 오른발 안짱다리로 역시 반 뼘 정도 끌어온다. 셋째, 자세를 낮추며 오른발을 상대의 다리 사이로 깊숙이 넣어 디딘다. 동시에 양손으로는 상대의 오금을 감아 챈다. 또한 머리를 왼쪽으로 비껴낸 채로 어깨를 상대의 복부 중앙에 댄다. 넷째, 어깨로 상대의 복부를 힘껏 밀며 전방을 향해 튕겨 나아간다. 동시에 양손으로는 상대의 오금을 당겨 올린다. 아랫대가 안전하게 넘어진 후에는 원래 자리로 돌아와 무릎을 번갈아 밀며 아랫대의 순서를 시작한다.

1	2	3-1

③ Woo Ahn-jang-dah-ree-ha-goh Ahn-ah-jae-bee

Woo Ahn-jang-dah-ree-ha-goh Ahn-ah-jae-bee is a movement in which you pulled the opponent's right leg with Ahn-jang-dah-ree, and then grab the back of the opponent's two knees with your hands and push him/her over with your shoulder.

First, push each other's knees in turn, then push the right knee a little deeper at the command of 'Suht-da' to move the opponent's weight back. Second, move your left foot back about half a handspan, and use the rebound to draw the opponent's right foot about half a handspan with a right foot Ahn-jang-dah-ree. Third, lower your posture and put your right foot down between the opponent's feet. At the same time, grab the opponent's back of the knees with your both hands. Also, lean your head to the left and place your shoulder in the center of the opponent's abdomen. Fourth, push the opponent's abdomen with your shoulder and bounce forward. At the same time, pull up on the back of the opponent's knees with both hands. After Ah-raet-dae falls safely, return to the original position and alternate pushing each other's knees to start Ah-raet-dae's turn.

3-2

4-1

4-2

안아잽이를 할 때, 주의할 점은 상대를 들어 올리지 않아야 한다는 것이다. 물론 힘이 센 사람들은 상대를 들어 올려 넘기기도 하지만, 이는 매우 어려운 일이다. 따라서 어깨로 상대의 몸을 뒤로 튕기듯 밀어내며, 양 손으로 두 다리를 잡아채, 다리가 몸을 따라가지 못하도록 만들어 넘어뜨리는 것이다.
또 한 가지 주의할 점은 상대의 몸이 밀리지 않은 상태에서는 다리를 잡아당기기가 매우 어렵다는 것이다. 두 다리에 상대의 체중이 온전하게 남아있기 때문이다. 따라서 안아잽이를 할 때에는 상대의 몸을 먼저 밀고나가며 다리를 채 와야 한다는 점을 명심해야 한다
효과적인 안아잽이 방법은 양 오금을 잡아채는 것이다. 그러나 초대 인간문화재 송암 신한승선생께서는 양 오금을 잡는 것은 기술이 깨끗하지 못하고, 이것에 익숙해지면 다른 기술에 대한 수련이 부족해지므로, 한 손은 오금을 잡고 다른 한 손은 어깨를 붙인 허리를 잡고 연습하게 하기도 하였다.

When you're performing Ahn-ah-jae-bee, take care you don't lift your opponent up. Of course, strong people can lift their opponents up and throw them down, but this is very difficult. Therefore, you push the opponent's body back with your shoulder and grab the opponent's both legs with your hands to make sure the legs can't follow his/her body, and throw him/her down to the ground.
Another thing to note is that it is very difficult to pull the opponent's legs when his/her body is not pushed. This is because the opponent's weight remains intact on his/her both legs. Therefore, it is important to keep in mind that you have to push your opponent's body as you grab his/her legs when you perform Ahn-ah-jae-bee.
The most effective execution of Ahn-ah-jae-bee is snatching the back of both knees. But GM Shin Han-seung, the first Human Cultural Asset, sometimes let trainees practice with one hand on the back of knee and the other (of the same side while the shoulder pushes the stomach) on the waist, because he thought grabbing both back of knees was not gentle, and also getting used to the first method prevented the training of other skills.